HUMAN ECOLOGY: 2nd edition

by
SIR GEORGE STAPLEDON
F.R.S., M.A., D.Sc., C.B.E., etc.
(1882 – 1960)

edited and introduced by

ROBERT WALLER

Second edition

CHARLES KNIGHT & CO. LTD.
LONDON
1971

First edition published in 1964
by Faber and Faber Limited

Republished by The Soil Association
in 1968 (limited edition)

This revised, second edition is published by
Charles Knight & Company Limited
11/12 Bury Street, London E.C.3

Printed in Great Britain by William Lewis (Printers) Ltd., Cardiff
A member of the Brown Knight and Truscott group

SBN 85314 071 5

Dedicated
to
Victor Bonham-Carter
by the editor

'A new era has been rendered inevitable by the practical and compelling manner in which time, space and energy have revealed their harmonic and universal attributes.'

Sir George Stapledon

ACKNOWLEDGEMENTS

To Lady Stapledon who bequeathed me the copyright and for every help and encouragement.

To Conant Brodribb for reading the manuscript with his invariable kindness.

Oxford,
1963

To The Soil Association for its generous support of Stapledon's work.

Haughley,
Stowmarket,
Suffolk,
1970

This book is the greater part of a manuscript left unfinished by Sir George Stapledon when he died in 1960. It was written during 1946-48. He referred to it as 'my book on Human Ecology'. Although he left some draft chapters for extending it, it makes a completed whole.

CONTENTS

Contents

Contents

... concentration
Without elimination, both a new world
And the old made explicit ...

T. S. ELIOT, *Burnt Norton*

This was not acknowledged except by a very few in 1946 – 48 when Stapledon wrote his book. It is only now now that his posthumous work can have a receptive public. Indeed, he left it unfinished when he died in 1960 because he despaired of public interest and because, when he was depressed, he wondered if the damage being done by technology with gathering momentum could ever be arrested in time, especially in our own country. 'Ours is a time paroxysmal outburst,' he said. 'But when nature indulges in such periods of variation and change, she generally counterbalances them with much longer periods of stability. Probably no species, least of all man, can live under the perpetual stress of paroxysmal outburst without dire harm to itself.'

The element of stability has already disappeared from American civilisation which has now accepted the dogma that mankind must adapt itself to perpetual change. If survival depends upon endless expansion and ever increasing production, then the form of society cannot remain constant. From the biological point of view change and stability should be balanced. In the cells of the body, for example, constant activity maintains unchanging form – homeostasis. In the growth of vegetation, there is constant change but the pattern is always repeated in the cycles of growth. The human consequence of trying to keep pace with the ever changing complexities of disordered shapeless growth is mental fatigue. American speech with its abstract jargon already reveals that the American is losing contact with the individual object and deals only with the process of production. Reality therefore is ever more and more remote as 'progress' continues. The capacity to make sound decisions that depend upon personal relations in individual situations weakens: artistic perception, which is essentially particular and individual, is lost. People have the sense of losing grip on real life and of living in a blue print. All western civilization is moving in this direction.

A good human ecologist would assess situations in terms of their effects on the vitality and practical ability of human beings: he would ask whether the policy pursued gave people more or less chance to cope with and control what was likely to happen and to make sound decisions. Above all he would ask whether anticipated developments strengthened or weak-

2

ened the tree of life itself, the health of the population and the fertility of the soil. Although this seems an obvious way of assessing policies, it has not been given priority. Stapledon told me, for example, that too much had been done under the stress of war without adequate research into long term effects. Then, instead of pausing to take stock, we allowed new technological developments to drive onwards 'too far, too fast.'

Stapledon felt isolated from the professional agricultural world, so largely consisting of specialists and so lacking in natural philosophers, what he called integrators. He himself suffered from being called the 'prophet of grass.' He was praised for his achievements as Director of the Welsh Plant Breeding Station: but his insistence that scientists should study history, art and philosophy in order to counterbalance their specialisms and prevent the abuse of their specific knowledge by ill-advised technology, was talked about as if it were an endearing eccentricity. When he said at public meetings that the arts had as much to offer in shaping and guiding society as the sciences and that science in a world of declining artistic perception could only increase ugliness, it aroused silent resentment among many of his colleagues. One of them is reputed to have said, when he learned that Stapledon wrote poetry, that he no longer trusted his scientific judgment; another told me (discussing Stapledon's cri de coeur to a grass-land society conference, that in backing science we were putting our money on a runaway horse): 'We all get a bit senile as we get older.'

Scientific method and the philosophy supporting it, admirable in their place, can create fanatics just as narrow as the Puritans, who in so many ways the scientists resemble. 'The scientific conscience' would often let us all die rather than issue a warning about, say, a pesticide whose toxicity has not been proven by current scientific methods. Scientific pride in these matters is almost pathological and the scientific outlook as straight and narrow as the road to Paradise: indeed one suspects that many scientists believe that salvation has been sacrificed if an empirical fact is treated as a proven one. Scientists are loath to admit things which, though obvious to a layman, have not been scientifically proved. They are terrified of becoming involved in the vague interacting states

3

of dynamic equilibrium which constitute that total state of dynamic equilibrium which we call nature. The complexity of life outside the experimental situation cannot be reduced to a condition in which there is only one variable and consequently nothing can be 'proved'. And yet this is reality and without a willingness to face these real problems scientists can never be ecologists. One famous scientist is reported as saying that he would never study ecology because there are no Nobel prizes awarded for it. A very revealing confession. We shall have to realize there is more than one kind of proof.

This prudery is not of course only true of scientists: they are not the only specialists afraid to be seen walking out with people of dubious reputation. This is a malady of the fragmented culture of our time which breeds such snobbery. Alexander Solzhenitzyn gave bitter offence to his fellow writers when he described them in *The First Circle* as churning out the conventional state dogmas in order to curry favour with authority. The writers responded by expelling him from the Writers' Union: they acknowledged his genius, but were delighted to save their own faces by having his work censored. Anyone who believes that this impulse does not exist in democracies is deceiving himself. The heretic is not censored: he is simply ignored or turned into a pleasant joke. The prevailing dogmas on agricultural husbandry and in particular on 'the necessity of higher yields at lower cost' have never been fairly examined in official circles: the alternatives have not been given the same serious consideration, but dismissed as cranky. 'Whatever is the most profitable is the best husbandry' has become a tacit assumption likely to have disastrous effects on the nations land and livestock, but one which it makes life easier to accept. Patronage can be bestowed on those who say the right things in Britain as much as in Russia.

Stapledon was one of the few successful scientists who not only thought for himself but said what he thought. He did not let his mind yield to the dominant economic doctrines. He did not agree that it was a sign of efficiency to have fewer and fewer men on the land: he did not agree that the best farmers were those who produced the highest yields at the lowest cost: he did not accept that more and more fertiliser and more and more sprays should be used without long term investigation of their effects on the health of soil, plant, animal and man. But despite his prestige, Authority took no notice when he challenged the dogmas. In those days no one could stand up to the hysterical faith in economic efficiency. It is perhaps worthwhile pointing out here that this interpretation of efficiency is not accepted by the philosophically minded economists, but only by the accountant type of economists who serve industry and government. A good economist will tell you that efficiency is reckoned in terms of the end in view. A monetary efficiency may be an ecological disaster, and in farming usually is. In other words, economics and science have been brought into disrepute by the renegade technologists and scientists who have been the servile hand-maids of commerce and government. It is, however, harder to ignore Stapledon today than when he was alive. In his books we see a Stapledon about which his contemporaries knew very little. We understand why he deliberately wrote for the future — which is ridiculously inefficient and foolish from the materialist's point of view. What can the future do for me? So why should I work for it? Just think how different the attitude would have been of the Chinese with their ancestor worship, when everyone hoped to be a revered ancestor! We may laugh at such superstition: but how superior it is to our own slavery to the moment!

The supreme biological law is diversity: without diversity neither nature nor society can survive. We have lived in an age of single-purpose men who have pursued monocultural, totalitarian objectives by purging their critics and opponents: and they have purged nature and the landscape too in pursuit of the single-purpose of economic efficiency. The men of power are predators who attempt to monopolise ideas so they can control action. This is justified on the pseudo scientific theory that it conforms to evolution — the survival of the fittest and so on. But Stapledon pointed out that, if we model society on nature, then nature gives us as many examples of co-operation and harmony as of competition: and indeed competition itself has balance and harmony as its aim. Thus it reconciles conflicts that seem to man irreconcilable. The conflicts in nature are of great diversity: their object is not the victory of a few species over all the others — the nonsense of world

B

5

domination that obsesses our nationalist politics — but the survival of all. Animals do not indulge in genocide: species do not prey on their own kind except when they are perverse. Species prey on other species, but the outcome is population control and a balance of forces.

The result of following these antiquated pseudo-scientific economic doctrines of the 19th century is that we live on the brink of ecological disaster. Our politicians spend money on supersonic flight and rockets to the moon: they build larger lorries and oil tankers and airplanes and encourage ever vaster industrial and political amalgamations. Instead of reconciling the conflict between man and nature, we weigh the scales in favour of man's ambitions: all balance is then lost.

With the increase of pollution and contamination, with constant stench and noise in the air and with ever more remote control over their lives, the people themselves begin to turn, intuitively, against industry and government. As we negotiate to enter the Common Market, separatist movements spring up in Wales, Scotland and Brittany. Regional government begins to arouse more emotional allegiance than national government. Students turn in bewilderment, anger and distrust towards another and simpler way of life. They reject the sciences: they scorn technology: they turn to their inner life, their emotions, their instincts, within, and to nature in the wild, without — exactly as Stapledon predicted. For this they are called permissive. But they can retort that a generation which in the name of laissez-faire — do what you like — has plundered the earth of its riches with less conscience than any other generation in history has set them no example of self-control. They can put their thumbs to their noses and it is only by hypocrisy that we can continue to preach at them; we would do better to repent. The time has come to set them an example of wiser behaviour.

This revolt will gather momentum and perhaps reach revolutionary proportions, unless we heed the lessons of human ecology as Stapledon has propounded them — not in detail, not in masses of facts, but in search of the underlying principles that enable every man to apply a new scale of priorities to what is allowed in his name by politicians and employers. We must counterbalance the urban and material with the biological whatever the cost, however stupendous the cost, for the cost cannot be greater than the cost of what we are already doing that is wrong, than the fantastic waste of our expansionist society that takes, makes and breaks unrestrained by social ethics.

Modern man is the most prodigal son of history: he is spending the vast capital bequeathed to him both by his own ancestors and by the evolution of the earth itself. If the earth were a bank in which the generations invested energy in the form of fossil fuels and minerals, then one century may well spend all that now remains in extravagant living and internecine struggles for world domination. This may not seem to be the case to those who do it — indeed they have interpreted their spoliation and robbery as the fulfillment of ideals — but those who see it in perspective will write of our time as the Israelites wrote about Babylon — and to the underdeveloped nations whom we rob for the sake of trade by keeping down the costs of raw materials, it already seems a Babylonian unrighteousness.

A moment's detachment will show us that the writing is on the wall. We are dependant upon oil for the greater part of our industrial energy and for locomotion. Oil will be exhausted within at the most 70 years. Already the price is rising because of the cost of finding new sources. Even when many of our natural resources still exist in large quantities, the inexpensive sources have been exhausted and the more expensive ones now have to be worked. The result will be galloping inflation; for the masses will not accept the true ecological cost of maintaining the standards of modern civilisation. They have been told by all parties that conditions will improve and that everyone, thanks to modern technology, will become richer. We have forgotten that the limiting factor is raw materials; that even synthetic substitutes require raw materials and the processes by which they are made have to be fuelled. Even on the farm the high yields of today are the result of energy brought onto the land from outside — chemicals, fertilisers and the fuels for the machines. These are dwindling resources. There can only be one lasting basis for a secure civilisation — the maximum use of renewable resources and the maximum restraint on expendable resources. And renewable resources must not be

7

used at a greater rate than we can renew them. California uses a thousand times more water than the hydrological cycle provides: it has to steal from other states to maintain its orgiastic use of water.

Rampant inflation may for a time hide from us the temporary nature of our wealth and that we are getting poorer. But in the end it will intensify the ultimate disillusionment and reveal with starker indignation the fool's paradise which our rulers offer us. Stapledon aims to open our eyes to the biological realities on which all life depends for survival. But even he scarcely guessed how grave the situation would become. We have evidence.

That the population cannot go on doubling exponentially is plain commonsense: long before there is standing room only — which is the arithmetical outcome of what is taking place now — there will be an ecological catastrophe that will adjust population to the level which the earth can sustain, not only in terms of food but goods and even æsthetically and spiritually. The population of the world already exceeds the number that can be nourished in a human way. Dehumanisation has already set in as in the shanty towns of Africa and S.America. And yet out greatest need is to rehumanise ourselves.

Capitalism contains built into it the inevitability of its own destruction, for it does not impose order on production and expansion but pursues them for their own sake — for the sake of so-called economic efficiency. Socialism and Communism are both products of the same pseudo-scientific positivism as created capitalism and do not transcend its materialism. Yet in our tradition there is the residue of an older world which respected the earth, a conservatism which, unlike capitalism, thought of man as God's steward of the earth's resources. It is indeed harder to conserve than to progress. The Christian tradition considered that usury was a sin, though men sinned. But in our time the older sins have become virtues. We have made wealth an end in itself which is diabolical. Mammon dominates half the pages of our newspapers, especially the advertisements. Of money there must always be more: usury demands it. The end of this philosophy of life will be that the Great Powers will fight each other for possession of the remaining major natural resources — for without them we are no longer able to conceive of existence as worthwhile. We shall have to relearn what really gives joy in life and makes it worth having, otherwise our despair and rage will lead to our destruction. It is in the long run then a religious problem. We shall be thrown back on ourselves.

Surely the readers of this book will see that it offers them a way of salvation that is both material and spiritual. The society of endless production destroys man as well as the earth — it exhausts them both. Ideas must be changed: and to begin with at least the change can only be brought about by a general recognition of the need to think in terms of human ecology. We are not all the wealthy children of industrial millionaires, though we would like to think so. We are the children of the earth. Necessity is ecological. Economics is man-made.

The first chapter of this book is concerned with expounding a philosophy of integration that could save us from ecological disaster. We have arrived at a turning point in our thinking about economics and production: instead of realizing that, we intensify the old modes of thought and thereby accelerate the onset of social tragedy.

How did Stapledon, on the face of it just another of the many able scientists of our era who pursue their work undisturbed by non-scientific considerations, come to concern himself so passionately about the uses of science?

II

Reginald George Stapledon was born in North Devon in 1882. He came from the family which, in the thirteenth century, had produced a Lord Chancellor of England, the bishop who founded Exeter College, Oxford. For seven hundred years the Stapledons always seem to have returned to Devonshire wherever their work took them or to have lived on their estates there. Our Stapledon's father followed in the tradition. Already a master mariner in charge of his own ship when he was only twenty-three, he married into the family that built the last wooden ships in the yards at Appledore. Then, when he was just forty, he gambled on the potentialities of the Suez Canal and abandoned the sea to open a shipping agency at Port Said. In a few years he was rich enough to supervise offices in Liverpool and Paris from his own home, the large house at Lakenham where George Stapledon was born — born, one might say, at the very crossroads of the nineteenth century, for though the family lived in pre-industrial Devon, their income was derived from the new world of free trade.

Stapledon has recorded that the strongest influences on his childhood were his mother and the servants: John Dennis, the coachman, for example: 'One of those grand countrymen who could turn his hand to everything and make a tidy job of everything he attempted. . . . He was illiterate, but because of him, even as a boy, I began to ponder the rival merits of illiteracy and book learning.' Referring to the servants as a whole, he wrote: 'Everybody was skilled with his hands and active. Pride in one's work, no matter what the work was, and pride in the establishment for which one worked, was a ruling passion. Slack or slovenly work was not tolerated by the servants themselves. Pride, friendship, loyalty, skill, that was the atmosphere under which I spent my boyhood.'

A. L. Rowse, whose father was a china clay worker in Cornwall, describes[1] his parents and the surrounding working-class families in the same terms. Rowse, like Stapledon, took with him into the urban-industrial world, and into the world of contemporary thought and scholarship, the memory of that earlier world and its virtues and skills. This memory of their early life was to create in both of them a tension and a dilemma. In the Stapledon household, however, the two worlds interpenetrated, the new one enriching the old. There was no reason to suppose that these two cultures were incompatible or could lead to a division within the personality. The new industrial prosperity arising from his father's business activities in Suez appeared as a new dimension to an old society: so did the ideas on which this prosperity was based. Its long-term consequences were hidden from view, particularly in the slow-moving West Country.

Neither at home nor school was there anything to turn Stapledon into a rebel or make him question his environment.

[1] *A Cornish Childhood*. Cape.

He had good reason to feel a conservative attitude to life. The United Services College, Westward Ho! which he attended as a day boy, prepared its pupils for Sandhurst and Woolwich: as much stress was laid on character training as on academic achievements. Loyalty, respect for discipline, the ability both to command and obey were part of its *training*. The headmaster, Cornell Price, believed that his duty was not so much to teach his pupils as to train them. He did not dissociate the mind from the other functions of the personality: he told the boys that he believed each one developed at his own rate and the late developers were often the most successful in the long run. Stapledon remembered this, for he was to be a very late developer himself. The headmaster evidently had the power of evoking respect for his beliefs, for Kipling dedicated 'Stalky and Co' to him.

> *And we all praise famous men—*
> *Ancients of the College;*
> *For they taught us common sense —*
> *Tried to teach us common sense—*
> *Truth and God's own Common Sense*
> *Which is more than knowledge.*

Stapledon was far too sophisticated and far too careful and logical in his thinking to use phrases like 'God's own common sense' — whatever that may be. But when he was still quite young he realized that our knowledge could never encompass what might be termed ultimate truth: that what we do not know will always surround and engulf what we do. Consequently we cannot live by knowledge alone: there will always come a point at which character, the intuitive sense of the right way to act trained through long experience, will be more important than knowing the limited and contradictory facts that in theory bear upon any problem or situation. We create our character to a large extent in the same way as we learn a craft or a trade, by following the example of those who have great characters, just as the apprentice follows the example of the master craftsman. This is the idea behind Kipling's poem: it is the famous men, the ancients, who set an example of common sense and character that is more valuable than the knowledge learnt by heart in the classroom. In the old world the

young were apprentice characters as well as apprentice craftsmen: leadership was a responsible role which the adult was
proud to accept. At school and at home Stapledon imbibed
this tradition. He lived to see it crumble under the stress of
the rational and technological world which was taking its
place, with its underlying assumption that everything can be
achieved by the intellect. He tried to counter this tendency by
insisting that teaching alone was not enough: that the school
must provide good training in practical crafts and good conditioning as well. The whole environment of the school must
appeal to the pupils' senses and enliven them. Stapledon once
maintained that the greatest educational reform of his time
was school milk – because it showed that the authorities were
at last alive, however feebly, to the fact that you cannot teach
a child whose stomach and senses are deprived of essential
nourishment.

Stapledon was probably lucky in being a day boy. School
learning was blended with an intimate experience of the everyday life of country people. His brother Ernest was a land agent
and he travelled around with him in his gig when he visited
farms:

'The dialogues with farmer, woodman, gamekeeper, mason
or carpenter were masterpieces in the thinking up and expression of ideas. Always the aim was to achieve essential and often
difficult ends with limited and often primitive means. Neither
the landlord nor tenant could afford to waste a shilling: men
thought slowly in those days but they did think.'

When we read Stapledon's last book it is not difficult to
trace the genesis of Chapters 6, 7 and 8. They are concerned
with contrasting the way that we actually learn difficult skills
and insights with the way that they are consciously taught in
our modern educational system. Our intellectual methods
frequently create a self-consciousness that breaks down the
unity of head, hand and eye, instead of knitting them together: in the same way, in the more intellectual spheres, the
head and the heart are divided, the senses and the intellect
treated separately. Looking back to his experiences as a boy
and comparing them to his experiences in modern universities
and schools, he could not but reflect on the manner in which
specialization has impoverished character and turned crafts-

men into machine operators. In Stapledon's youth the intellectual world was already becoming highly segregated and specialized: the industrial worker was an automaton, but Stapledon himself was fortunate enough to experience what remained of the old traditional world of unselfconscious, apprenticed craftsmanship: a world integrated by tradition. It was Stapledon's view that we should respect and study this ancient world wherever it still thrives – especially in the peasant countries of Europe: once it has been destroyed by progress, we may find that we have lost important insights into living that we may never be able to recover.

Although they did not realize it, men such as Stapledon's father were breaking up the homely communities on which they depended for so much of their personal happiness. Stapledon observed that his father behaved differently at home to the way he behaved at work. 'My father lavished all his virtues in full measure on his wife, his family, his friends and the servants of his household.' On the other hand: 'The man who had become redundant (in business) or who, in any way, whether his own fault or not, stood in the way of the job in hand was deserving of scant attention. My father's attitude to his crew when they were sick, or my father-in-law's attitude to poachers, was ruthless.'

Stapledon ascribed this split attitude to life as a characteristic of the Victorians arising from their abrupt break with history. They were able to justify two contradictory ways of behaving, one way at home and another way at work. On behalf of a special business morality identified with patriotism respectable men became gangsters. Even religious people believed in two kinds of providence: one the providence of God, the other the providence of economics. Free economic expansion was believed to be a benevolent force. It became, as it is in America today, a heresy to oppose it. This tension in society – which contradicts its declared ideals – was strengthened by the emergence into the personal life of impersonal scientific concepts, a new kind of dogma more effective and real than religious dogma. Capitalism and Communism – both economic fanaticisms – subjected the personal life of the Christian world to an impersonal functionalism. The guiding hand of economic progress was raised to the status of

13

a divine providence: and this diabolic creed still drives men of all political parties and none to participate unwittingly in the undermining of religion, culture and communal life. It is an evil so woven into the fabric of our existence that we do not recognise that it is there.

While Stapledon was still at school his father died. This left him still more under the influence of his mother, who was perhaps over-devoted to him. She was a remarkable woman: one of those self-taught, individualistic Victorians who reconciled religion and science in a private philosophy:

'She gloried in evolution and read into it not only accident and chance, but purpose. She saw herself as a humble part of the "Great Invention". Always for her the theme was the same — the wonders of Nature and the littleness of Man.'

In this way she tempered the arrogance latent in a materialist interpretation of life with an emotion that has its roots in religious tradition. She communicated this feeling to her son: 'Thus very early in life I realized to the depth of my being that no matter how hard I might work to acquire knowledge, there would always remain much that would be a closed book, not only to myself but to the scientists of every generation. Scientific arrogance was never likely to hamper my outlook.'

Stapledon went up to Cambridge with the outlook of his family. He admired the enterprise of his father: his mother's contemplative rationalism: the craftsmanship, loyalty and simplicity of the servants: the sturdy self-reliance and skill of the rural community. He had yet to experience the defective morality of political systems. It was only in retrospect, studying his father's notebooks and recalling the incidents of his father's commercial life — they were never allowed to intrude into his home life — that he realized something was wrong with business morality.

As he did not need qualifications to assure himself of what is called a future, he was able to take his science Tripos at Cambridge at leisure. After additional coaching in botany — the subject in which he was afterwards to hold a chair — he obtained his B.Sc. He made no friends among the undergraduates who were afterwards to become celebrated scientists. With never a thought of postgraduate research he departed for Suez.

When he was a professor and an F.R.S. he asked himself with amazement: Why was I bored at Cambridge? His answer was: because the teaching was neither sufficiently practical nor sufficiently philosophical. If it had been philosophical it would also have been practical: it would have demonstrated the connections between one science and another and between science and the practical problems of society. It would have described the place of science within the general culture. Instead of that all the teaching was pure, specialized and departmentalized. The organization of the university had grown up around this specialized attitude to knowledge, so that each subject had its professor with his own jealously guarded empire. Learning was concerned with subjects, not with problems or trying to see life as a whole. It analysed reality into chemical substances and could not restore its character by demonstrating the interrelationship of the different sciences. The world is not botany, geology and chemistry: the world is what we experience with our five senses and our innermost sense of Self. It infinitely exceeds the parts into which we break it up: yet there is not, except in name, even such a composite science as biology. Those who have a strong, instinctive sense of being part of the unity of life feel a repugnance for the way in which science is taught and organized. Stapledon developed a love-hate attitude toward the profession that he honoured and which brought him so much honour. As a boy, proud of his vegetable garden, he had learnt that the primary function of the soil is creative: to assist and sustain its activity should be the object of research. In the laboratory and the study, the creativeness of man and soil alike tend to become shadowy mental concepts. It is this that makes education boring.

His first critical reaction to society was provoked by education. It was in terms of his own depressing experience that he worked out the programme of educational reforms in this book. Chapters 6 to 9 stress that teaching cannot be separated from the conditions of the pupil's own life, including his home background. Stapledon considered that to make examinations the object of the educational system was a confession of its failure: it standardized and mechanized education. Once interest is aroused a man educates himself, and he will to a large extent devise his own methods of learning to suit his own goals. Such a system of education was devised for bullying the unwilling through a syllabus. Stapledon was shocked that he could have left Cambridge officially qualified and yet with his intellectual powers and his imagination unawakened. Such things should not be possible, and a society in which they are possible is uninspired.

Suez was far more exciting than Cambridge — ships, sailors and all the intense activity of international trade:

". . . many of the feats of speed in coaling and trans-shipping cargoes were positively amazing. The scenes at night were thrilling. Lights everywhere . . . ponder the frantic and hurried toiling of our age of smoke and light-hearted squandering of the patient labouring of natural forces: nature unhampered creates and replenishes: man destroys. . . .'

'I was made to feel (though not understanding all the consequences and ramifications) the magnitude of densely populated England's dependence on her overseas trade and on her shipping. . . . It has never ceased to agitate me . . . other nations might not always be prepared to adjust their affairs to suit our economy.'

As a shipping clerk Stapledon — for obvious reasons — was not a success. He had ideas about how he would like to run the business and came into friendly conflict with his elder brother, who sent him back home to look for a career more suited to his temperament. While he was in the East he spent ten days in the Lebanon where, as letters to his mother reveal, he took a keen interest in the techniques used by the peasants to grow corn on the stony mountainsides — a foreshadowing of his own work in Wales.

His mother had the good sense to realize that he was marking time until he discovered his true vocation. He worked for a while in a market garden in Kent: if he liked the work he was to start one of his own in Devon. But the commercial side and the hard physical grind ran counter to his natural impulse to reflection. As he wrote: 'In these days of marking time I was learning the important lesson of what I did *not* want to do.' It was on this market garden that he became friendly with the 'farm labourers' whose cause he was to champion for the rest of his life. 'Labourer, indeed, as applied to craftsman and artist! The term is erroneous and has done immense harm. To be certain on a matter so fundamental was worth a year wasted in Kent.'

The year was far from wasted: he took to wandering about by himself and frequently strayed off the farm to study the flora and butterflies of the district. He began to make what was in effect an ecological study of the various fields and orchards in relation to cropping and management. 'I found myself much more interested in the natural history aspects of fruit and vegetable production than in the business aspect.' His inner life was beginning to take control. On his twenty-fifth birthday he sent his mother a letter of seventy pages filled with observations on the tints of spring. This essay attempts to describe the emergent colours of spring poetically, scientifically and philosophically. It displays the integral manner in which the mind works when it is not over-disciplined by scientific techniques.

Stapledon was to struggle desperately all his life for a larger framework within which to express his ideas than even the highest scientific appointments could provide. He began to consider himself a luckless mongrel inheriting two incompatible strains, one artistic and the other scientific. It was late in life that he realized he was an extreme example of a dualism within all contemporary people and that it was western culture itself that was at fault.

This fully human interest in life, averse to specialization, perhaps accounts for the remarkable fact that even in Kent he did not yet realize that 'agriculture was to be the thing'. No doubt many careers were open to a man of such protean imagination and an element of accident decided the final choice. At first he thought he would like to become a school-master so that he could follow his interests in both science and the arts: and with this in view he went back to Cambridge to consult with his old tutor, Sir Albert Seward.

The Department of Agriculture was at that time being re-formed and re-inspired by Professor T. B. Woods who was determined to apply the pure sciences to practical agricultural problems. Seward had the acumen to realize that this would appeal to Stapledon's temperament and that he might be able to unify his many interests within the vast framework of agriculture – which is a science, an art and an industry. He was even rash enough to suggest that Stapledon might gate-crash lectures on ecology and forestry although they were not included within the syllabus. Stapledon could not help wondering what difference it would have made to him if this advice had been given in his undergraduate days: then he reflected that in those days Seward would not have dared to give this advice: 'No blame attaches to Seward. The whole system would collapse if students were advised, or permitted, to gate-crash at will. This experience is a good example of what happens when any institution great or small permits itself to be dominated by an overruling principle. . . . All forms of domination are incompatible with freedom. It is begging the question to say that conditions and circumstances make it inevitable. . . . Man needs to be constantly weighing up what he is losing under the system he adopts and always to believe it possible that the losses may be greater than the gains. Flexibility in action and not rigidity best accords with the heart-beat of life.'

He left Cambridge with a Diploma in Agriculture. While he was there he also acquired his M.A. for which he qualified by residence: he ironically observed that this was how all degrees should be awarded: 'It would be a liberal education for the university authorities to be shown how well, and in what a serene state of mind, men would work when not infected by the examination virus.' Why had studying for the Diploma in Agriculture been so much more interesting than studying for the B.Sc.? 'I was twenty-six and had not had facts ruthlessly pumped into me regardless of whether my phychosomatic condition was in a sufficiently receptive condition to digest them. . . . Every single fact is a mental enzyme.'

Even so, the university authorities had not observed in him a promising research worker and he was not invited to stay on for post-diploma research. 'I think this was providential in view of what I was to do later: it meant I was not brimful of preconceived notions as to technique borne of vigorous laboratory training.'

At the suggestion of Professor Woods he was appointed to the staff of the Royal Agricultural College, Cirencester. His two years on the college staff were crucial: they were to determine

18

the course of his life and justified his wayward approach to a vocation.

His first summer at Cirencester, 1910, was perfect for the production of grass: but the second ended in a severe drought. Stapledon, for whom botany was both a scientific pursuit and an artistic joy, had encouraged his pupils to go on rambles observing the flora of the Cotswolds. His aim was to instil the idea that nature is an organic whole with far more inter-relationships at work than it is possible to describe in the class room, observe in the laboratory or reproduce on the controlled plot. He wanted his students to acquire an imaginative feeling for the way in which nature works as a whole: this is not possible if they are only onlookers incapable of emotional participation in the scene spread out before the eye, spontaneously integrating the attitudes of science and art. In the dry summer days of 1911, the leys sown by the farmers began to die out while the wild grasses in the hedgerows, ditches and roadside verges remained green. So Stapledon dug up some of these roots and replanted them in a kitchen garden. He also observed that plants tended to remain green longer in proportion to the depth of the soil. 'Nature laid on this experiment for me: I could not have done it on such a vast scale.' Interpreting nature's own experiments and learning from them how to experiment oneself, by guiding and re-fining upon what actually happens in the outdoor scene, be-came a firm Stapledonian principle. It requires an artistic sense of the character of place and a willingness to allow for chance and circumstance in assessing the potentialities and characteristics of growth.

At Cirencester he reorganized the manurial grassland experi-ments by asking the questions: Which species of plant life thrive and which die away under various treatments, whether they are sown or appear of their own accord? What is the effect on the overall sward of the competition between different kinds of grasses? He directed attention to the effect on the individual plant of the conditions of its existence within the plant community.

This ecological approach was related to the history of the landscape around him: a landscape which shocked him into investigating its past. How was it that this grand Cotswold country had declined into a rural slum, the fields full of buttercups, dandelions and daises, beautiful but unproductive, the villages derelict — beautiful but unfit to live in? The countryside seemed abandoned by the nation, segregated from the thriving urban life. The answer came to him — it was the dark side to the furious activity and growing wealth of the international trade he had seen at Suez: even the explanation of the leys dying out in the drought was that the seeds the farmers put in their fields were imported and no experiments had been undertaken to find out if they were suited to Cotswold conditions. The nation (without any regard for the real needs of the farmer) imported seeds to help pay for manufactured exports. Seeds were simply seeds: their ecological relationship to the environment in which they were used was subordinated to the part they played in the international balance of payments. To the public all grass was roughly the same and many farmers had sunk to such a low condition that they assessed grass by its cheapness. The great estates on the Cotswolds were mainly used by their owners for sport: farming was a secondary consideration — and this two years before a great war in which we were nearly starved into defeat. 'Vegetation accurately read', wrote Stapledon, 'is a remorseless and wholly objective historian.' Although Stapledon did not yet grasp all the details and remifications of what he saw around him on the Cotswolds, his Suez experience had given him a clue. He began to place the rural decline in perspective.

At first he encountered the situation as a technical challenge to the agricultural scientist rather than as a political problem: then he gradually related the two problems and saw them as one. Underlying this book is an integral vision of agriculture, industry, village, town, landscape and political policy. The seeds of the chapters 'Urbanising the Rural' and 'Ruralising the Urban' had been sown thirty years before they grew into a book. Basically, the philosophy of integration means that nothing is sufficient unto itself and can live alone. The urban was mistaken in thinking that it could be independent of the rural: and so were those rural sentimentalists who thought that country life could settle down into thatched cottages and polo, hunting, shooting and fishing: or even that farming could continue in a countryside excluded from every modern development. Similarly, art and science cannot continue indefinitely as segregated cultures.

In 1912 Stapledon was appointed to the agricultural department of the University College of Wales at Aberystwyth with the joint task of advising farmers and taking part as a botanist in a survey of the Welsh hills. Everything that he observed in his work confirmed the judgments he had begun to form at Cambridge and Cirencester. In the university he was scornful of the mad passion to pass examinations — exacerbated in Wales by the poverty of the students who depended on academic qualifications to rise above their peasant background. He was appalled by the dire struggle for existence that confronted the hill farmer: at the same time he responded to his character and that of his student sons at the college with passionate admiration. He fell in love with Wales. The depopulation of the hill farms, the spread of moorland into areas that had once been cultivated: the desertion of hamlets and death of villages filled him with anger. He resolved to devote all his scientific knowledge to finding means of re-populating the hills and restoring prosperity to the country-side in the most practical way possible. In this sense he belonged to the important tradition of practical administrators in this country with an urge to reform, men who have in varying degrees succeeded without the backing of party politics or even mass discontent. Although Stapledon could not alter political policies or make blind men see, he did a wonderful lot to persuade governments to back agricultural research: and when, in due course, the policies changed, the research was there to give them reality.

In 1912 the task that confronted Stapledon in Wales was similar to the struggle to increase production that we find today in the underdeveloped countries. He saw himself as a social engineer. He saw in technology the weapon of reconstruction. It is important to recall that by the time Stapledon began this book in 1946, scientific techniques which did not exist in 1912 were having effects that he had not anticipated and did not like. In *Human Ecology* he takes these changes into account and assesses the new situation in the light of his original vision of the ends which techniques ought to serve. When the technical means began to determine the social ends,

Stapledon's enthusiasm for technology began to wane and even to turn to horror: but in 1912 he was all enthusiasm for new techniques and new knowledge – and with good reason. It would be grossly misleading, unecological and unjust to dissociate his ideas from the conditions in which he applied them. It must be rare of course for conditions to have changed so rapidly in one man's lifetime: it was remarkable that he was able to keep pace with them in his thinking. Other people did not: and it was this that left him as much a solitary figure in his last stage as he had been for a time in his first.

His work on the hill survey convinced him that two misconceptions held back the progress of cultivation: one was rigid traditional notions of what constituted fertile land and the other was seeds and seed mixtures. Good seed is fundamental to all biological life: the idea of the seed was held in religious veneration in the ancient world – good seed and good ground. For example, the Parable of the Sower transfers the husbandry of the biological seed to the husbandry of the spirit: the fertility of the land and of the mind have many parallels. The capacity to transfer a generalization from one sphere of life to illuminate another was highly developed in Stapledon; in an overspecialized life this great gift tends to lie unused.

Following up his observations at Cirencester, Stapledon realized that the poor quality of the leys sown by the Welsh farmers was in large part due to unsuitable seeds and seed mixtures. So he undertook, single-handed, the prodigious, meticulous and boring task of testing samples of all the seeds sold to the Welsh farms. Simple though the technique was for doing this, he believed that it was the most important way that he could apply science for the benefit of the community. The report (published in 1914) had an immediate effect. The farming community learnt that for years their seeds had brought pernicious weeds with them: when the low percentage of germination is also taken into account, the seeds were not so cheap as they seemed. And the foreign seeds lacked persistence because they were not suited to Welsh conditions. 'I should never have realized the extent of this evil if I had not seen it in the field as well as the laboratory.' A report on the condition of the seed trade in England by Professor Biffen came out at the same time. It was generally thought that the irrefutable evidence of these two reports would lead to Government action. But nothing was done. The trade and the commercial principle were too strong. The indifference of the Government made Stapledon aware that he was living in an era of drift: this was the beginning of his castigations of the governments in power between the wars. These feelings are reflected in this book when he deals with the planning of the balance of town and country. Although improvised chaos is perhaps preferable to State domination, freedom should not be made an excuse for allowing a piecemeal strangulation of the national life.

A bright journalist could have turned these reports on the seed trade into the exposure of a scandal: in fact, the state of agricultural knowledge was so low that few people involved in the transactions could be accused of knowing what they were doing. Stapledon was the first trained agronomist to come to the aid of the Welsh farmer, study his means and methods and use the results of his investigations to give practical help.

The object of cultivation in rough and hill country is to raise the level of fertility well above that chosen by nature for its own survival. Good cultivation can extend the grazing season and lift the nutritive value of the grass – and any other crop that may follow it. Welsh hill farmers had rigid notions, defined by the traditional layout of fences, trees, ditches and other barriers, as to the degree of fertility of their fields and mountain grazings. They had little idea that these barriers were often artificial and that new methods of cultivation could raise land regarded as hopelessly infertile to more productive uses. Often the neglected land on one side of a wall or fence was potentially as good as the land on the other side which was constantly employed: an arbitrary, traditional barrier had been given the status of a qualitative or class division. All over England Stapledon found what he called two-department farming – permanent and neglected grass on one side of a farm and arable cultivation on the other. The possibility of treating the farm as an organic whole and taking the plough right round did not seem to have occurred to anybody. Stapledon reflected that this dividing up into separate departments (segregation) of activities that ought to be interrelated (integrated) and which were capable of enriching each other, was an attitude that infected our whole society: it arose out of an ingrained state of mind. It made many problems far more complex than they need be by dividing them up into parts: science had its rigid classifications; education divided up knowledge into subjects; above all, society itself was divided up into classes which seldom reflected the real merits of individuals. Sex barriers, colour bars and many forms of academic differentiation made it difficult to assess individual character and potentialities. On top of that were the national or tribal divisions that divided up the human race into groups. Stapledon became so excited by this theme that he burst into verse about it:

> *The boundary walls and buffer states*
> *That man sets up through greed or fear*
> *'Tis just because they are not real*
> *They count as if in truth they were.*

The most remarkable of these unnatural barriers seemed to him the one dividing the conscious from the unconscious mind:

> *The human mind has boundary walls,*
> *All ill-defined and hard to draw.*
> *They may be here, they may be there,*
> *So little makes or masks a flaw.*

The dynamic fluidity of nature as compared to the rigid and geometrical manner with which man tried to contain and understand it was impressed upon Stapledon by his long walks on the Welsh hills and solitary meditations upon what he called the moods and tenses of nature. Everywhere he saw states of transition, one kind of vegetation overlapping with another. The rigid classifications of the text-books could never be applied to what he actually observed. A survey could never be other than approximate: nature was always on the move, and when man and his beasts intervened new conditions were created that required close and constant study. He devised for himself the philosophy of patches. Why were good grasses sometimes found existing in patches even when man had not intervened? Could not man create for himself deliberately the conditions which nature itself had found suitable for a

24

higher level of fertility? The manner in which a man focuses his attention on the natural scene spread out before him makes a vital difference to what he sees and understands — to what he reads and interprets: to what he hears when nature speaks to him. Generally speaking, the modern scientists never considers the idea of 'nature speaking to him': he is a cold and detached onlooker searching for means of controlling and manipulating a slave. The integral, as contrasted to the analytic, 'eye' involves a shift of consciousness. A new attitude to experience may well involve the development of latent powers of consciousness; it is not only physical nature that evolves, but consciousness as well. Stapledon stressed again and again after his long period of relative solitude in the Welsh hills that our manner of consciousness and our depth of insight is affected by the conditions in which we live: that a wholly urban environment, or a wholly scientific environment of laboratory and office, is insufficient to evoke and stimulate many of our finer feelings *upon which the refinement and delicacy of our ideas may well depend.* The natural world has a living and vital relation to ourselves: the consequences of cutting ourselves off from it and substituting a concrete environment of our own choosing may have incalculable consequences involving the loss of some of mankind's most cherished powers and experiences. It may produce a depression of consciousness far worse than any economic depression.

Among the most dangerous of all the barriers wilfully erected by man is the barrier between town and country: many artificial barriers have fallen since the beginning of this century with the emergence of a more democratic and informal age: but the barrier between town and country has in many ways grown stronger as a consequence of the haphazard control of the expansion of industry and population. It begins to appear as if it is too late to regain a proper integration. Much as we cherish the right of individuals to manage their own affairs, the cost of freedom in this aspect of social planning may well turn out to be so great that it cancels out all the other benefits of freedom, in the sense that it leads to a society in which most of the citizens are spiritually and emotionally undernourished in the midst of affluence. If this is followed by a breakdown both of the will to live and to work, then even the affluence will finally be sacrificed.

The classic collapses of civilizations that seem so baffling when looked at from outside with the detached eye of the objective historian are much more explicable if we try to enter in to the feelings of the people of the time. Then we get a glimpse of the changes of consciousness that have led to a collapse (or a renewal) of the will to create – that is, the will to relish life. Consciousness rests upon an inner fountain of life and it is the joy in that fountain which determines, in the long run, how long a society will survive. A society may win wars, create great empires and crumble, while a poorer society with a balanced economy of town and country, trades and professions, science and arts, a pattern reflecting the wholeness of man, will continue. It may not be brilliant or powerful, but it is nearer to the secret of social persistence. It can survive defeat and ill-chance. A society that achieves wealth and power through a one-sided development of its capacities is giving perilous hostages to fortune as England did when it set itself the aim of becoming the workshop of the world and sacrificed its agriculture to that end. From the community's point of view a true profit is only made when the goods provided by an industry are not cancelled out by the 'bads' of social imbalance, pollution of the environment and so on. The prosperity of one basic industry gained at the expense of another is not real prosperity at all. The profit of one industry must be balanced against the loss in the industry with which it competes. In other words, it is communal welfare that matters. The manufacturer's welfare is not intrinsically more important than the farmer's. When farming can only be kept viable by massive subsidies, it is not the farmer who is to blame: there is a mortal sickness at the heart of society. Food and many raw materials are only cheap because society has to pay the real bill – the cost in ill-health, soil deterioration and general environmental deterioration which results from the methods used to keep down prices.

That is why Stapledon saw nothing comic in writing the chapter 'Food Considered as a Criterion of Good Government' an essay which I have put in the appendix. The reader who is not interested in scientific breeding for quality and utility can skip these pages: but the close relation between diet and culture, between quality and freshness, and between quality and traditions of skill and place reveals in greater detail the devastation wrought in society by letting its pattern become the victim of economic development for its own sake, a runaway economy.

In 1917 the Government recruited Stapledon for the Food Production Department in London. In the meantime, fretting with impatience and anxiety to help in the war effort, he assisted a wealthy friend to grow more food off the inherently poor land of his estate in Wales. Bligh was a London barrister who wrote books on psychology. At the outbreak of the war he returned to his estate at Builth Wells with the intention of doing his bit by intensive farming of his land. By a stroke of good luck, Stapledon was the man on the spot called in to advise him: thus began a most fruitful partnership in agricultural history, not in terms of output of food but in adventurous experiment and stimulating reflection. Stapledon was immensely impressed by Bligh's freeminded attitude toward techniques: 'Technique is not the prerogative of science: poetry and literature are equally concerned with it. But the scientist is I think far more inclined to let himself become a slave to it. In a discussion on technique, literature and science meet on common and equal ground. This is likely to impress the young scientist: the influence of Bligh was far reaching in this respect.'

After they had finished working in the fields, Stapledon and the Blighs and their friends would 'sit in high-backed chairs drinking Spanish claret or Bristol Cream until well after midnight' interrelating problems of science, literature and politics: often Mrs.Bligh would read poetry — Yeats was her favourite. ('Are poetry and research more closely related than the generality of technological scientists would suppose?') Here Stapledon got a fascinating taste of the quality of life that he admired: a philosophical and yet active atmosphere in which the potentialities of man were brought to bear upon the problems of living the full life. Here was a culture that did not make the practical man reach for his gun or drive the poet out into the cold — an integrated culture. After the war Bligh's estate was to play the part of almost a sub-station in the affairs of the Welsh Plant Breeding Station. Stapledon wanted Bligh's influence to spread to the young scientist under his command.

This is not the place to discuss in detail the experiments undertaken on Bligh's estate. Stapledon tells us that it was here he learnt the uselessness of haphazard experiments. He resolved that he must plan experiments within the framework of a definite philosophy directed from a central point, preferably a research station where control experiments could be conducted at the same time. It was on Bligh's land that Stapledon discovered it was possible to plough up land and re-seed it with grass without an intervening arable crop: 'So there was Bligh in 1919 adopting methods that are now current practice.' Stapledon was also impressed by the fact that Bligh did all this without any Government help or encouragement. 'I always like to think Bligh turned the first war furrow and stubbed the first gorse bush in the interest of winning the war. And still there was no purposeful action on the part of the Government.' This experience led Stapledon to conclude that while government must plan overall action, it must at the same time leave the inventive pioneering types like Bligh free to do a great deal on their own initiative. Stapledon sometimes suspected that Government departments were jealous of such pioneers — for they never seemed to incorporate their work into their own or even acknowledge their achievements. He himself, when an administrator, always tried to harness the work of the pioneer to that of the official research station. He advocated a two-way flow, each learning from the other, in order to break down the separation of the research station from the farm.

The Government of 1914 made little or no attempt to organize the brains of the country for war. 'It is easy to organize bodies just to fill gaps, incredibly difficult to organize brains.' Stapledon was disillusioned by the Food Production Department: it was a high example of bureaucratic muddle. But several things emerged from it of great value to Stapledon — though far too late to help in the war effort. He was sent touring the countryside to report on the best methods of raising productivity, and advised ploughing up the sacred fatting pastures of the Midlands and re-seeding them. 'This was equivalent to dropping a bomb on Whitehall.' It was called impracticable – an accusation which, in time, Stapledon learnt to anticipate and treat ironically. Nevertheless it was impracticable at that time, for good seed did not exist in adequate quantities to sow the pastures down again. Despite the national emergency the old seeds scandal continued: and then, suddenly, authority became convinced of the need to act: 'For a few short weeks it seemed to me I was given command of the whole resources of His Majesty's Government. Fancy waiting until the end of a great war to do it. And then it was done through the influence of a layman – Sir Lawrence Weaver.'

Stapledon extemporized a seeds testing station – in effect the first national seeds testing station, and Stapledon was its first director. A committee was formed to draw up a Testing of Seeds Order. There were twenty representatives of the trade and twelve representing science and Government – 'a nice majority for the trade', Stapledon commented. It was, as can be imagined, a long drawn-out affair with every clause strongly debated: 'a liberal education and something of a shock to a purist and an enthusiast.'

This was the only series of committee meetings that Stapledon ever attended without defaulting, he was so convinced of the need to bring the testing of seeds under legal control. In our own time the control of agricultural chemicals – subject only to a voluntary scheme of testing – provides a parallel. In August 1920 'quite a sensible' Seeds Act found a place on the Statute Book.

The lack of national purpose between the wars was reflected in the absence of a vital relationship between government and commerce. The Government was absorbed in its own – debatable – affairs, while commerce went its undebated way. The combined effect of these two separate activities on the nation as a whole was little regarded. Stapledon wrote (in *Disraeli and the New Age*): 'There had been at least some pretence of aim and purpose during the war. The post-war period was to prove one of hectic endeavour to no particular purpose – hectic and masterly drift.'

He had an intuitive feeling that this lack of sane purpose and creative enthusiasm was in part due to man's increasing alienation from the land and husbandry. He resolved to devote himself to the soil: 'Men and nations could shout themselves hoarse and pull the old order to shreds and tatters, yet the foundation of the new needs must be dug where always foundations must be dug – in the soil itself. . . . I knew that sooner or later even statesmen and reformers would be driven back to mother earth for inspiration and nourishment: in the meantime I was not going to exhaust myself in fruitless and nerve-shattering attempts to keep pace with the march of events.'

Land plays a part in the satisfaction of almost every human need. It provides food and fuel and mineral resources: it is the foundation of our villages and towns and our physical recreations: it gives aesthetic enjoyment. The problems posed by the need to reconcile these conflicting demands upon the land surface challenge the whole cultural values of nations. Our politicians have shown few signs of understanding the urgent priorities involved. When they do (if ever in our age), they will call for a survey of the use of land in terms of human ecology.

In April 1919, when he was thirty-six, Stapledon returned to Aberystwyth to become the first director of the Welsh Plant Breeding Station. 'Although the Government was not interested in helping farming', he observed, 'research was the thing.' And research was largely carried on in the laboratory for its intrinsic interest, expanding like a cancer according to its own Parkinsonian laws, undisciplined by needs beyond its own walls or the uses to which it should be put. An ivory tower research station seemed harmless enough and was a sop to the conscience of those who did not want to see a revival in farming.

Stapledon had very different ideas. He wanted his station to be ecological, staffed with a team of experts who would share knowledge with each other for the purpose of tackling problems: he was not content with the essential specialists. He also wanted to get out of the laboratory into the fields and try out the results of research on the farms amid the multiform influences of nature: he wanted to find out what the farmer needed and suggest what he could do. He wanted a network of vital relationships between research, farming, commerce and Government. Yes, particularly Government, for changes in farming techniques and methods change the shape

30

of villages and affect the lives of country people. Would this progress be integrated into a sane and balanced pattern of living, or would it be allowed to continue the prevailing haphazard growth — expansion without form — that results from always giving way to the greatest pressure, which is usually the profit from land speculation? For example, would new methods be directed to repopulating or depopulating the hills still further? For, as we have seen, if improved methods of production are used to increase output with fewer men, then, from the ecological point of view, the situation is worse than it was before the new methods were discovered. The proper alternative to this would be that where cultivated land falls into disuse as a result of technical changes, the land is preserved in the most suitable rural form for the benefit of visitors. This is an ecological use of land in terms of human need. But the abuse of science and technology by the unrestrained search for profitable commercial applications leaves humanity at the mercy of its ever changing environment. Until new techniques have been considered in terms of human ecology by teams of qualified people from many fields of life, the progress of science is likely to intensify human misery faster than it alleviates it. Man's control of his environment has now reached a point in which man becomes his own problem and his own enemy to a greater extent than nature was ever his problem and his enemy.

For twenty-five years Stapledon struggled to impose upon research and Government policy an ecological philosophy. He attacked on two fronts, by showing what he could do with limited means and by constant lecturing and talking and writing. In shaping his own research work he turned a blind eye to official directives, often spending money assigned for one project on another. He integrated administration with research. He chose his staff personally and refused to advertise or hold appointment boards — he had refused to accept the post of director if he was appointed in this way. He considered that direct appointment was a gesture of confidence of inestimable value in establishing good staff relations. His staff were chosen from among the sons of Welsh farmers who knew how to handle a plough as well as pass an examination; who were practically acquainted from childhood with the problems of the land where they would work. Most of them passed through the school of botany at the University College where he was able to form a personal judgment of their character and capabilities. In this way he built up a team that was inspired by intense personal loyalty to him, to the research station and to the aims of its work. During the whole period of his director-ship only one key man left — and his place was taken by his brother. Stapledon took a keen interest in the relationship of administration to creative work: he doubted if an admin-istrator who did not take part in some branch of the work himself was capable of creative administration. The pure administrator had the same defects as the pure scientist. To keep his hand and eye in and to retain the feel of research work so that he could sympathize with the problems of his staff, he continued with his own cocksfoot breeding even when the station began to expand. He suspected that if an organization became so large that the chief administrators were cut off from the practical work of the organization, it would gradually begin to lose its creative zest and degenerate into safe jobs and sinecures masked by a proliferation of specialized scientific publications. 'Everything bores me in research', he wrote, 'unless I can see the aim that it serves.' He tried to unify the station as it were by a threefold knot that held together research, administration and rural life, which included the farmer's problems and the distribution of new varieties of seed through the trade.

It was obvious that a research station of this kind would soon enter into competition with the trade: no one seemed to have the slightest idea how the new strains of grasses, clovers and cereals should be distributed. Stapledon got the impres-sion that the Government considered that research should be an academic exercise and that to bring it into contact with commerce was indecent. Even the problem of growing on new stocks involved contracts with farmers, that is, contact with private enterprise, and the Government frowned upon it. There is no time here to relate the long and amusing story of how Stapledon wriggled his way round all the difficulties, but it is one more example of following the path from segregation to integration. By means of *ad hoc* organizations such as seeds associations miracles of improvisation were performed that turned a blind eye to official regulations.

What in fact did the Welsh Plant Breeding Station do, and what was its plan of campaign? First of all, it is important to note that this was a virgin field of research: everything had to be done from scratch. Nevertheless the movement toward this kind of research was spreading all over Europe, especially the investigation of the genetic aspects of plant life. Stapledon had already visited research stations in Sweden. The emphasis in the Welsh Plant Breeding Station was upon grass and its place within methods of husbandry. We have already seen how this problem attracted Stapledon's attention in the Cotswolds where he first became interested in the individual plant, its history and its relation to its environment. This was followed by his experience of the operation of nature in the wild, semi-wild and cultivated state on a vast scale in Wales, then by his experience of seed testing. All this varied experience began to form into a pattern of action for co-ordinating the activities of man and nature for the purpose of raising the fertility and productivity of the land to its optimum.[1] Even before he joined the Food Production Department in 1917 he had experimented on his own with plant breeding: it was an experiment with the seeds of red clover that gave him 'one of those shocks without which nobody ever really learns'. He has left a fascinating description of this in a lecture 'Ecology and the Breeding of Herbage Plants', that he gave to his students at Aberystwyth in 1935 — published in *The Way of the Land*. 'When I was just a student', he told them, 'cocksfoot was just cocksfoot and red clover just red clover, and for several years I taught students and lectured to farmers on this fantastically false foundation. Then (in 1917) I had the shock of my life and in one short half-hour I acquired the modern biological outlook and realized that living things if at all highly organized are true to pattern, yes, but only within limits. I was made to realize that within themselves they are unique, individualistic, and, one might almost say, egotistical, in all their more subtle and vital characteristics.'

He had arranged for a big set-out of single plants of different lots of seed of red clover. Shortly afterwards he was seconded

1 The most that can be produced consistent with lasting fertility. Hence not the same as maximum.

to the Food Production Department in London. When he came back to Aberystwyth for a week-end visit he looked at his plants: 'That was my shock. That was my first acquaintance with Montgomery red clover as a clover apart and unto itself unique. Unique as a group and a class, mind you, for no two plants of Montgomery clover are precisely and absolutely the same.' He went on: 'I am determined to make you appreciate this matter of uniqueness and difference, for it is the great biological truth upon which all progress and all fun depend. Life is only tolerable, and learning only possible, because we are different.'

Similarity: difference — the biological contrary. To treat all men as the same (equal) is as absurd as treating them all as absolutely different. Thus the administrative problem of integrating the antithesis, function: personality. In the highly systematized modern world function is suppressing personality. Men and plants are both subject to this biological antithesis. The function of a new individual plant may not be immediately apparent: or a new plant may suggest a new function: or a new function may be needed and no plant as yet exist with the individual characteristics capable of fulfilling it. 'Hunt the exception,' said Stapledon, 'it may contain the genes you need.' That applies to persons as well as to plants.

The plant breeding programme was, then, based upon integrating plant individuality with agricultural function. Previously plants had been forced into function and left to survive and produce as best they could — just as people are forced into functions in large organizations with little respect for the idea of adapting the function to the personality. I mention this to show the interplay of biological thought between the husbandry of the fields and the husbandry of the files. In the same way examinations standardize — they do not reveal — personality. Men and grasses are both cross-fertile: their infinite genetic variety offers untold opportunity to the creators of culture and society as well as to agriculturalists. Creative progress is arrested by imposing the conscious rules of man rigidly upon his unknown potentialities. The methods by which we assess each other are out of tune with our human nature.

The theory of evolution was based upon the simple observation that plants and animals adapt themselves to localities in order to survive. Recent genetic theory suggests that the limits of adaptation are more narrow than was previously assumed. When too great a change is required too quickly the species is more likely to die out than to conform. Nevertheless varied environments can produce new strains within a basic variety. Stapledon made the existence of different strains within varieties of plant bearing the same name the basis of his search for new plant individualities to satisfy the needs of the farmer. (He alludes to his methods in the essay in the appendix.) Nature, man and animal working together sort out various groups with defined tendencies, known as ecotypes.

So Stapledon grew plants of the same variety but from different localities in groups of 500. These groups were large enough for it to be possible to discern the characteristic manner in which the plants as groups differed from one another. Plants that looked likely to provide a useful strain were propagated again. Without a clear knowledge of what the farmer needed, Stapledon considered that all the wizardry of genetics would lead nowhere. There would be no aim and no criteria for selection. It is true that Stapledon accepted a measure of selfimposed specialization when he concentrated the work of the station on the improvement and management of grassland. But he had already seen the disastrous consequences of two-department farming with its permanent grass mentality. Grass was related to the whole surrounding environment and to the crops grown before and after it. Thus, on a basis of alternate husbandry with oats as a nurse crop, he undertook cereal breeding.

The permanent grass mentality in farming is analogous to the permanent staff mentality which also tends to two-department husbandry: administration on one side and creative workers on the other, and no alternate husbandry. A deadly monoculture blights organizations with the permanent staff philosophy.[1]

The immense success of the station in breeding the now famous Aberystwyth strains of grasses and oats culminated in

[1] There has been an immense improvement in the management of permanent grass since Stapledon's time. Stapledon's major point is that grass should never be taken for granted. Ploughing-up should not be a dogma.

the Fourth International Grassland Congress, with Stapledon as president, which was held in Aberystwyth in 1937. This was in many respects the end of the grassland revolution: it had become accepted practice; it was constitutional. Tributes came to Stapledon from all over the world. The grassland revolution of the twentieth century had a nexus of causes, but this can be said of Stapledon, that no one else was so successful in showing how all these forces could be interrelated and made to serve mankind. This was generally acknowledged and made him the symbolic leader of the transformation. A year later, with war inevitable, the Government called belatedly for a British Grassland Survey under Stapledon's direction. The results gave them a shock. Stapledon left Wales in 1940 and took over the direction of the Grassland Improvement Station on the clay soils of the Midlands. From there he led the plough-up campaign, touring round the country and addressing mass meetings of farmers. Farming had scarcely improved between the wars: there was as much permanent grass in 1938 as in 1914, but the difference was that agricultural research combined with the experience of the last war — which had taught some members of the Government that agriculture must be brought under a measure of direction — now made it possible to go into planned action and throw the resources of agriculture as it were into the battle line. With a more far-seeing Government a great deal more might have been done. However, in terms of British economic policy everyone who understood the situation breathed a sigh of relief that anything truly constructive was done by the Government at all.

Stapledon was immensely impressed by the work of the War Agricultural Committees in solving the problems of combining freedom with direction and centralization with work on the spot. He saw the immense value of combining elected members with appointed Government officials together in a team. After the war when the W.A.E.C.s were disbanded he conside.'ed that they had given a remarkable example of inspiration and work that might be copied in peace time to solve many of the vast problems of social reconstruction that remain to be done — as urgent in many ways as those of war. The secrets of co-operation without dictatorship that had been discovered in the war were allowed to lapse in peace time when the country no longer had any unifying aims, and political squabbles among ourselves lost us the opportunity to give the lead to Europe in reconstructing itself as an integrated society. 'We were great enough', wrote Stapledon, 'to have given the lead to Europe. Instead of that, we simply squabbled among ourselves.'

At the end of the war Stapledon was weary of technological work. His mind was distracted by his conviction that we should prepare imaginatively for the new age of integration that should renew and inspire Western civilization after the war. He wrote *Disraeli and the New Age* working late into the night. The only official work that would have tempted him would have been to direct a vast research station that integrated rural life, rural industry, farming, holiday camps and a national park together in one vast enterprise on a basis of human ecology. He had striven for years to raise the money to do this on a part private and part government basis. As he observed sardonically: 'It had not the glamour of the profit motive: if it had, I might have succeeded.' It was in this great agro-social experiment that his heart really lay. In his book *The Land: Today and Tomorrow* he had outlined his plans and made an appeal to large industrial firms to co-operate in bringing industry into the countryside in such a way as to allow for holiday camps and country interests to be encouraged among their workers. He believed that this partial dispersal of industry could be made to pay as well as providing a healthy solution to the over-concentration of urban development. In his chapters in this book on integration he carries these ideas forward into the whole countryside, as apart from the special areas that could be designated as national parks. His idea of the national park was not that of an area kept as a rural museum: it was an experiment in rural reconstruction. And as we can now see, he was right. It is going to be impossible to immobilize national parks as pleasure grounds. It is far better to plan them from the first in dynamic terms before piecemeal development ruins them from every point of view. In one of his essays in 'The Way of the Land' Stapledon points out that the frustration of the need for wild and open countryside in modern man is as great as that of his sexual frustration and will in time probably become considerably greater. It is this frustration which accounts for as much neurosis as anything else in our neurosis-ridden age. To bring town and country close together again without losing the character of either, to give the industrial worker the access to countryside that he had in mediaeval times, will be to restore a healthy psyche to contemporary man, renew his will to work and break down the massive and menacing consolidation of a proletariat that pursues affluence for its own sake because it has no means of satisfying the basic emotions on which man, without realizing it, has depended since time immemorial for his happiness. These basic emotions are largely instinctive and related to the unconscious. As he grew older and read widely in every field of science and history and literature, Stapledon was convinced that one of the most destructive of the many barriers that man had raised was the barrier between the conscious and the unconscious. This had the effect of segregating and cutting off from use the instinctive powers of his nature: they had become an enemy instead of a friend, something archaic and dangerous instead of something inspiring and useful. The reinstatement of the instinctive became one of his primary aims and he devised techniques for integrating the conscious and un-conscious in his own life. (See Chapter 4, *Nature of Progress.*) Nothing should be investigated as complete-in-itself because part of its nature is likely to be latent and not manifested. When the latent becomes manifest, the surrounding causal nexus (with which science is concerned in making its predictions) is changed and possibilities hitherto considered inconceivable become possible. Stapledon's growing conversion to the importance of the unconscious and instinctive was a consequence of experiences in his personal life, one of which I have described in my biography of him.

In a sense, this observation of Stapledon's brings his thought back to the centre. The last chapter of this book is a postscript in which he describes his hopes for what he calls his dream of a re-created Britain. This dream is the dream of a very practical man who knew something about turning dreams into realities: his grassland revolution was a dream that became real, or perhaps it would be better to say that it was part of a dream that became manifest, while the rest remains latent. The element of dream is the latent element in a practical proposition, and it is real or unreal, sentimental or practical, to the extent that the dreamer is in touch with the depths of human nature. I am sure myself that Stapledon's dream is the suppressed dream of those who are being engulfed by conurbia. If that is the case two courses remain open to governments: one is to take account of the dream and try to find practical means of satisfying it: the other is to adopt an attitude of wanton obliviousness and wait for the suppressed passions of mankind to explode. A revolution of the explosive kind brings as much ill as good in its train: what is needed is a far-sighted and constructive revolution based upon understanding, and this book gives us some ecological principles to civilize our revolution. This brings me to a point that will worry a great many people who have had experience of unconscious surges overwhelming the conscious life of individuals and nations. This can be so terrifying that surely no one in their senses should advocate that we encourage it? Now anyone who reads Chapter 4 carefully will see that it suggests the only way in which these horrors can be exorcised from the history of mankind — that is by training the unconscious, so that it is no longer a mad, unwieldy beast but a sensitive, enthralling and magical servant. Many of the fairy stories of antiquity are concerned with the secrets of this. The unconscious is a flow of genius, good or evil according to how it is used, which is required to carry men and nations into the realization of impracticable achievements. It is bound up with love and the community spirit: its negative expression is hate and the comradeship of hate. Unfortunately, for the majority of people this inspiration is felt only in moments of eroticism or in the comradeship of war. What is needed now is a constructive philosophy of the instinctive which will enable us to evoke and train this element in our lives which has been variously called mystical, supernatural, occult and psychic, because it wells over the threshold of the unconscious and seems to take the conscious mind into its possession. Those who have trained themselves to cope with this element, and who are not afraid of it, expand their conscious apprehension of life, increase their spontaneity and, because they learn to be expansive rather than depressed, they attain to reason and wisdom beyond the reach of most of us.

The Situation Now.

The underground currents of ecology have now broken through into news: last year, for the first time, the word ecology appeared in newspapers without parenthetical explanations of what it meant. Like all words that pass into current speech, it now has so many intellectual and emotional associations that it is beyond exact definition: whatever the purists may think that is so much the better. It has now acquired the power to suggest an attitude of mind: it is crystalising into an ideal, though presented as a science. People begin to understand that we must reassess our world from the ecological point of view, even though they can only vaguely tell us what that is. They feel that ecology stands for being more human, more concerned with the beauty and healthiness of life, less about profit and economic expansion for its own sake. The infiltration of ecology into our thinking has made us realise that economic expansion is not necessarily the solution to our ills: indeed it may be creating our ills. The 'goods' promised us by industry may be accompanied by so many 'bads' that even economically we lose out. Chemical labour saving techniques on the farm may be more expensive in the long run than taking men out of the chemical factories and putting them back on the land. That is why ecology is becoming a battle-cry and rallying thoughtful and sensitive people in a demand for change. Ecology is becoming a focus for those with religious, scientific and political vocations who have observed that their interests overlap in the need to create and conserve an environment in which the human spirit flourishes. Has a time come, we wonder, when it is not so much man that is wrongly made as his new environment? Ecology is the flag under which people who believe this is true can gather, however far apart their daily lives. Human ecology means seeing things whole and that means co-operative effort in which everyone pools his particular insight.

We have had an industrial revolution, we must have a human revolution. We have heard of the brave attempt to humanise the face of communism. Is it not the case that all the industrial civilisations need humanising? Or should we say rehumanising? — brought back to the original ideal of the industrial revolution as a means of increasing the freedom of the ordinary man and adding to his major satisfactions — not increasing his secondary ones at their expense.

Faith in unrestrained productivity and ecology are incompatible. We must learn now how to create and order a stable state on an ecological model. As explained at the beginning of this introduction, the earth's non-renewable resources are being mined to extinction. Consequently we must use them with thrift, allocating careful priorities if we are to keep our productivity at a tolerable level: otherwise we shall go back to the 18th century without the beauty of the 18th century and with a 20th century population. Our present industrial methods cannot last another hundred years at the present rate of consumption of fuels, minerals, and even renewable resources which are not given time to restore what has been taken from them — as with whales, wild life and so on. The biological cycle is disregarded in the lust for profit.

When large numbers of people suddenly realise they are threatened, they will become desperate and angry: that is how violent revolutions start. We must hope that the ecological revolution will be a revolution of persuasion by ideas: but if it is not, it will be a revolution of the traditional kind. A class of people will be removed, often, no doubt, with injustice, who are thought to stand in the way of the welfare and survival of the rest of mankind.

Already in America 'Ecology Action' has become a slogan for student revolutionaries. The British Society for Social Responsibility in Science, mainly young people, seems to have established itself. These young people are, after all, the next generation who will suffer more than my generation for the mistakes we have made. As far as I can see, the only chance my generation — the middle aged — has of saving the day without earning the scorn and contempt of its children, is to support the voluntary associations concerned with environmental conservation. These associations are uniting at last, thanks to the leadership of the Duke of Edinburgh, who has realised the urgency of the situation and spoken out bravely, often at the risk of offending the complacent. The voluntary associations (such as the Soil Association, which ever since the war has urged the ecological outlook now become fashionable and been dubbed 'cranky' for it) are mostly composed of middle class people with liberal or conservative views and a christian conscience. They believe in reason, in order and democratic change. If governments do not listen to them, it will be their fault if the inevitable revolution becomes destructive as well as constructive.

The Countryside in 1970 Conference which the Duke inaugurated has given birth to CoEnCo – the Committee for Environmental Conservation – which has 18 outstanding representatives who in turn speak for several hundred voluntary bodies. They should be a powerful and law abiding pressure group bringing informed opinion to bear on the government of the day. They have set up several committees of investigation into environmental problems for this reason.

The government usually listens first to the economic arguments and the interests of the major industries and only later to ordinary intelligence and humanity and authentic science as opposed to government science policies. Therefore the public, as the representative of human feeling and truth, must speak up and protest against the inhumanities of the ambitious and their distortion of reality – as Stapledon discusses this in the chapter 'Hand and Eye, Head and Heart'. They can only do this through voluntary societies founded for that purpose. Then the government must listen to human ecology not to inhuman economics.

Those who believe in human ecology must speak up, protest and attack. The survival of our humanness depends on it; more than that, ours is the age with the greatest cause of all time – the survival of the planet earth itself from destruction by a dehumanised mankind.

beer, all products of the soil, had to be cheap, no matter where or how the parent crops were grown, no matter at all if the very character of the farmer was destroyed.

The soil is not the only raw material that is limited in quantity, but it is unique in two quantitative respects. If we were to denude the world of certain raw materials – of gold, for instance – of truth we should not be any the worse for it. In the case of a large number of raw materials, if driven to it, we should be able to devise substitutes. Already we see opening before us prospects of 'manufacturing' energy on a scale undreamed of, and by processes which foreshadow a revolution in all our modes and methods. With this rising surge of new knowledge and new technique, no man can see an end to the possibilities of substitution; but the manufacture of a substitute for the soil on a sufficiently large scale is hardly likely to be within human competency. It is true that the method of growing crops by water culture – the so-called hydroponics – is gaining ground and may well become a considerable commercial undertaking: but it would require great optimism and a far-ranging imagination to envisage hydroponics rendering the cultivation of the soil unnecessary. Even so plants must have food, and supplies of some of the necessary elements are not unlimited, it we are willing to think in terms of thousands of years ahead. Thus, as a raw material, the soil does stand in a class to itself, and not only in virtue of its inherent characteristics. Food, including water, it will be generally conceded, is the first need of man and therefore the soil must be man's most treasured possession: so he who tends the soil wisely and with care is assuredly the foremost among men. This care of the soil emphasizes another striking difference between the good earth and the great majority of raw materials. The husbandman sees his product through to a finish, nearer to the finally retailed commodity than is given to most of those who win raw materials from quarry, pit or mine, from the atmosphere or water. This creates interest in the daily task and invites the exercise of the imagination, which is of high importance in influencing the character of those concerned. The skilful coalminer works his bountiful seam to the end: the thrifty husbandman wins his crop and creates yet more bounty in the process. What a world of difference: the one

44

man with his own hands only destructive: the other, if destructive (he garners his crop but usually when it has run its course) also and always constructive.

The mainspring of my argument is that agriculture implies so vastly more than the growing of crops, the care of livestock and the production of food. Food matters profoundly. Human nutrition, it is at last realized, is at the core of human health and happiness, and probably is also not far from the core of social and national stability. In a sane world food would be the background against which all international arrangements were made. In private life food is used not only to feed the inner man, but to nourish cordiality, hospitality, good-will and friendship. We live in a dark age with fitful gleams of light penetrating to the depths of human conscience. No gleam is brighter than that which has reflected the conscience of the United Nations in creating the Food and Agriculture Organization, a tangible and visible picture of representatives from upwards of twenty nations joined in permanent conclave to make proposals of an international character relative to food and agriculture. If this is earnest of a change of heart in international relations, and if at last man has learned to be guided in his international actions by the same feelings that have created what is best in domestic life and social intercourse, then indeed there is some hope for the world. There is no hope whatsoever for the rural-agricultural of any country, unless all countries understand precisely what is at stake in every respect, and unless world arrangements make possible a sound food policy and a balanced agriculture in each separate country of the world. In this crucial matter, great and small, we stand or fall together. Agriculture as such, the agriculture potential of this country, methods and systems of farming, certain aspects of modern technique, human nutrition, food in times of war – all these subjects and many besides will need to be considered in no mean detail: but I shall propose to deal with them in sympathy with what I consider to be an overruling necessity: a better balancing between the rural-agricultural and the urban-industrial and on an entirely new basis the world over. I continually harp upon the theme 'the world over'; but, at the risk of jarring reiteration, this theme, of necessity, will run like a connecting thread through most of my chapters: for I am convinced that no one country can hope to achieve for itself an ideal agricultural-rural-industrial-urban balance, unless all countries are like-minded; and, without an all-round willingness to assist rather than thwart, suffering humanity is unlikely to reach beyond good ideas and noble words.

Nothing in life is more difficult than to achieve balance: it is easy to talk glibly about a balanced mind, a just balance of interests, or of the use of one's time and energies. I fully realize this, and I am painfully aware that I have set myself an exceedingly difficult task; but I can at least attempt to express opinions, based on deep conviction, supported by considerable experience in some directions, and by a long period in which my mind has been engrossed, now in agitated thinking, now in quite contemplation, on all that is implied by 'balance'. I am persuaded that if a man has devoted his life to a certain line of work and to a certain trend of thought, and if this work and thought culminate in deep conviction, then that deep conviction as such means something: means more perhaps than the facts and arguments brought forward on paper in support of the conviction.

The question we shall have to try and answer is what precisely it is that we want to balance, and why? and, then, how?

We have two chief aspects of the problem to consider: firstly, the just and balanced use of the land surface of a country, and, secondly, the just and balanced use of the man-power of a country. Even rural land is not the sole prerogative of the farmer and the countryman; we have to ensure balance between the needs of the farmer, the needs of industry and the needs of the people at large: and most important of all we have to try and seek ways and means of making those needs as far as possible compatible — that is the way to attain balance. Ours is a small island with a very large population and it has been man-ridden and man-handled from end to end for centuries; consequently balance is now doubly hard to realize and we have lost beyond all hope of repair much of the natural beauty and wild life proper to our beautiful country. Against this we have to set the fact that the British Commonwealth is large and contains huge areas still in a natural condition, and that distance is now to be measured not in miles but in hours. Land balance could therefore be arranged to much better advantage on a Commonwealth-wide than on an England-Scotland-Wales-wide basis. But probably to attempt this on a comprehensive scale is no longer possible, except, perhaps, in one direction: to use the Commonwealth as a holiday ground. We are air-minded and air-borne, and there is something in our blood that cries out for the exhilaration to be derived from the unalloyed contemplation of glorious scenery, of open spaces and wild life, something that drives us to escape for a while from the works of man and to commune with species other than our own, and with the natural scene. The opportunities that exist within the Commonwealth for safeguarding areas as nature reserves and sanctuaries, and as national parks on a grand scale, are of an entirely different order from those now open to us in Great Britain itself. Directly or indirectly the hand of man has touched every yard of country here at home and vandalism has swept like a devastating fire through the length and breadth of the land. Not a moment is to be lost if we are to nourish one of our most compelling and one of our most character-forming urges. Reserves sufficiently large to meet biological requirements to the full are still a possibility in lands overseas, while selection of suitable tracts could be made from a wide enough range of characteristic types of country fairly to represent the grandeur and fickleness of nature's moods and tenses. From the travel point of view the Commonwealth grows 'smaller' every day and already it is no larger in travel hours than Britain was a hundred and fifty years ago.

In our discussion on land for holidays and for reserves, we shall obviously be driven to consider overseas resources as well as those at home. To do so will, however, also be essential for this further reason: because a better balancing of the urban and rural in Great Britain will call for a drastic intensification of farming practices on our marginal and waste lands. This will become apparent as we develop our theme.

The crux of the human problem is the just and balanced use of man- and woman-power: it is from this point of view that agriculture and certain other related industries and callings appear to me to assume their greatest importance. We (if 'we' are human and interested in the sort of lives human individuals live) should assuredly judge the value of any particular employment by two entirely different standards of comparison — shall we say the vertical and the horizontal — and then as far as is possible arrive at a fair 'weighted' ('weighted' it must be) average between our two methods of assessment.

By the vertical I mean the influence on the individual, as a person and as a member of society, of the occupation to which he devotes his working hours. By the horizontal I mean the value to the community of the work done by the individual. This differentiation raises a host of issues every one of which is fundamental to human progress, human happiness and human stability. It raises questions affecting our ideas as to education, character, reason and instinct: as to what we mean by progress, by useful, by the good life, by the full life. Abruptly we are brought up against fateful questions. In what direction are we heading, in what direction do we wish to head, in what direction is it desirable that we should head? All these difficult matters and questions will need to be explored, because our attitude towards them all influences, or should profoundly influence, our attitude towards agriculture and the land. I do not wish unduly to anticipate, but a few points by way of introduction to what is to follow can usefully be made at this juncture. By all accounts the age that is dawning is to be one of all-round and perpetual employment — employment at all costs and at any price. At the outset then we should be wise to realize that every trade, profession and occupation goes a very long way — some further than others — to imposing a way of life upon those engaged in it. Let us realize further that the character, morale and purposefulness of a people is determined to an overwhelming degree by the sum of the ways of life of the population.

This raises three questions in particular: the first, the desirability of intense research as to the influence of the manifold employments on ways of life. Most certainly it would be found that some occupations made for satisfactory ways of life, others for ways so utterly unsatisfactory that the products or services giving the employment should if possible be discarded.

Thus the second question: Of the products and services that almost of necessity engender sub-human ways of life, which are really essential to the full life of the community as a whole? The third question is this: Is it in sober truth possible by means of formal education and welfare services to counter satisfactorily what may be evil and soul-destroying in the less desirable ways of life imposed by modern needs and whims?

Formal education and acute experience are as poles apart. Character, good or bad, is built, not on class and lecture-room education, but on acute experience; and acute experience is an everyday and an all-day affair, a lifelong affair, an affair of our way of life.

Even in the absence of the necessary research, we can still make certain important distinctions. We can, for example, classify occupations: (*a*) According to the extent to which the machine dominates the man, or *vice versa*. (*b*) Whether the worker is wholly or mostly out of doors, or wholly or mainly indoors. (*c*) If out of doors, whether the worker is (1) merely subjected to the vagaries of the weather, like the roadman, or those whose care is railway lines: or (2) only contends with the forces of nature, like the seafaring man, or those who quarry surface minerals: or (3) consciously manipulates the forces of nature to creative ends like the farmer and the forester.

We shall argue, and with considerable factual support, that acute experience is favoured by consciously manipulating or actively contending with the forces of nature, and is deadened in proportion as the worker is dominated by the machine. We shall pursue the implications of these deductions in a number of directions, most of which will bring us back to the soil and agriculture.

I would wish strongly to emphasize that my approach to the problems under discussion is advisedly a-economic: this does not mean that economic aspects will not be considered, but it does mean this: there are certain issues that should not be decided solely on economic grounds. For example, suppose it were proved that in the human interest and on vertical grounds certain occupations (as a hypothetical case those connected with agriculture) should be extended, then economic arguments ought not to be permitted to come into the question: only direct and factual economic necessity should be allowed to count. Surely, in our consideration of ways of life, we should be acutely alive to the fact that the full potentiality of human character and human greatness can never be cast from a single mould or from comparatively few and remarkably similar moulds? We shall have come to a sorry pass when human beings consist of two dominant classes: one that sits all day at office tables and the other at factory benches. That in very truth answers my earlier question as to 'the direction in which we are heading'.

In this introductory chapter I have no more than tried to indicate (and with the minimum of anticipation) what this book is about, what I am aiming at, and the fields that I shall have to cover.

To sum up, I think it all boils down to this: How to steer a middle course between the all-out, and in itself immensely attractive, ruralism and craftsmanship of the countryside as depicted and advocated by deep thinking and keenly observant men like H. J. Massingham and Rolf Gardiner[1] and those who march in step with them, and the all-out mechanization of agriculture and industrialization and urbanization of rural areas. That is the problem, a problem which, in my view, is the most important of all the manifold problems which confront this country, as it does almost every other country of the world today. To find the correct answer is as difficult as it is urgent: it is doubly difficult because, in the last resort, it depends not only upon a wiser and probably a more guarded exploitation of natural and artificial resources, but equally on the cultivation of a new attitude of mind toward exploitation. The future of civilization and the destiny of man tremble in the balance. In the one scale, the soil, the natural and the spirit: in the other, concrete, the artificial and creature comfort. The master problem before mankind is, I repeat, to achieve a correct balance between the rural-agricultural and the urban-industrial. To endeavour to help define 'correct' is the heavy burden of my book. The substantiation of the case for a better balancing of the rural and urban, and also some indication as to the wisest means of attempting to achieve this end are to be sought in a fuller understanding of the

[1] Now Chairman European Landscape Committee.

forces at work within ourselves, and of those forces operating in the complicated environments in which we now live. To which of these forces is man compelled to submit, from which can he escape and which can he control? Holding strongly that the biological approach can throw a flood of light on these subjects, I deem it essential to devote a large proportion — unduly large, some may think — of my book to a fairly detailed consideration of the human situation as it appears to a biologist looked at against the background of environment.

CHAPTER 2

THE METHOD AND PURPOSE OF HUMAN ECOLOGY

The principle of balance and integration demands research into man's whole nature and all its interrelationships with the environment

---

' 'Tis but a part we see, and not a whole.'

ALEXANDER POPE

'There is a unity of the body with the environment, as well as a unity of the body and soul into one person.'

A. N. WHITEHEAD

MY PRIMARY interest is the proper use of land surface in relation to human life, and the influence of association with nature in the raw on human behaviour and character. So this book is deeply concerned with humanism. H. V. Routh has said: 'By humanism I mean the study of man as revealed in men. . . .' Jacques Maritain takes us a little further along the road I wish to explore. He says: 'Humanism tends essentially to render man more human and to manifest his original greatness by enabling him to partake of everything in nature and in history capable of enriching him. It requires both that man develops the latent tendencies he possesses, his creative powers and the life of reason, and that he works to transform into instruments of his liberty the forces of the physical universe.'

Man cannot understand himself, or reveal his potentialities, unless he realizes that his environment is a part of himself and he himself but a part of his environment. This statement introduces the biological point of view, which suggests that Maritain has perhaps not gone quite far enough. No concept of humanism, I believe, can be complete, unless the two-way influence of environment is stressed. If this is so, we must think of human affairs in terms of human ecology. To do so is to study man as revealed in his infinite responses to the manifold stimuli of environment. The myriad possibilities within man himself and the myriad influences of his environment constitute an all-embracing flux, in which man persists in regarding himself as the central figure. He is the central figure only in so far as the onus of coming to satisfactory terms with his environment is placed upon himself by virtue of his reason, creativeness, will and spiritual intuition. Man is not immune from environmental conditions, be he sage, saint or reprobate. He can isolate himself from many natural impacts, and create for himself almost any number of new and artificial impacts, but from environment he can never escape. It is hard for man to draw up a reliable debit and credit account of the gains and losses which result from his wilful tampering with his natural surroundings. On biological grounds one would expect signs of maladjustment to reveal themselves if the environmental conditions are made to differ too much from those to which man was originally heir. We must, however, make generous allowance for the creative faculty, perhaps the most compelling of man's attributes, and for his remarkable powers of adaptability.

Even granted this compensation, it is the bounden duty of the biologist to put up the warning finger and peremptorily to command: *Not too far too fast.* Any unbiased study of social conditions suggests that the pace at which man is tampering with his environment has completely outstripped his capacity for adjustment. He must slacken his pace. He must cry halt to all fundamental research in the physical sciences, or learn, while yet there is time, how to adjust himself more quickly to ever-changing conditions. No matter what the outcome, there is high inspiration in the fact that his actions are so dominated by the creative impulse, that *Homo* would willingly commit suicide rather than abandon any of his adventures in the fields of the unknown.

It is therefore only to adjustment that we can look for salvation. This adjustment can be sought in two directions, the one by so altering the environment that harmful impacts are counterbalanced, the other by developing further powers of adaptability within ourselves. Broadly speaking, all the

E

53

tremendous changes that man has wrought in his environment in recent times have arisen from research in the physical sciences and from clever exploitation of the new knowledge. The changes have been physical and material rather than biological and vital. The internal combustion engine, with tractor, motor-car and airplane has followed too rapidly in the wake of the steam-engine: wireless too rapidly in the wake of the telephone; new alloys too rapidly in the wake of steel; concrete and fabricated materials too rapidly in the wake of bricks and mortar. At last the sheer weight of physical and material impacts has caused us, almost subconsciously (and this is in itself a measure of the danger) to assess human progress in terms of comfort and gadgets. Here, then, perhaps, is the key to all our troubles, and at least a partial answer to the questions which by implication I put forward in my first chapter. First, to take long and research views, we see the need for strengthening the resources of the biological sciences by every means in our power and for bringing man himself more definitely under the purview of these sciences. Quite recently, however, physics has given biology a lead in the matter of technique appropriate to the study of life: the great and frightening advances in physics have been due to a growing tendency to break away from a rigid fragmentation and to bring together in a single, harmonious and well coordinated team men working in apparently disconnected fields. Biological sciences can only make the stupendous progress necessary, if man is to keep pace with the advances made by the physical sciences, by an altogether closer integration between its branches, and by a greater willingness to study *problems* rather than *subjects*. Since man himself is deeply involved — man who, because of his conscious mind, has always before his mind a mirror, blurred and misty at present, of what goes on within himself — no science is of equal importance to psychology. Consequently, in the realms of research likely to assist man to achieve the best mutual adjustment between himself and his environment, results of unprecedented fruitfulness must follow from a closer integration of psychology with other (and I say 'other' advisedly) branches of biology.

We must here note a fundamental difference between the

physical and biological sciences as they influence the affairs of man; particularly as they affect the methods he uses in handling the soil, plants, animals and himself. In the physical field we need have no exaggerated fears as to the validity of our facts and assumptions and no allowance need be made for what we do not know. If mistakes are made and false assumptions acted upon, the lines of inquiry concerned will not yield results in terms of new knowledge that can be made to contribute something additional to the physical content of the environment. In the physical sciences it is the end stages of pure and technical research that directly influence man: the radio, high explosives, the aeroplane. Bad science – organized ignorance – and bad reasoning may delay the appearance of these and kindred masterpieces of ingenuity, but the bad science and bad reasoning carry within themselves no danger to humanity: it is not they that are lethal. In parenthesis we may here remark that because good physical sciences and inspired reasoning have resulted in high explosives, and other inventions with equally dangerous properties, it is not to be laid at the door of this science if man misuses them. If the blame can legitimately be laid at the door of any science, that science is the infant psychology, which has not yet accumulated enough evidence to show man how to control the more vicious of his urges.

Now the facts and assumptions of biology cannot with safety be left to stand alone. To date most of these facts and assumptions have resulted from the well-tried method of fragmentation. Life is, however, maintained by the delicate interaction of myriads of factors; it follows, therefore, that results arrived at by the study of factors *in vacuo* (or, for that matter, *in vitro*) may not be entirely applicable to life in action. It is the intricate interplay between thousands, nay millions, of factors operating under the totality of the conditions in which each individual organism has its being that makes it difficult to arrive at a reliable technique for biology and which, failing such a technique, renders suspect so many of its facts, findings, and assumptions. Adequately to study the natural interplay of factors under normal conditions, and by accepted scientific methods which demand control and counter-observations, may not prove to be possible. It is, therefore,

scarcely thinkable that man will ever be able to devise sufficiently reliable experiments *accurately* to study the interplay
between *all* factors under *all* conditions. There is hard irony
in this: for it is only by a full knowledge of the interaction of
all factors that man can reach safe conclusions about the control of environments most favourable to his animals and crop
plants. Such favourable environments are necessary to promote his own health and the unfolding of his potentialities in
directions advantageous to his progress — to his stability as a
species or a race and to his wholeness as an individual in a
society of individuals. There can be no escaping the fact that
there are latent in all the facts and assumptions of biology
(and in all biology it is far more difficult to prove the correctness of a 'fact' or an assumption than in the physical sciences)
seeds of lethal consequences to mankind and man's domesticated animals and plants. Further than this, lethal consequences are all too likely to follow from the unguarded and
wholesale application of the most tried and trusted facts of
biology to man and the higher organisms generally, unless we
are prepared to pay great deference to what we do not know.
We must freely admit, however, when we aspire to know all
about the complicated actions and interactions that constantly operate within the flux of which man is a part, that we
are today only at the threshold. Such lethal consequences as
may lie latent in some of the current facts and assumptions of
biology are likely to act rapidly, but if false facts and assumptions are long retained as authoritative biological dicta and
generally acted upon, then the consequences might well be
lethal in the extreme, and culminate in the premature extinction of man, or of his domestic animals and plants, or of all
three together. Reasoning of this general character animates
the work and utterances of those who go the whole way, or
even most of the way, with Sir Albert Howard in their
strenuous advocacy of natural manures and of composting
and in their abhorrence of chemical fertilizers. They are on
the soundest of biological grounds in so far as they make
generous allowances for what we do not know; but unfortunately their admirable enthusiams carries them far beyond their
facts. It is anathema to the scientific mind to make too
sweeping allowances for what we do not know: but in the

eyes of the scientist it is a crime of the first magnitude to accept as fact that which has not been well and truly proven by *current* scientific methods. It has *not* been well and truly proven that chemical fertilizers properly used have any short- or long-term lethal action on plant growth or human life, *nor* has it been proved beyond all shadow of doubt that lethal properties do *not* lurk in some of them. We should exercise great care and be on the alert; that is as far as it is reasonable to go at present. The compost case is merely mentioned as a good example of the *dilemmas* in which biology cannot escape from being involved and because it is a live issue today.

This somewhat lengthy reference to research and to the physical and biological sciences has been necessary for two chief reasons. In the first place, since we have been dealing with man from the biological standpoint, it is essential to emphasize the limitations of that science, and the more so because it is of such importance to add to the fund of exact biological knowledge. In the second place, the need to take both long- and short-term views of man's future should not be overlooked.

What are we to say about adjustment in the light of our present knowledge and from the ecological standpoint? If our environment is overweighted with the products of the physical world, it would seem to be common sense to introduce a counter-balance charge from the biological world, to get nearer to life, and to what I have described, and can best describe, as nature in the raw. To do this requires a closer contact with the country and with those occupations which involve active contention with the forces of nature, or which involve their partial and conscious control. Hence, then, the supreme importance to our national life, national character and national stature of the shipping and fishing industries, of agriculture, horticulture and forestry. Hence, too, the value of holidays spent in close contact with the country, and the pursuits and occupations of the country, in contradistinction to the holiday merely spent in the country. In considering the human problem we are at all times thrown into dilemmas; our dilemma here is to draw a balance between the rival claims of the individual and the group — whether community or state. The modern tendency is for the individual always to come off second best. From the point of view of a state in which the great majority of the population live in environments surcharged with the physical or material, it might well be that national adjustment and compensation could be brought about merely by increasing the numbers employed in environments highly charged with the biological.

This perhaps would be the simplest way now open to us: a way which would justify a great extension of agricultural and shipping activities, provided only that the economic consequences did not prove disastrous after every attempt had been made to adjust the economic to the sterner dictates of the human-ecological. Such a solution would only be a second best, for not enough individuals could be affected; yet, from the state's point of view, national stature and character are almost certainly a function of the number of individuals living full, useful and worthy lives.

Two difficulties immediately present themselves. We must reach some agreement as to what precisely is meant respectively by a 'full', 'useful' and 'worthy' life, and decide if it could be made possible to organize industry (the physical side) and agriculture (the biological side) so that the majority of the population came sufficiently under biological influence during most days of the week, and not merely during holidays. This problem will crop up again and again in subsequent chapters and be brought to a climax when my theme has sufficiently matured. My immediate concern is to apply the ecological method of thought and inquiry to the problem of the quality — useful, interesting, good, bad — of the life of individuals. The content of the environment in its fundamental importance and influence can be likened to the soil, for it is within the power of man to add to and take away from its ingredients; but for healthy development he must always maintain a proper balance of ingredients. Man, however, unlike the plant, which is spotbound, can exercise a very high degree of selectivity as to the ingredients that he will select to impinge most forcibly on his inner self. Man has his being in an environment within an environment. There are ingredients which are essential to his existence, and must be within his reach. There are others, many in no wise essential, and numbers of them bordering on the lethal, from which a particular man in particular circumstances can never, or never for long, escape. There are still others from which he can shut himself off completely, or which do not come within the reach of all men. The consequence is that the effective environment in which each one of us lives is as individualistic and unique as is our own inherent personality. It is this uniqueness which cannot be overstressed. The quality of a man's life will be revealed in the manner in which he, with his unique will and reasoning power, unique sensitivity and intuition, reacts to his unique environment. Again we have the two-way action; for his urges will influence the quality of his sensitivity as applied to his environment, and his environment will influence his urges. It is this, the immense influence of environment, that it is the province of ecology to study. The influence of environment applies as much to man as to any other living creature: indeed, I will go further and say that it applies with greater force, just because it is within the power of man to manipulate his own environment.

All this is fundamental to my thesis, for it is fundamental to any comprehensive view of life and education. Education we shall be forced to consider because modes of adjustment to environment count for more in human progress and happiness than does the accumulation of knowledge acquired only through the medium of the class and lecture-room. That being so, how shall we manipulate environment and to what ends? We must broaden the whole scope of education; but, at the best, education can do no more than direct experience along certain channels. This serves to remind us that everything intended to cater for the mind, the senses or the emotions becomes, like formal education, part of the environment. Books of all kinds, music, poetry, drama, works of art, the theatre, the cinema, the night-club, the stadium, the race-course, are all additional ingredients from which the individual can select, and the stimuli assimilated will react upon his thoughts and actions. Equally the personality, manner, method and appearance of a teacher, actor or athlete become absorbed into the environment, often to penetrate deeply and arouse acute reactions. The environment of man, like that of all living things, is ever changing. The more complex the organism, the greater the range of manifest and operative change. Man, therefore, lives under an environment subject to greater hourly, daily, weekly and yearly change than any other creature.

Because man is influenced by the sum of all the subtle shades of changing environment to which he has been subjected from conception, and because *subconscious* memory may be regarded as the thread which binds these long-lost environments to his developing personality, I think it is the more necessary to insist upon the influence of *conscious* memory on the continuing development of adult man. The subconscious memory is a store house, the keys to all the chambers of which the individual may never find; but the doors to all the chambers of the conscious memory are wide open and may be entered at will. This point is worth making since, in my view, psychology is so deeply absorbed in probing into the subconscious that it does not pay sufficient deference to the ever-growing conscious memory of the adult. Here we have what is perhaps the master cell in man's delicately tuned instrument of selectivity. He can and does choose for himself certain outstanding memories which he uses, and very largely consciously uses, as catalysts to enliven and direct — for good or for evil — the unfolding melody of his personality. To have been happy, useful, free — to have been in love or in danger, to have responded acutely to beauty or to a vision — may exercise a profound conscious influence on a man's subsequent way of life.

CHAPTER 3

HUMAN AND BIOLOGICAL ANTITHESES

The contraries inherent in nature's processes of development suggest a way of solving our human dilemmas

---

'Without contraries is no progression.'

WM. BLAKE

'WE CANNOT have it both ways,' says the common-sense man who prides himself on his practical wisdom. The fact is entirely otherwise: life in all its manifestations is ever trembling on the brink of irretrievable disaster, disaster which would be absolute and final if 'one' rather than the 'other' gained complete mastery. The very spirit of life is drawn from apparently irreconcilable opposites — antitheses that the organism needs must resolve if the species which it represents is to persist and the individual members of the species remain healthy and vigorous.

The fundamental laws of biology are at first sight puzzling. They seem to place insuperable barriers in the way of any rational organization of our mode of life here and now, and even greater difficulties in the way of any conscious attempt to take care of the future destiny of the species of which we are the contemporary guardians. Always we are set the task of harmonizing the incompatible. This is the task which nature triumphantly achieves on behalf of every species but man. Man (by nature or by the gods or by whatever genius guides the dice of fate) has been paid the delicate compliment of being considered worthy, and presumably capable, of resolving almost unaided the fundamental biological antitheses peculiar to his own station, for himself and by himself, through the medium of his conscious mind. He is but little assisted by the play of automatic and instinctive reactions or, as perhaps

61

we should say, in the language of the thoroughgoing intellectual, he is not 'hampered by such rudiments of instinct as are
left to him' — left to him, aye! in this grand age of the dominance of the intellect and perversion of the instincts, emotions
and the senses. So here is the fundamental of the essentially
human antitheses we shall have to consider: *intellect—instinct*.
There are others which are actively and manifestly inter-
twined with man's daily life, with his conscious powers of
reaction and selection, such as: *good—evil: love—hate*. Most
fundamental of all, however, are the essentially biological
antitheses, those which affect equally all organisms including
man: indeed those go to the very root of man's life and fate.
To name a few we have: *segregation—integration, inertia—
change, complex—simple, lethal—enlivening*.

Man would seem to have been set down in a world of disordered opposites, out of which he must needs make at least
some pretence of order. We have to conclude that strain and
tension are a necessary to life; with increased complexity in
the organism, the number of strains and tensions to which it
is subjected are correspondingly increased. These strains and
tensions may be likened to a fire; perhaps, like a raging
furnace, they release energy — that vital energy whose constant expenditure alone keeps organisms alive, and men not
only alive, but actively and mentally alert. 'Energy is eternal
delight.' It would seem to be a reasonable hypothesis that the
act of resolving antitheses should release energy. Many a man
does his best work, or at all events develops the most energy,
under high tension. The waging of war, for instance, is in
essence a matter of resolving incompatibilities; witness the
prodigious energy and capacity of work that this releases in
successful war leaders. These biological and human antitheses
are a part of man's life, both necessary in themselves, and,
taken together, perhaps the very driving force of life itself,
that force which gives to life its elasticity, rhythm and adaptability. Thus man, subjected to more strains and stresses than
any other species, can pride himself on being incomparably
the most elastic and adaptable of them all.

To be elastic and adaptable is one thing; to use these
attainments to the best advantage of the individual, of society
and the species, is quite another. To follow the complexity of

the human situation we must consider man's reactions to each of the main antitheses separately. The starting point is *segregation—integration*, for the breath of life of every individual man results from the most intricate acts of segregation. To these he owes 'the chance' of the particular internal and unique armament of potential forces with which he will be equipped to adjust himself to his environment and to tame his environment to his will. With the development and growth of the individual begins that intricate and marvellous balancing of segregation (the allocation of particular, and we might say grosser, functions to particular organs) and integration (the bringing together of all the functions in united and beautifully co-ordinated interaction and interdependence) through which alone life can be sustained.

Man stands at the peak of that self-organized, self-repairing and self-reproducing complexity which distinguished the organic from the inorganic world. This organized complexity which is life derives its being from what E. S. Russell has so well described as its 'directive activity', an activity which is born of the power to co-ordinate and integrate. It is extraordinary therefore that man, who must necessarily be endowed with exceptional powers of functional co-ordination and integration, has so little developed these virtues as a conscious habit. This is perhaps as Russell insists, 'because he is by nature a mechanist', or because most men are more interested in playing tricks with the environment and with each other, than they are in natural philosophy and the natural dignity of man — the truth and the fitness of things. Whatever the reason, there can be no denying the fact that man has happened upon exploring the alluring path of segregation. This has been the easier path; because he has followed it fearlessly, though unwisely and too far, man's achievements, within their own limitations, have been staggering — so staggering to himself that instead of being in a natural and healthy state of *imbalance,* he is now in an unnatural and unhealthy state of *unbalance.* This state of unbalanced and unco-ordinated endeavour has led to an immense accumulation of facts, undreamed of advances in the sciences, and incredible inventions: in short, to a stock-in-trade so vast and a departmentalization carried to such lengths, that long since, in sad

63

truth, man has not been able to see the wood for the trees: assuredly he has lost his way in the forest. The historian of the future, however little biologically minded, looking back on the era which closed with the fall of France in 1940, will realize that then ended the era of segregation carried to baneful extremes: for end it must if our civilization is to survive and our species persist. A new era, the first lights of which are to be seen on the horizon, has been rendered inevitable by the practical and compelling manner in which time, space and energy have revealed their harmonic and universal attributes. They have done so with a completeness and to an extent which would have seemed incredible to those who were the chief architects and to those who later were the driving force of the era of segregation.

It is the era of integration that has in fact dawned; it is an age in which man will learn to harmonize all his activities and to use his vast stock-in-trade in accord with biological laws; and so will dawn a society and a civilization pulsating with the breath of life as opposed to one in which robot men wander aimlessly in a world of dangerous toys. Behold the lengths to which segregation has been carried: segregation of the classes, the interests, the sciences, the arts, and probably the most baneful of all, the complete segregation of town and country. The tragedy of it is that the age of segregation (and consequently specialization) invited all men, brilliant and dull alike, to chase hares, and invited none to look at its problems whole and large. At last the very men who should have held the citadel of wholeness – the poets, the sculptors, the painters – joined headlong in the mad chase. So that now all men alike, men of science, men of affairs, men of art, have to start at the very beginning and learn a new language, the language of integration. There is a compelling tolerance in the laws that govern life, and a readiness to forgive marks all the sentences passed on us here on earth, for truly: 'In nature everything has a meaning. And everything is forgiven. And it would be strange not to forgive.'

Thus we may transgress against these hard rules of antithetical adjustment by going too far in one direction and yet, if we realize it in time, we can atone by turning, and maybe for long periods, in the direction we have neglected. Such in-

64

deed, as we shall see, is nature's own way of regaining a state of equilibrium after episodes of unbalance and upheaval. This brings us to grips with the immensely significant and all-pervading antitheses, *inertia—change,* the *static—dynamic,* which dominates the whole life process and which in manifold and subtle disguises influences man in his conduct of great and petty affairs. The two together, *segregation—integration* and *inertia—change,* are the great incompatibilities over which man has stumbled through the centuries, but sustained evolutionary development and contemporary equipoise alike depend upon the degree of success with which man can reconcile them in his mode of life.

All advance is based upon variation and change. Stability depends upon inertia. Every single new birth is an act of variation. With each new individual new potentialities are brought into the world. The mixing of individuals of different ages — of experience with youth — brings stability to bear upon the Social mass. The newborn are necessary, so is death. If men lived for ever the weight of inertia would be intolerable. If all parents died as soon as their children reached adolescence, the speed of change would break the elastic that holds society together. The balanced mingling of individuals of a full range of ages is to be deemed a biological prerequisite of any healthy society. The changes of nature herself are as a rule slow; favourable mutants of a species are not frequent and have to justify themselves, since the inertia of the old forms presses heavily upon the new. The ways of nature are sometimes exceedingly violent. Change may rule supreme for long periods of time, and thus we have what the geologists of an older order with fine enthusiasm termed periods of paroxysmal outburst. But when nature indulges in such periods of variation and change, she generally counterbalances them with much longer periods of stability. The lesson is obvious and final. Probably no species, least of all man, can live under the perpetual stress of paroxysmal outburst without dire harm to itself. Man, we must remember, reacts hypersensitively to environmental conditions, and he lives in an environment surcharged with lethal as well as favourable forces. It is difficult to estimate whether the environment as influenced by man's own inventions and innovations, or his attitude toward life, is changing the more rapidly. The truth is that everything is in a state of paroxysmal outburst, and has been for so long that man is lost in a maze of changing ideas, changing devices and changing conditions.

These biological considerations would suggest that what man needs most today — in politics, in science, in the arts, and even in education — is a long period of rest in which calmly and unhurriedly he can take stock of the situation as a whole, without inviting further muddled thinking by initiating premature changes in all directions. Meanwhile the life of the countryman has much to teach us. It is an antidote to the excitements of the city and to the fervid exchange of opinions so dear to those of the intelligentsia who live chiefly in a world of their own, their 'minds steeped in the provinciality' of their particular school of thought, their environment dominated by a constant torrent of words.

Indolence—activity is a variant of *inertia—change*; thus many animals and most of the higher plants hibernate more or less completely during the winter. No individual man, any more than a society or nation, can stand more than a certain amount of tension for an indefinite period without tiredness or reaction revealing itself in a thousand different ways. These ways depend upon the uniqueness of each individual, the character of a society or nation and the circumstances of the time. We have seen that war tends to generate great energy in successful leaders; but if the tension is sufficiently long continued it must in the end lead to some form of fatigue that may not appear until suddenly revealed by reaction after the 'cease fire'. The fact that tiredness, or the need for a period of indolence shows itself in so many forms, tends to mask its lethal significance. A great man, a successful man, an energetic man, may expend more energy, and often does, when he is tired than when he is not, and will frequently get through a prodigious amount of work, possibly more than usual. Close contact with such a man will, however, reveal certain changes in his method and in his outlook. It may not be that he will have lost grip or decisiveness; most likely he will have become more decisive and more autocratic, these peculiarities exhibiting themselves as subconscious defence measures. It is easier to be 'certain' and to give instructions than to think again and consult with others. Tiredness bears upon the final success or failure of democracy and should serve as a peremptory warning against going too far and too fast in the pursuit of change. The speed is now so great that it tends to make tired men of all Cabinet ministers, all senior Civil servants and all those who have to make fatal decisions. Such men will tend, unwillingly and unwittingly, to act too decisively and too autocratically. They may therefore be driven to act undemocratically. Another defence measure is to consider the expedient at the expense of principle, the tendency being discreetly to shelve the real issue. Here again in tiredness there lurks a great danger to democracy: democracy is nothing if it is not a matter of fine principles. Nature left to her own devices takes subtle precautions against tiredness; she appreciates the significance of inertia. A cat is a perfect object-lesson in the supremely important art of relaxation. Tiredness is a symptom of man's neglect to adjust himself to the rhythm of indolence and activity.

Interestingly enough, certain men of genius instinctively understand the antitheses we are discussing, for high imagination and indolence may almost be regarded as linked characteristics. The man of the highest imagination needs and demands rest, and he sees no crime in a period of extreme indolence — a period in which, shall we say, his subconscious is able unhampered and undirected to do its momentous work. The genius will not force the pace or drive himself prematurely into activity; the incubation period of apparent sloth will be allowed to run its course.

Both the practical man of affairs and the strenuous idealist contend that owing to the confused state of the world today no time should be lost in effecting such changes and adjustments as they consider appropriate. To which the biologist is compelled to reply, not without irony, that danger lurks in excessive effort, while non-stop activity may defeat its own ends. This is a hard saying: life is hard.

Organisms with a psyche less well developed than that of man tend to respond decisively to even the more complex of the natural situations in which they may find themselves: they have a remarkable facility for responding unerringly. Man is called upon to respond to much more complicated situations than any other creatures, but he also has to bring a much more complicated and massive ego to bear upon the situation. The result is, he is more likely to hesitate than be decisive. He is, as it were, unable to grasp a highly complicated situation at a glance, and equally unable to bring to bear upon that situation the whole of himself and all the stored memories of his being. The fatal consequence is that he has lost, or very largely lost, the ability to reach a master decision with lightning speed and then automatically and instantaneously to take the right action. In proportion as actions are the result of master decisions, so they will tend to be simple and direct. The animal is an artist in master decisions and in simple actions; in any set of circumstances, and emphatically in a crisis, he is actuated by a single dominant urge which for the time being completely suppresses all other urges.

The animal, with its less complex psyche, behaves in much closer accord with the manner of working of its functional activities than does man. Functional activities in their totality constitute the act of living: it is well to emphasize again that all organisms, including man, sustain themselves and perpetuate their species by virtue of their 'directive activity': an activity which, as E. S. Russell has so convincingly argued, calls into play the correct means with which to achieve an end. The ends to be achieved are almost beyond computation and vary, for example, from the constant and seemingly automatic performance of the necessary life functions, to strenuous efforts to heal wounds, to subsist for as long as possible on starvation diets, or to make do with too little water. To achieve these ends is essential if living creatures are to be held to the prime task of fulfilling their biological destiny.

The human psyche, if it is to attain wholeness, must embrace ideals. This involves aims, many of which may be unattainable in any finite sense, or which can only be satisfied after long periods of time. These aims are very different from the more strictly biological ends on which life itself depends and which satisfy the animal world. None the less, the 'aims' and 'ends' as here differentiated may well be essentially similar in their operation as stimuli. This view, I think, is supported by A. N. Whitehead: in discussing the higher manifestations of life, he writes: '*Aim* evidently involves the attainment of the purely ideal so as to be directive of the creative process.' He also insists that 'We are *directly* conscious of the purposes as *directive* of our actions.' The immediate point at issue is that the animal's method of response to complex situations is different from that of man: this difference is no less real if the impulses involved vary rather in degree than in kind. I do not wish to seem to be arguing that the animal method, as such, is sufficient to meet the case of man. It is important to realize, however, that the more complex of the mobile organisms are to some degree involved in affairs: they have scope, if only within strict limits, to go here or there, or to do this or that. In these daily affairs they normally behave as if directive activity applied to the working of their psyche almost as strongly and decisively as to their bodily functionings.

Therefore I argue that the animal method has many inherent virtues; virtues to which man should be fully alive and which, perhaps, improved or amended, he should be at pains to cultivate. If directive activity operates upon the psyche of man and animal alike, and if the difference in the mode of reaction is one rather of degree than of kind (which would seem to be highly probable), then it would follow that man has latent within himself a faculty which he has failed to utilize or to train.

Suppose man was suddenly possessed of the aim of developing this potent faculty to the full, consciously bringing it to bear upon his complex affairs — international arrangements and equity, central and local government, education and personal integrity. What then?

In order to emphasize and justify my opinions on 'what then', I must make one more pertinent comment on directive activity in action. The conscious reaction to this activity is that highly complex processes are made to appear simple, but not only that: in their action they are made simplicity itself to the individual. It is no difficult matter to breathe: it is easy to devour a meal: to digest, assimilate and excrete are all child's play. Yet the chemical, physical and functional processes involved are of a complexity to match the most intricate ramifications of international and social relationships. The way of nature is by wonderful feats of co-ordination and

F

integration to make all overt action simple. Man has tacitly assumed that to segregate is to simplify. This may be true, or partially true, in so far as the physical world is concerned, and so far as, up to a point, to pursue both learning and research in departments is necessary. But in the art of living to segregate is to complicate. To integrate is the only possible means of effecting direct, decisive and spontaneous actions: that is to say, to compel social man and individual man to perform complicated actions and to resolve complicated issues with ease and simplicity. In the complicated world of today, the most complicated of all acts is to govern with far-seeing wisdom and with justice to all men. It is only by integration of the highest order at all stages that complicated issues and situations can be brought to a common denominator and reduced to their essence. In the last resort, if government is to be effective, then the edicts of government must be relatively few, absolutely to the point and simple: then, and only then, will the response of the governed be willing and spontaneous and therefore FREE. Governments have long since fallen into the habit of meeting situations of growing complexity by setting up ever more complicated machinery (segregating problems), and by the enactment of ever more involved and far-reaching legislation. This procedure, as it seems to me, is anti-biological: consequently it is anti-social. It is probably the root cause of the growing chaos and indecision that is everywhere apparent in the world today.

I have tried to approach the fascinating and frightening tangle of human affairs from what, with justice, I may describe as the standpoint of natural philosophy. In a word, I have been driven to the conclusion that salvation is only to be found in simplification. Simplification in affairs can, however, only be achieved by much closer adherence to the biological method of integration. I do not think it is too much to say, as a matter of general experience, that decisions reached by an intelligent and conscious consideration of a great number of conflicting facts are likely to be complex and erroneous, while decisions intuitively reached are usually simple and correct.

Today an intolerable weight of anxiety presses heavily on mankind: those whose duty it is to bring cohesion and design into man's waygoing are almost beside themselves to decide how best to act. Never before has there been greater conflict between views honestly held: never before has the great game of statecraft been played with so many pieces on boards of such intricate design and under rules more hampering to the evolution of tactics and strategy most likely to avoid stalemate. Goaded by necessity and by the overwhelming amount of business to be transacted, statesmen and men of affairs are forced to seek — or, more accurately perhaps, have blindly fallen into the habit of seeking — solutions to their problems by a process of unbridled talking. This is indeed the age of committees run riot. The net result is that men tend to juggle with facts and opinions with the aim of reaching some sort of decision at any cost, rather than to brood over their problems with the master aim of reaching decisions pregnant with creative drive and in keeping with the dignity, spirit and deeper human needs of man. Men have come to trust overmuch to their ability to collect and marshal facts, and to their powers of arguing and reasoning, and hardly at all to their intuitions of which they are, perhaps, afraid. Thus, gradually, and without malice aforethought, man has dropped into the easier course of attempting to direct his affairs by the method of segregation. He has almost completely neglected the great guiding principle of integration.

Mere accident cannot be held sufficient to account for the fact that the conclusions to which I have been driven by thinking in biological terms are strikingly paralleled in the opinions of an elder statesman of wide experience in Cabinet and Parliament, who has had to grapple at first hand with the everyday problems of policy and administration. The Rt. Hon. L. S. Amery[1] emphasizes in his book *Thoughts on the Constitution*, the distinction between policy and administration: he shows conclusively that policy, which is essentially a matter of integration, has tended to be shelved at Cabinet meetings because of the claims of the departments, or, in other words, because of the results of segregation. To obviate this fatal defect Amery 'would have a Cabinet of about half a dozen, all entirely free from ordinary departmental duties'. I need not follow him in all the detailed suggestions he makes

1 Later Lord Amery

for the setting up of standing policy committees and other matters. The crucial point is the need for a functional group-ing of the several departments, and for putting each group under the aegis of a member of the Cabinet who would be policy minister, no more and no less, 'for his group of depart-ments'. Such a plan is in complete accord with biological principles, for integration cannot be undertaken in the last resort by large numbers of men working in conclave. It is in essence a function for individuals to perform, individuals of the highest ability, trained to their supreme task and armed with all essential facts appropriately marshalled. Within the living organism integration is of the nature of a two-way action. Orders are given impartially from the higher to the lower and from the lower to the higher: whichever way they are directed they are obeyed with equal precision. In our efforts to improve the machinery of governments, we cannot aspire to reach quite these heights of democratic perfection: but we can at least accept nature as our guide. Amery's plan would enormously facilitate this vital (vital in the literal sense) two-way action.

The Prime Minister is integrator-in-chief: he needs by every possible means to foster two-way action between himself, his Cabinet ministers and the departments. His own views and wishes must permeate the whole machine: but if his views are to be sound and creative, he must himself be equally permeated by the detailed knowledge and views of all his departments. I cannot believe that a heterogeneous Cabinet consisting of a large number of heads of departments could under any circum-stances even approach to the biological ideal. The essence of two-way action and integration is to individualize the whole process. The policy ministers would know all about the heads of departments with which they were concerned in order to fulfil their function as channels for the necessary two-way action. It would be far easier for the Prime Minister to know all about all his departments and to impress himself upon them if he had only to deal with a handful of informed policy ministers, than if he had for ever to deal with all ministers separately. Policy ministers are themselves integrators by definition with time to brood over their problems. Amery's plan would not only make thinking more leisurely and easy for the Prime Minister — who by definition should be the nation's greatest thinker! — but also for his Cabinet. It is inconceivable that any policy born of hasty thinking, that has not allowed time for brooding and integration of the highest order, could be convincing and still less in the best interests of the nation. Much would of course depend upon the correctness of the functional groupings of the departments. For my own part, I would regard agriculture (including fisheries), forestry, food and town and country planning as departments which should constitute a single functional group. Nothing can be more important in this small country than high-class integration in respect of the use to which our limited land surface is put. It follows that the policy minister concerned with this group should have power to influence the policy of the fighting services and other departments (transport and supply) that make heavy demands on land. In other words, policy ministers in respect of certain defined matters should probably have some authority beyond the group of departments which is their primary concern.

Amery is rather attracted to the idea of setting up a Lower House, or sub-parliament of industry, as suggested some years ago by Churchill. At first sight the idea has its attractions as a means of furthering two-way action: in this case between Parliament proper and the various national interests, business, trades and professions. A properly reformed House of Lords with added rather then reduced powers would, however, better fulfil this need. A reformed House of Lords, given a status acceptable to all men and fully representative of all national interests — cultural, scientific, social and industrial — itself a part of Parliament, could be made to bring the informed opinion of the interests as such to bear powerfully and without undue political bias upon the Government of the day.

In my view, however, the task of a reformed and acceptable Upper House should be to effect a truly functional two-way action within Parliament itself between the more essentially party tenets and aspirations and those which arouse little political antagonism yet which go to the core of man's human needs and spiritual gaiety.

Essential as it is to improve and strengthen the working of central government, it is vastly more important to widen and strengthen the machinery of self-government, and to carry this to the lengths of regional devolution in respect of some affairs. Amery clearly favours such a course, though, as I understand him, primarily to ease the heavy burdens of the Cabinet and Parliament. As I see it there is far more to it than that. In proportion as local government is rendered alive and responsible, so should we achieve a closer functional two-way action between central government — the final arbiter of our fate — and local committees. The closer the two-way action between Westminster — Whitehall, by that much the closer are we to a real, organic two-way action between 'they' who govern and 'we' who submit. The extreme psychological and biological importance of local self-government implies that nothing less than social cohesion and an enduring civilization depend upon organizing the peoples of the world into comparatively small and truly homogeneous communities. Today, we all tend to think and act as individuals or as members of large disparate groups. A nation should be a heterogeneous patchwork of homogeneous groups, each group self-sufficient in many important respects, but dependent on other groups in other respects. The will of the people would thus function through the co-ordinated interaction of all groups. We should make a supreme endeavour to bring about a closer contact in all directions between the indigenous customs and ways of thought of the man of several localities, and between these customs and the disciplines born of national cohesion, and the obligations of the shires and parishes to the state. To attain this would come closer to the biological pattern of functioning and give society that organic harmony which it now so sadly lacks. I am sure it is only through vitalizing local self-government right through from every parish and ward (which of itself would go far to add warmth and strength of purpose to local patriotism) that we can advance toward this ideal. For too long we have tried to build from the top (London and the central government) downwards. No Government can be world-wide or nation-wise, strong or virile, if it only derives its mandate from the votes of individuals cast in the mould of party. A truly representative Government needs, too, the wholehearted mandate of the shires and parishes as such: that is, a classless and patriotic mandate of the character which carried Sir Winston Churchill and his National Government to victory in the war. Witness the Home Guard, a compelling example of latent local homogeneity and patriotism rendered dynamic and vocal. Witness, too, how wantonly we throw away the hard-won fruits of creative spontaneity. It is high time to begin to experiment in building from the foundations (the parishes and wards, the counties, the regions and local self-government) upwards.

To conclude this chapter I will wholeheartedly endorse Amery's opinion that 'the time has come ... for a new and far-reaching Reform Act'. First, please, let us set up a Royal Commission with the widest possible terms of reference to report on the means of strengthening the machinery of government (ultra-local, regional and central) of this country, the better to handle the affairs of state and play fair by the people during this era of frightening complexity and truly unprecedented change. Such a Royal Commission should be of the old-fashioned type with unlimited time to accumulate facts, and still more time to brood over facts and problems. Times have so greatly altered that no commission could be adequate to deal with the issues at stake were it to consist only of statesmen, sociologists, Civil servants and economists; the field of selection needs to be considerably widened.

It is not only on account of its biological interest that I have discussed the machinery of government, but also because, when dealing with agriculture, I shall have much to say about regionalization. The feasibility of the regionalization of agriculture on anything approaching a workable basis must be determined by the general orientation of the Government, particularly by the extent to which the orientation permits regional and local differentiation and freedom of action. I shall have more to say about local self-government in the next chapter. By a rather different approach I shall, I think, be able to strengthen the case I have so far made.

CHAPTER 4

THE NATURE OF PROGRESS

Man's adaptability enables him to fulfil an unlimited number of purposes: in this way he is free to progress. But his very adaptability has allowed him to create an environment that threatens to swallow him up. How can he know whether he is progressing or destroying himself?

'The conscious mind, that greedy thing which eats so much that is bad for it, and seeks out so many inventions.'

JOHN MASEFIELD

'Man is above all a leader charged with survival of the "values" which are in his keeping. Man's leadership cannot be tyranny since that would be to forget the "values".'

SIR CHARLES SHERRINGTON

IN THE last chapter the discussion of the *simple-complex* antithesis was carried some way. We shall now have to extend our inquiry to lead up to a consideration of what precisely we are to mean by progress.

Quite broadly speaking, the evolutionary process has proceeded from the simple to the more complex, and from the less to the more adaptable. Man is by no means the most highly specialized species; man is something vastly different and vastly more exciting, for he is incomparably the most adaptable species. Man's peculiar and unique adaptability turns upon his power to harness his faculties to the fulfilling of what, in practice, amounts to an unlimited number of purposes. For example, if *Homo*, in a fit of lunacy, decided to eliminate all trees from the face of this planet, he could do so. No other species has powers of this order developed to anything like the same degree. By virtue of his very adaptability man has, however, contrived for himself an environment of such extreme complexity that he is in the gravest danger of being swallowed up by his own innovations. He has been excessively adaptable in some directions and insufficiently adaptable in others; so that we should be in error to judge human progress by the degree of complexity of man's achievements and of the environment which he has made for himself. Not only has man to learn the biological lesson of how to react simply to complexity, but he must also take heed of his spiritual and moral aspects. No definition of human progress which ignores these can be complete. From the biological point of view, these attributes of man must be considered as forces and functions equally with his grosser forces and functions. We need not be religious or virtuous, or in any high degree spiritually minded, to realize, if only dimly, that altruism and universal love are all-pervading, if latent, qualities of man: qualities which are probably as necessary to man's continued existence and balanced development as his creative or any other activity. At this juncture it is enough to say that increasing complexity with decreasing altruism and love could not justly be regarded as human progress. A more positive definition will emerge in due course.

The implications of the *simple-complex* antithesis are far reaching. We are faced with this drawn-out sequence of complexity and this chain of increasingly difficult antitheses to resolve: *the individual — the family — the pack — the herd — the community — the society — the race — the nation — the species*. We have a more or less parallel sequence in the realm of ideas, leading finally to politics, platforms, programmes and propaganda. On the face of it there is no valid reason why the ideas forced upon us by these antitheses should necessarily culminate in politics, programmes and propaganda, or that the three 'p's' should necessarily lead (as they invariably do) to excessive centralization of civil power and excessive organization of the affairs of men. Perhaps this is a partial explanation of why man is not more successful in his methods of resolving his social antitheses.

We have now reached a stage when the power exercised by a highly organized central government has profoundly influenced the life of every individual. This tendency has greatly loosened the ties of the family and of community: today literally millions of people have no community life at all, in the sense of community as an organic and more or less self-contained whole. This gives the individual a freedom which is won, however, at the expense of becoming a slave to remoter ties and controls — ties and controls which largely command his life and, since they emanate from organizations and officialdom, do so unnaturally: they are not vitalized by the warmth and intimacy of human contacts. Our human contacts with inspectors, collectors, food officers and fuel controllers, and others of the official fraternity, are at best distant and lukewarm. We have seldom any idea where these people live or what their homes are like: our contacts are mostly *paper* contacts. The net result is that psychically the individual gains a number of freedoms of doubtful worth at the cost of losing certain family and social ties of the utmost importance to his personal happiness and well-being, and of even greater importance (and here is irony once more) to society at large — to the state. This aspect of centralization must be faced: it is the human aspect. We are moving — although slowly at present — toward a more rational organization of world affairs. It is perhaps inevitable that sooner or later some central authority will be set up with powers to impose its will on all countries of the world. In this event, and unless sufficiently strong off-setting measures are found and enacted, we are likely to accentuate tendencies already gnawing at the heart of our humanhood and which are bound to endanger our precarious civilization. In our efforts to strengthen the material and political foundations on which man builds his castles, we need ever to be on guard against further exhausting the springs of his spiritual development.

In a word, the problem which now faces mankind is how to build a sufficiently strong human foundation to carry the heavy superstructure of all this paper-made centralization. Should we not begin rather at the bottom — the individual and the family and the compact community — than at the top? Should we not also realize more acutely that centralization must always have the inherent weakness that in proportion to its completeness (degrees of excellence as some would argue) all major and essential decisions are by definition taken by an ever decreasing number of persons? This can only have the effect of narrowing the range of individual opinion and experience in the conduct of our affairs, and of canalizing, and therefore stultifying, the scope of human development. The fallacy of relying on the potency of centralization built without human foundation is that it presupposes that a mere handful of men can be all-wise and be responsive to the environmental conditions and human reactions of all men in all places — a supposition which is as arrogant as it is foolish. The human foundation can only be the family and the organic community. We can only achieve social answers to social problems if the state consists of an harmonious and well-knit assemblage of strong local communities. Only when communities know their own minds and their own needs, and have definite local aspirations, will a nation be in a position to support the weight of centralization. These communities would then be strong enough to influence the activities of the central government: they would be organic partners. Under these conditions central authority would be concerned with its legitimate responsibility — principles: the local authorities with ways and means.

The urgent problem is, then, greatly to strengthen community life in this country and then to awaken a new surge of interest in local and ultra-local affairs and in local and ultra-local self-government. Although there are hopeful signs, the organization of the whole life of the nation in groups of organic communities is made daily more difficult by the annihilation of distance, and by the authoritive voice of London and of a few — all too few — other great cities booming over the radio. These issues are in themselves at the heart of our theme: the more so because rural effort, rural experience and the unobtrusive activities of simple people in country districts indicates that the community spirit still exists in this country. It is starved, but not dead.

These considerations also bear upon the international situation. The truth is that nothing can be settled and righted unless international affairs are settled and righted. Moreover, international understanding and stability never will be achieved unless all local communities bring their several voices — truly human voices — to bear upon the seemingly insoluble problems that hold the Governments of the nations apart. The dilemma is tragic, for these communities are not yet ready to lend a helping hand, so that a terrible onus is placed on the central Governments. Today as never before man is called upon to think and to act both with parochial and international understanding and zeal: as General Smuts said, the peace of the world is in the hands of the ordinary men and women of the world. Peace, I would contend, lies in the hands of the 'parishes' of the world, for every homogeneous community could and should have a voice capable of making itself felt — not so every individual as such.

Only by a great surge of local patriotism and community feeling shall we be able to bring a measure of simple humanity to bear upon our problems and perhaps begin to look for solutions in terms other than those of politics, platforms and propaganda. Very disturbing, therefore, is the tendency for local government elections to be conducted on political platforms. I regard this as one of the most unhealthy of modern trends: it represents a further development of the idea of centralization, the more dangerous because it is insidious. Some powerful counter to the political approach, which is a necessarily biased, if not actually a prejudiced, approach to every problem, is a biological necessity. The great law of opposites is not to be denied in any sphere of human endeavour: it is not conceivable, therefore, that all problems, or, for that matter, any single problem connected with the lives of real men, can be solved by a single method of approach and of assessment.

The view to which I have been driven seems to me to be supported by Sherrington in all that he says about the social-predatory antinomy. Man as a social species can only attain to his full dignity if carried on the crest of an ever broadening human fellowship. Human fellowship, to be harmonious and creative, must be born of deep understanding and sympathy between individuals. 'The cement of fellowship is altruism, for that is truth to fellowship.' Altruism is a propensity of the individual, so is predacity. Individual men and groups of men who are predatory are a danger to society and to the species beyond anything known among other species — predacious men prey upon other men. There is a strong element of predacity in politics and in party — a tendency which all must admit grows stronger and not weaker. It is ideas —

man's crowning glory — that the predatory politician wishes, in effect, to capture. He sets out by methods which savour but little of the altruistic to graft his own ideas on to the heads of others and then to seduce these others to add strength to his citadel by the direction in which their votes are cast. I am not so simple as to suppose that democracy can attain to democratic ends without politics and party. Unbridled politics and party, however, little mellowed by the warmth of altruism, are pregnant with the dangers inherent in predacity. I fear, too, that men in the mass, carried away by the hysteria of mass emotion, are less altruistic even than individual men. Yet nature with all her seeming anomalies has strong currents of altruism. This is shown by any close study (such as that of Hornaday) of animals under natural, or more or less natural, as opposed to experimental, conditions. Evolution has shown an altruistic tendency. In the multicellular organisms, millions of cells work together in incredible harmony for the good of the organism; the differentiation of sex in separate individuals made additional demands on altruism and gave scope for the further growth of this virtue in new and, in embryo at all events, social directions. In all this there is perhaps to be found a key to the human need, and to the means of adjusting social organization in a manner that is best to meet that need. The way of evolution, as of growth and development, has been to work from within outwards and towards a closer cohesion of ever larger aggregates, shall we say from the cell to the individual, from the individual to the family, from the family to the small group, from the small group to the larger one and finally to the state. Only so can altruism and fellowship grow and develop sufficiently to permeate and cohere the greater aggregates of humans — the state and now the world.

In saying this I am repeating in different words a view to which Sir Richard Livingstone was driven, although he approached the matter from an entirely different angle: 'Men are born to four citizenships, they should be able to live as good members of their family, of their community, of their nation, and of the whole of human society.'

Political systems and modes of government everywhere are tending to run more and more counter to natural laws; for the state, through the central government (the offspring of politics and party) to permeate local committees (such as they are) and individuals rather than the reverse and natural (and therefore more wholesome) mode of action. Here then is a further argument — and one exceedingly difficult to counter — in support of my claim that the baneful influences of over-centralization (soulless and self-conscious) can only be countered, so that a more human centralization is established, by the powerful influence of small homogeneous communities infused with altruism and fellowship, and the will to achieve strong local self-government free from political bias. 'England', said Disraeli, 'should think more of the community and less of the government' — and the community is nothing if not local.

No discussion of the social antitheses would be complete without a detailed consideration of the lethal factors in the environment: we must now examine them in the light of the antithesis *lethal — stimulating*. Certain drugs, as is well known, are either lethal or stimulating according to the dosage. I am not concerned here with narcotics as a part of the environment — exceedingly important though they are: though I shall have something to say about tobacco and alcohol when discussing food and health. Drugs, narcotics and poisons are by no means the only lethal factors in our surroundings today; probably more important are a great number of stimuli and forces which are themselves the outcome of man's own inventiveness and which he does not even recognize as being lethal. Most of them are not killing individual men outright: in their immediate action they may be highly stimulating (although perhaps in pathological directions), but in the long run they are usually sufficiently enervating or destructive to cause grave malaise or even to contribute decisively to the suicide of the species. A variety of factors in the environment working in unison may create forces out of all proportion greater than the influence of any one of them operating alone: or, on the other hand, they may mutually counterbalance one another. Thus factors which are potentially lethal may be harmless as part of the sum of the forces operating at a particular time, but definitely lethal within a different sum of forces operating at a different time.

We get an insight into this from the study of genetics. Plants or animals may carry in their constitution a number of lethal factors without harm to themselves: by appropriate breeding methods, however, it is a simple matter to arrange the combination of factors so that those which are lethal dominate the newborn organism. Similarly, natural mutants may be the heirs to lethal factors and come to nothing. A predominance of lethal factors foredoom an organism to a precarious existence or an early death. Man is now faced with the urgent problem of discovering, if he can, the legacy of lethal factors operating outside of himself which his manifold inventions have bequeathed to the environment in which he lives. I know of no fundamental researches into this important and fascinating problem, so I shall have to confine myself to my own speculations. I should imagine that man's emotions would be most healthily nourished on simple social contacts, and on the contemplation of natural things and natural beauty: it might well be that the substitution of artificial for natural stimuli in these directions might introduce factors of an active, or potentially active, lethal character. I fancy that multitudes have substituted the social contacts depicted at the cinema and on television for real contacts of their own. We must beware of lethal factors that emanate from the artificiality of these sources of stimulation. Again we should ponder the influence of the machine on the man: it would be reasonable to suspect the operation of lethal factors, particularly in those cases where the machine completely dominates the operative. These explicit possibilities are mentioned as examples of the dangers which we have invited to prowl in our midst. No thoughtful person will have any difficulty — if he will face the situation squarely — in adding endlessly to the number of likely-to-be-lethal influences which have resulted from the proliferation of man's inventions.

Nevertheless this is not to go far enough: despite his wisest resolutions, man's creativeness will manufacture, if unconsciously, lethal as well as beneficial stimuli. Knowledge, as knowledge, has, inevitably, a lethal streak in it. This must be clearly recognized. Man organizes his individual, his social, his national and his international life, or, at least, he makes an effort to do so, on the basis of the sum of his knowledge; but this fund of knowledge can never be complete, and the use of incomplete knowledge is a dangerous weapon when dealing with life. The great danger is that the more man knows, the more he is tempted to act on the basis of his facts and to make decreasing allowance for what he does not know. If a man plays a highly complicated game without knowing all the rules, he will be 'offside' more often than a man who knows all the rules. This is our position today, greatly aggravated as it is by the dominance of science. Scientific knowledge carries a heavier and more vicious load of the lethal in its satchel than does any other type of knowledge. This must be recognized, recognized everywhere and recognized at once. We are on the threshold of tremendous advances in biology, in medicine and in biochemistry: and it is essential that we have the courage to invite these advances. But let these advances only become as spectacular and far-reaching as the recent advances in the physical sciences, and there will be no end to the mischief man can do to himself: and he will have greatly to mend his ways if the good is to outweigh the mischief. Already we know that drugs can do the strangest of things with men's brains; and that hormones, which can now be used medicinally, in certain cases have remarkable influences on the personality. Advances in these and similar directions put responsibilities on man which, grave as they are, are as nothing compared to those which discoveries in genetics and nutrition have placed, and will increasingly place, upon his shoulders. Towards the end of this chapter I will have something to say about our duties as ancestors.

Power, at best dangerous, is usually lethal. Man has lorded it over the plant and animal world, regardless, heedless. Sometimes his errors meet him half-way — witness the havoc caused by soil erosion: but he little knows what far more insidious seeds he may have sown. Has he already scattered the seeds of irreparable disaster? Complete dominance of man over man is lethal, although partial dominance is probably unavoidable and can be beneficial. Competition is unavoidable, stimulating and biologically necessary, but it carries a heavy load of lethal possibilities. Within limits it may be good for individuals or for comparatively large groups of men, but it is likely to be bad for other large groups and, carried to excess, will be lethal alike to state and species. 'Let states that aim at greatness take heed how their nobility and gentlemen do multiply too fast. For that maketh the common subject grow to a peasant and base swain, driven out of heart, and in effect, but the gentleman's labourer.' These prophetic words were spoken by Francis Bacon. The industrial revolution and the years thereafter have perhaps not greatly altered the *proportion* of master to man; but they have had the effect of turning too many masters into directors rather than into active working partners with those employed; while industrial wealth created a new and large class of men with independent means and no clearly defined responsibilities. The net result has been to create countless thousands of gentlemen (!) and in the process to make swains of millions of men. Every error in social dealings and arrangements comes home to roost: now we seem to be striving toward a dull uniformity when all men will be either gentlemen or base swains.

It is evident that it is beyond the competence of man to use his creative energy and his capacity for acquiring knowledge and, at the same time, to eliminate lethal factors from his environment. This is unfortunate, but it is an inevitable consequence of the ocean of antitheses through which man has to steer a course in search of secure anchorage. The *knowledge − ignorance* antitheses does not mean that the alternative for man is perpetually to vegetate. Adventure he needs must, for the spirit of adventure is in his blood and is as vital to his human existence and development as are the red corpuscles themselves. No! In the organization of his individual, his social and his international life man must face the antitheses of life with the determination to harmonize them. If he finds himself drifting too fast towards the north, he must halt, pause and veer to the south. In this age of unprecedented discovery, the urgent need is to bring to light the myriad of man-made lethal factors and, if possible, counterbalance their worst effects. It is just here that the dominance of the scientific outlook (considered apart from the findings of science) is most serious: for it is the function of science only to probe into the unknown in order to increase the stock-in-trade of the known. The function of art is entirely different: the life-blood of art is derived from the fact that it

G

accepts no barrier between the known and the unknown. Art takes equal heed of both: it serves ever to remind us of the power and infinitude of the unknown.

More than half of our modern troubles are assuredly due to a general decline in our artistic perception:[1] a decline which has been glaringly manifest in so much of our building, in our vandalism, in our neglect of craftsmanship. Blame must attach to the men of art whose province is to hold the citadel of artistic perception against all attack — direct and insidious alike. Today it is popular to blame science for our present ills. This is unjust: if we take the long view, it is true to say that bad art, or the total neglect of artistic perception, has done, and can do, far graver mischief to the human race than that for which science can fairly be held responsible. *Art — science* constitutes an antithesis, and one which like all others must be resolved. Developments in artistic perception are necessary counterweights to developments in science. It is ironical that good art will always serve the best interests of man, while good science in a society devoid of artistic perception has the power to cause irreparable harm. The irony is increased by the further fact that bad art can do harm, while bad science is harmless. It is only good science that can let loose lethal stimuli upon the world — the better the science the greater the danger.

I have now said enough to enable me to extend my definition of human progress, and to do so in terms not wholly negative, though my definition will still be incomplete. Human progress must necessarily imply an advance from one state of affairs to another, and probably always to a more complex state. But one of the most important conditions is that this advance must always carry with it a heightened power of control over lethal stimuli. Then, given advance in spiritual and moral standards and in the strength of artistic perception to match advance in knowledge and material achievements, we

---

[1] On a piece of paper clipped on to the manuscript of this page is written: 'If I had been a dramatist I should have wished my life's work to have centred around the theme that first and foremost our agriculture should be established on the firmest of footings and as far as possible be made capable of maintaining the maximum number of farmers and supporting the largest possible rural population. I should try to show the tragedy of failing to do this: I would try and dramatise how best to deal with this vast and intricate subject in separate and related plays.'

should have a comparatively simple definition of at least one aspect of progress. *Progress, indeed, largely depends on the individual and social adjustments which man makes to ensure that lethal stimuli shall not more than offset what he may gain in other respects from his growing knowledge of himself and increasing control of the forces of nature — that is, from the expansion of his internal (mental and sensual) and external environment.*

The base of most of man's difficulties — as of his aspirations and achievements — is his power of conscious reflection. In *reason — instinct* there stands forth an antithesis which is probably the most impelling of all. Intellectual man is a creature of strange conceits: he has permitted himself to think that his instincts are mere survival from remote ancestry because he sets such store upon his brain: he is beginning to assume that his instincts are useless or even handicaps to his reasoning powers. Man is not purely intellectual and would lose far more than he gains if he eventually trains himself to dispense with the services of his instincts. It may well be that the very dangers inherent in mental dominance have already been gravely accentuated by the scant respect paid to instinct. Instinct is nature's safety valve. Wholly to substitute such discipline as can be imposed by the will for that of the instinct would be dangerous in the extreme: to guard against one-sided developments should be man's first care. His constant aim ought to be to train, and to train on the right lines, every directive activity straining within him, every faculty, propensity and power of which he knows himself to be possessed. Thus, and only thus, can he attain to his full stature. Man, if whole, would progress beyond our powers of imagination: robot man, or man as thinking and talking machine, is bound to come to grief more quickly than even the most pessimistic could suppose. Man's instinct has not yet atrophied. Rudolf Jordan, in his analysis of the *reason — instinct* antithesis, states that, 'Today man has to rely altogether on his intellectual nervous tissues, on his conscious reflection for his existence.'

In other words, if his intellect leads him towards specific suicide, then suicide it must be. Jordan is probably premature in his estimate, particularly since mankind embraces all races, all classes, all employments. 'Altogether' is an overstatement. Man still derives essential help, and far more help than Jordan admits, from his safety valve of instinct. Man, by virtue of his capacity of conscious reflection, may well have the ability, alone of the species, to *reverse* tendencies. It is absurd to deny that it is well within the power of man to train his instincts: he could devote much less time to the acquisition of knowledge or the indulgence of his intellectual faculties.

We are apt to think in terms of the so-called primary instincts as limited to hunger, reproduction and protection, while the secondary instincts are generally deemed to be social and capable of being trained. These distinctions are arbitrary. On the one hand, man by mental interference has weakened his primary instincts – which, incidentally, suggests that by proper training he could strengthen them. On the other hand, if the secondary instincts are not, as such, inheritable, none the less the extent to which they are capable of being developed implies inheritance. *With both types of instinct we are really talking in terms of tendencies and potentialities:* it is potentialities rather than actualities that are inherited: so the implied difference between primary and secondary instincts is not fundamental. Instinct and intelligence are complementary and should not be antagonistic: like brothers they can be mutually helpful or mutually destructive. It is often true of individuals that 'the more intellect there is, the less instinct'. With a wide knowledge of simple countrymen, I deny categorically that the reverse is true: 'the more instinct, the less intellect'. As a broad generalization comparing the species *homo sapiens* with other species 'the more intellect, the less instinct' sounds convincing enough, but there is no proof that man has won his intellect at the cost of his instincts. All that is proved is that it has amused man to sharpen his wits and disparage his instincts.

It is commonly said – and such sayings, like those uttered in jest, are often devastatingly true – that particular men have the ability to do a variety of things instinctively. This common saying conceals a truth of great importance to the progress of the human race. Man can and must train his instincts. This is a major thesis in my general argument. It is through his instincts that man has it in his power to counterbalance the immense load of lethal stimuli for which his intellect is responsible. We can usefully regard the subconscious as being the vat in which the harvests of conscious reasoning, the instincts and the senses, are fermented, mellowed and matured to produce rare vintages of wisdom, foresight and purposeful action. We should be wise to assume that the subconscious is not beyond our reach, but an essential part of ourselves and that it, too, can be helped and trained to do its creative work creatively. This is the background to all I shall have to say about education, ways of life and balance. They should be an essential background to all planning, devising and organization intended to help contemporary man to live a worthwhile life and to foster the progress of the race.

The men of the day are 'the ancestors' and therefore the trustees of the human race and probably also in some measure the architects of the new species which will eventually replace or dominate *homo sapiens*. This is man's heaviest responsibility; and in his actions on behalf of posterity his artistic perception, wisdom and integrity are put to the greatest test.

I will deal with one aspect of what I may describe as the *immediate future − remote future* antithesis, the hereditary aspect. We can approach this problem from two points of view: firstly, the various actions, wise or foolish, we could take on the basis of modern knowledge and the further actions that are likely to become open to us as more facts are made available; secondly, to go beyond the known facts and the further kindred facts of the near future, and to speculate as to other and quite different means by which perhaps we can influence the development of our species and the trend of evolution.

If man so decided he could apply to himself the art of the cattle breeder and the findings of genetics. Within limits he may be compelled to do so. The real danger lurks in being carried away by the new possibilities and the dogma of science to such an extent that we try to breed the perfect man. What an absurd abstraction! There is not even such a thing as a perfect milch cow or a perfect wheat − and never can be. Man can only approach towards perfection through adaptability: that requires diversification of talents and points of view in individuals of vastly varied genetical qualities. To imagine a world of extreme but uniform complexity (which meddle-some man is well toward achieving) inhabited by a single type of man is to ridicule the whole idea of over-standardization and to pour scorn on any attempt to bring man himself within the grand idea: 'if all things were alike, all men alike, all thoughts alike, what pleasure, what interest, what anything could there be?' Once again we would be faced with the extreme danger of abstraction as applied to human life: 'but every abstraction neglects the influx of the factors omitted into the factors retained'. I have quoted this observation of Whitehead's out of its context: but the warning applies to those who would too lightly meddle with the genotypical make-up of man.

To try to control the breeding of manifestly defective types, doomed to misfortune and palpably genotypically harmful to the species, is one thing: to control human breeding so as to make man conform to a preconceived standard of perfection is another. In very general terms we can say that a gene that is potentially dangerous may do no harm to an individual; but if two such genes come together, one from the male parent the other from the female, then the new individual carrying both genes will, in all probability, be doomed to ill-health or some form or another of unbalance. If such a doomed person dies without passing on the genes to another generation, the bad genes will have been eliminated from the genetical tree and no lasting harm will have been done. If, on the other hand, such a doomed person is responsible for producing children, then these bad genes will further accumulate to the grave detriment of posterity. The danger has to be faced that, because of improved hygiene and medicine, a progressively increasing number of 'doomed' people are not only being kept alive but, by producing children, are endangering the tree of life. The practical problems to be solved are accentuated by the fact that many 'doomed' people under good conditions live happy, comparatively healthy and exceedingly useful lives. Some are men of the highest talent, even geniuses. Another difficulty is that 'doom' due to genetical causes is by no means easy to distinguish from 'doom' which has nothing to do with heredity. The problem must not be shelved, however, because 'it would . . . be many centuries before these genetical effects were fully manifest'. Potential ancestors cannot stand by and watch themselves knowingly, as if by slow poison, kill the tree of human life. We can see, quite objectively, the danger of pushing the findings of one branch of science too far in a practical direction before another, complementary branch, has the information to ensure that the action taken will be beneficial to contemporary man and posterity alike. In this there is a warning to be pondered deeply in all branches of human action. One answer to our immediate dilemma is to push forward with added zeal research into the genetical problems involved. At present the wicked migrant genes cannot be detected when alone in a healthy person, and not always when hunting in dangerous couples in a less healthy person. Let detection once be possible, then the problem should be as good as solved. If man's genetical make-up could be charted like the essential properties of his blood, then all men and women would know what genes to seek and what to avoid. In an enlightened age, men and women would be provided with charts of their genes, so that knowingly to endanger the tree of life would arouse moral condemnation. It would be something of which people would be ashamed. Of this I am quite certain, if the tree of human life is to be properly guarded, the guarding must be by enlightened volunteers. To attempt to do it by legal enactments and sterilization would be a negation of the principle of life — would be to despair of the strength of the human spirit and the human heart. From small beginnings, be they never so well intended, appalling ends can be reached. Make of sterilization a legal instrument, and where shall we end? With the sterilization of love and of altruism and the annihilation of the human spirit, I would surmise.

Contemporary man can stand guard over posterity by avoiding genetically unsatisfactory matings. Not all the hereditary ills are due to the wicked genes of the types we have been discussing; many are well understood and can be charted, so that already education and enlightenment should be sufficient to guard the tree of life from many dangers. A passion to keep the tree of life healthy for all should be a basic virtue of civilization. The pollution of the atmosphere and the poisoning of the soil and the indifference to beauty show that it is not: it is equally important that individuals should passionately desire to mate to the abiding gain of future generations. If man's material lusts could be mellowed to a passion for enlightenment, then indeed the tree of life could be greatly nourished as well as guarded by the voluntary actions of individuals. The life in the soil, the atmosphere and man himself is finite: it cannot be indefinitely abused to satisfy our immediate greeds. As ancestors do we wish to leave our posterity with nothing but waste, sterility and death?

The essence of love, like that of life itself, is spontaneity: therefore it is to the spontaneous passions of men and women to which alone we can look safely for genetical advances by selective mating. Some of the more humanly important characters of man develop late and then only fully develop under favourable environmental conditions. Characteristics which may have immense genetical importance to man may not reveal themselves in individuals until the second half of life. A couple of unusually sound genetical stuff may have a family of but one or two, and have brought this small family into the world, long before they realized that their union was one of outstanding genetical potentialities. If it is not too late, and if realization dawns upon them, it would be to the advantage of the tree of life if they embarked again on the great advanture of parenthood.

In what I have said I do not think I have gone beyond the tentative conclusion drawn by John Hammond: referring to the later developing characters in animals: 'Thus by controlling the environment, both mental and physical [I have assumed a good environment, and this is legitimate for there are excellent environments where still reside some of the best genotypes in the country] in which the next generation is reared [my man and wife were the next generation] man can direct by selection in this environment [I have asked for numbers from which naturally to 'select' and perpetuate the favourable genes] the future evolution not only of his domestic animals but also of himself.'

Muller guardedly suggests that researches now in progress may point the way to the possibility of controlling mutations and even of occasioning 'directed mutations'. If the latter were made possible by direct and conscious intervention, a

92

terrible responsibility would be placed on man, for in what direction would he, or should he, direct? I am emphatically of the opinion that on no account should he permit himself consciously to direct, rather he should concentrate all his researches on the means of preventing adverse mutations. No: if man is to control the direction of the development and on-ward evolution of his species, such control, in its incidence, must be subconscious. Is it to be conceived that such sub-conscious control is possible? And if it is possible, could it conceivably be influenced, although indirectly, by man's thinking, actions and behaviour?

I now come to my second point of view and enter a realm of pure speculation. I believe that directive activity is a force that operates in the psyche of man as well as in his bodily func-tions and functioning. This opinion, in one guise or another, is gaining ground. Directive activity implies purpose, and purpose implies attaining to ends. If directive activity operates during the lifetime of an organism, it would be only rational to sup-pose that it operates also in directing the development of species and the trend of evolution. If this were so, then the point at issue would be whether the species itself directs the course of its own development — the nature of its mutations and the trend of its evolution. Let it be supposed that all organisms be possessed of will power, a biological will power. In some this 'will' would be necessarily a-conscious, in others presumably subconscious, and in yet others the conscious would be expected to play some part. Suppose the 'will' re-acted to the sum of the environmental stimuli reaching the organism, and these reactions were passed on generation to generation, so that the influences of environment impinged upon the 'will' of individuals continuously and collectively as long as life on the planet persisted: the sum of the 'will' of all the individuals of a species would constitute the 'will' of the species. It would not demand a wild flight of the imagination to suppose that it was the 'will' of the species operating through individuals that directed and occasioned the precise character of 'that tiny minority of mutant genes having bio-logically progressive effects'. The 'will', it is to be understood, is nourished by the 'food' it receives from the environment; it would respond to that food according to how it 'digests' and 'assimilates' it. The 'command' of the 'will' to the genes would then be a function of the character of the 'food' provided and of the 'digesting' and 'assimilating' capacity of the 'will'. On this basis of this speculative hypothesis, the type of experimental mutant genes that any species throws up, may be — and may ultimately be proved to be — the reaction of the 'will' to the sum of the environmental stimuli operative over the life period of the species. The great naturalist Henry Walter Bates, a contemporary of A. R. Wallace and Charles Darwin, realized that in segregation (*i.e.*, heredity in operation) there was some more subtle agency at work than the direction operation of external forces.

To turn to man: since the subconscious is the storehouse alike of man's biological and affective memories, we must, I think, conceive of the subconscious as being the abiding place of man's biological will. The subconscious is, however, influenced to the strongest degree by all man thinks and says and does — by all his experiences. It would, therefore, be in keeping with my whole argument that this thinking and acting should have a decisive influence on the feeding and tone of man's biological will. This will, as it is an affair of the subconscious, would issue its orders to the genes so that the conscious mind would be oblivious to the whole complicated proceedings. Yet all man's conscious thoughts and acts would influence the orders given by the biological will to the genes. If there is a grain of reason and a glimmering of truth behind these apparently wild speculations, then man, by his thoughts and actions, by his behaviour towards his own and other species, would exert a profound influence on the development and evolution of his species. By right thinking and good actions he might 'will' an advance through exceptionally favourable mutant genes toward genotypically higher realms and by wrong thinking and bad actions 'will' his species to decadence and decay.

I can fittingly conclude this chapter with a general observation as to the moral antitheses and those antithetical moods which fill our daily lives. I mean, for example, to *good — evil*; *love — hate*; *altruism — predacity*; *drudgery — enjoyment*; *boredom — exuberance*. Without the bad and the boring, we could not realize the true essence of the good and the pleasing and we should have no incentive and little material for their study. 'Whereas', says Bacon, 'it is most unskilful to investigate the nature of anything in the thing itself: seeing that the same nature which appears in some things to be latent and hidden, is in others manifest and palpable.' Which shrewd observation is singularly applicable.

The issue emerging is stated by Macneile Dixon: 'When Heraclitus declared strife the keystone of existence, he spoke, or did not speak, the truth.' The biologist, as I have been at some pains to indicate, has no alternative but humbly to bow to Heraclitus who, about 2,400 years ago, saw where the truth lay.

If man would calmly accept conflict as inevitable and, since it is the fountain head of the flow of vital forces, essential to his existence and progress, he would have no grounds for despair. Rather he would respond to the implied challenge and set about understanding discord: even, as far as within him lies, set about devising ways and means of maintaining tensions in such a way that the brutalities and miseries that they so often occasion are eased.

Here then are the human reasons why man needs greatly to contend with nature in the raw. He does so when he sails the seven seas and flies the nine heavens. He does so when he dares to repair the ravages of his own folly: when he turns with devotion to the soil and seeks with zeal to break the barriers of space and time. Always he can adventure in ideas and fight against fear and dishonesty in facing the facts of life. Love is the pith and pulse of humanity, well learned at the price of hate. How grows the pith? What feels the pulse? Does evil, equally with good, play a vital if equally obscure part?

We stand dazed and expectant at the brink of a new age when insight will be free and unfettered. We already feel that in justice we owe a greater tolerance to those who have fallen by the way under a crushing burden of hate and evil. Because they have fallen, others are driven to aspire.

CHAPTER 5

THE QUALITIES AND WAYS OF LIFE

No single individual can possibly respond to all the stimuli within human range. What, then, is the criterion of the full life?

'None can usurp this height. . . .
But those to whom the miseries of the world
Are misery and will not let them rest.'

KEATS

'To live reasonably is not to live by reason alone — the mistake is easy, and, if carried far, disastrous. . . .'

I. A. RICHARDS

'The right of education, if we could find it, would be to work up this creative faculty of delight into all its branching possibilities of knowledge, wisdom and nobility. Of all three it is the beginning, condition, or raw material.'

C. E. MONTAGUE

TO CONTINUE the argument in proper sequence, I must now define the qualities of life as far as is possible in terms I have used so far. To live a full life in the biological sense would demand intimate contact with a high proportion of the stimuli to which man is capable of reacting; it would demand, too, that each and all of these forces should have been assimilated and aroused to effect the individual's responsiveness. Although he can widen, by means of travel and varied interests, the range of his environmental influences, he cannot aspire to feel *acutely* all the myriad stimuli that make up the sum of the forces acting upon the species as a whole. This is impossible, no matter how varied an individual's experiences, how encyclo-paedic his knowledge, how retentive his memory or highly tuned his sensitivity. A man would need to have travelled into every corner of the globe, experienced every conceivable kind

96

of adventure, mastered all the arts and sciences, been sports-man and athlete, musician, poet and inventor and known *all* the sorrows and joys of life; participated in all the actions — all the glories and horrors — of which man is capable; would need to have witnessed and felt much more beside, more than anybody could possibly call to mind, before he could claim to have even approached a full life in the biological sense. Impossible: no man has ever lived or ever will live a *truly* full life, although there are men who spend all their time in the attempt to feel, see or know all life has to offer. Paradoxically enough, the only organisms which live full lives in the bio-logical sense are those which must respond to all the factors of the environment to which they are capable of responding or perish. Not so man: we must look further if we wish to define the full life in practical terms applicable to ourselves.

The will and ability to create is perhaps the greatest dy-namic force peculiar to man: unless that force is active, the full life is impossible. This ability is, however, prone to lie fallow and can only be aroused by the awakening of interest. Interest may be regarded as the forerunner of the creative force in action and, because of man's mental selectivity, it will be directed along certain channels in particular. Interest and selectivity are assuredly the forebears of creative flores-cence. In practical terms, the first essential to a full, creative life is enthusiasm or the 'creative faculty of delight' directed to particular ends. The second essential is adaptability: the ability to assimilate and utilize environmental forces for the ends ardently sought. It follows that determination of pur-pose, will power, is also essential to the full life: so too is opportunity. A full life is not possible on a starvation environ-mental diet. Some are so placed that despite strenuous effort, they cannot sufficiently widen their experience of environ-mental influences in the directions most desired: thus neuroses and empty lives.

My analysis shows that what may be a full life for one individual, may be a narrow life for another. In general terms, the opportunities for living a full life would be great in propor-tion to the number of environmental stimuli to which an in-dividual was subjected. The fullness of the life would be determined by the number of the stimuli helpful to the purposes he fervently desired, his energy and ability and the acuteness of his response. From the social point of view a full life, as thus defined, may be judged useful, good, worthy, noble or harmful, wasted, bad. Nevertheless it is the necessary foundation on which alone a life can be built that fulfils individual potentialities, which includes potentialities of goodness and nobility, etc. But it is well nigh impossible to those working long hours, who are tired during their scant hours of leisure, unless their daily work in some degree captures the imagination, and unless something akin to delight is felt in the performance of daily tasks. In my view contemporary society denies to multitudes of people the possibility of living a good life, because it denies them any glimmer of a full one.

The useful life calls for exertion, adaptability and determination of purpose. The good life (or worthy or noble) will also be permeated by wisdom. Wisdom, that strange quality, delicate and robust, which learning seems unable to create, but which, if present, can either be nourished and widened, or wounded and narrowed, by human contacts and experiences. Wisdom enables a man to rise superior to himself, and superior to environmental conditions. Wisdom is nothing more and nothing less than inspired selectivity, the power to sense what is beautiful, right and good. Wisdom, if it is to be more than passive, demands sustained effort of the highest order directed to assimilating and seeking those environmental forces most helpful to the spiritual needs of man. Wisdom takes heed of biological laws, and recognizes the need to make allowances for antitheses. Further, in the words of D. H. Lawrence: 'It is the state wherein we know our wholeness and the complete, manifold nature of our whole being.' Wisdom and expediency can seldom be partners, for wisdom looks rather to the future of the species than to the needs of the day.

Wisdom must not be confused with character. A man of character might almost be defined as a man who is true to himself — such a man might be devoid of wisdom and a bad character; if bad, he would be bad in proportion to his courage and will power — both necessary ingredients in character. Purposefulness is inherent in character. Good characters devote themselves to purposes and aims that do not injure others: the greatest characters by accident or design, will benefit humanity, enrich society, and further the cause of the species. *Great* character is, therefore, impossible without wisdom, 'the insight and the vision' that directs purposefulness, almost subconsciously, towards good and great ends: nor is it possible without will and courage to inhibit such personal tendencies as may interfere with the thought and action necessary to achieve the ends to which a man of high character is driven.

I suspect that at least the germs of sound character are incipient in far more individuals than are the germs of wisdom; by training it should be possible to develop the character of large numbers of individuals in directions favourable to themselves, to human fellowship, and to mankind. Great character is another matter: but if the germs of wisdom are more widespread than our present modes of life render manifest, then by thinking, educating, and organizing with wisdom and character in view, rather than striving after barren knowledge, material comfort and artificial 'equality', we might hope to nourish what is most humanly necessary to the real progress of mankind.

I have written in terms of what might be described as 'the higher usefulness', and perhaps I have implied that it is open to all men to choose for themselves their own way of life. Unfortunately, as things are, the majority of men, if useful at all, are largely so by accident, and only on a lower plane, in so far as their work is connected with material products, commodities or services which are judged essential or useful to society as organized at present. How can an individual committed to long hours of work on a lower plane of usefulness attain a higher, dynamic and satisfying plane? The only road which leads to a higher plane is that of interest. As I. A. Richards has well said: 'What an individual responds to is not the whole situation, but a selection from it. . . . What is selected, and thus the relevant environment, is decided by the organization of the individual's interests.' And there lies the difficulty: for if an industrial working day unduly curtails the range of the environment, the scope for selection may be pathologically limited. It may not present any features that arouse interest, or only features which tend to arouse morbid and anti-social interests and the craving for an environment to satisfy these morbid and anti-social interests. This brings us

face to face with the real sociological purpose of education —
to create among individuals the capacity to become interested
in the work they may be called upon to do.

Outside interests may be good or ill, but are likely only to
be ill if they tend to make the individual more than ever dissatisfied with his workaday hours. Work still remains from the
human-ecological point of view the great uninvestigated subject. Intended to enrich society, for the great part it steadily
destroys humanity. Interest may derive from the moral or
social value of work, from its actual performance or from
both. No doubt some gain real interest from their good fortune in being engaged directly or indirectly in tasks which are
essential to the life or material welfare of man. Such tasks include the winning of food and the sinews of energy, the making of clothes, the building and maintenance of houses, the
manufacture of furniture and the running of essential services.
It is, however, unfortunately true that there may be more
scope for arousing interest in employments which are concerned with the production or dissemination of lethal stimuli
than in many of the truly essential employments. Here there
is need for critical research.

I would argue that the good life should necessarily be a full
life in the sense in which I have outlined it. Shelley's definition appeals to me and is in accord with my biological view-
point. 'A man to be greatly good', says Shelley, 'must imagine
intensely and comprehensively; he must put himself in the
place of another and many others; the pains and pleasures of
his species must become his own.' Our views on what is useful
or reasonable must be a function of our contemporary situation. The good, on the other hand, is timeless; but its detailed manifestations are hard to define in terms acceptable to
all men whatever their creed or mode of thought.

After love and altruism, I would place next in my scale of
values that quality of tolerance and forgiveness associated with
serenity rather than with humility. But the more man achieves
in the intellectual sphere, the greater his need for humility towards life and its eternal values. There is no greater danger
than conceit born of mental arrogance toward the unknown,
and towards schools of thought and of learning with which
one has little sympathy or about the details of which one is

ignorant. Just pride in a particular accomplishment is another matter, but as G. K. Chesterton has said, it does a man 'most harm to value himself for the most valuable thing on Earth — goodness'. Whatever views are held as to our spiritual life, and whatever a man's religious beliefs, our bodies and, effectively, our minds are fleeting tenants of this planet. Since we are endowed with intelligence, it would seem to be no less than our *spiritual* duty to take comprehensive views, and to learn all we can about ourselves and about the environment in which, for the moment, we have our being. This is the least we can do to justify the compliment we have been paid by the gift of so many freedoms.

In an earlier chapter I made a distinction between what I called the vertical and horizontal ways of life; we must look more closely into this matter. No pattern of human life can be adequate unless the family looms large in the picture. We can, however, make too much of the fact that man is a social species. Thus I. A. Richards goes rather far in saying: 'that only as a dehumanizing fiction, do we regard him as an individual', although it is perfectly true that: 'a momentary individual good has often to be sacrificed for the sake of a later or general good'. Similarly in regarding the family 'as a live functioning organism', the point of view which has been the basis of the significant Peckham experiment, we are, perhaps, although adopting a sensible and legitimate biological attitude, not being quite true to the whole teaching of biology. We must be careful to pay sufficient deference to the individual, for the individual is unique. I would rather regard the family, not as a functional unit, but as an amalgam of closely knit and interdependent individuals and a healthy society as an amalgam of closely knit and interdependent families.

'The goal of life', said D. H. Lawrence, 'is the coming to perfection of each single individual.' This I believe to be true of man, though not necessarily applicable to other forms of life. The truth of the matter undoubtedly is that the individual cannot come to perfection in a society where neither the family, nor the society itself, approach perfection. We shall perfect ourselves only along the road which leads to integration, firstly of the individual within himself, secondly of the

H
101

individual into the family, and thirdly of the family into society. The family is therefore of crucial importance. Happy and united families cast their radiance over all who are fortunate enough to come under their influence. Indeed, we can almost go so far as to define human progress in terms of increasing numbers of happy and united families. In the antithesis *individual — species* a reconciliation of the opposites is achieved through the family, and in the case of man, as we have seen, neither the individual nor the species can achieve perfection except through the society or community. Indeed the individual and the species appear to be contraries, and actually become contraries, when this other factor is denied its proper function.

In assessing the work done by the Peckham Health Centre, it is important to take long views. We must remember that the success of that experiment was partly due to the low ebb to which family life had sunk in the large centres of population. In making further plans for the future, there lurks a danger in any institutionalization of our family life. Our researches should be carried right into the family circle, and we shall perhaps learn more of lasting value by the study of happy and successful family life than by the study of those whose family circumstances have been less fortunate.

If we look around us, what conditions have we found among such happy and united families as it may have been our good fortune to meet? In the first place there has generally been elbow room — a garden, or something more than a garden. In the second place, the children will usually have taken some part in the work of the household: they will not merely have been amused, they will actually have helped in the care of plants or small animals, will have fetched and carried, and in some way will have been concerned with the activities of their parents and therefore of real life. They will have been given food for their creative activities, and early familiarized with the demands made upon the personality by the performance of useful jobs. They will have learned to enjoy simple things. It is an advantage when the mother and father work responsibly together in some undertaking, and perhaps particularly when the older children help with the work upon which the family income depends. There can be little doubt that family life has deteriorated in direct proportion as the influence of the father has waned. The real trouble began when the man went out to work, went far from home to work, worked long hours, acquired outside interests, came home late, came home tired. This is the position in most homes today. Women have worked at tasks other than the care of the home from time immemorial, but until comparatively recently they worked at or near the home — in the fields, for example. There can be no real family life — except that of an institutional character — if both parents work long hours away from home. It is essential that the father should associate himself actively with the lives of his children. If he leaves the house early and returns late, his only chance to be an active parent occurs at the week-end. His weekday experiences are unlikely to have been connected with the family: he will perhaps have made friends and acquired interests, either good or bad in themselves, which tend to remove him further from his family. This applies to all classes. The wife and the children will never have seen the breadwinner at work and will have no idea how he spends his away-from-home-time — by far the larger proportion of his waking hours. All too frequently the only interest of the family in the father is 'the bread', a most unhealthy state of affairs — a state of affairs which tends to make the father lead one kind of social life in one place, while the mother and children lead another kind of life elsewhere, the interests and friends of each being different. Under such conditions the family can have no proper roots. There is little scope for the happy mingling on friendly terms of children, adolescents and adults which is an essential part of family life, and an equally essential part of the social life of a compact district, itself a community of families.

It is platitudinous to say that the deterioration in family and community life is the outcome of ever-increasing specialization and of improved methods of transport, which make it possible for workers of all classes to live further and yer further from their homes. Platitudinous or not, the real point to be faced is that segregation of the individual from the family, and of the family from the community, has been carried to dangerous, not to say lethal, lengths; and it would seem that modern trends will accentuate that segregation. This is one of the chief reasons why, in my view, we must achieve a new and better balance between town and country, and attempt to achieve this despite the dangers inherent in such an attempt. We must organize our social lives in terms of smaller and more homogeneous units, based on sharper and wider diversification of interests. By sharper diversification I mean that appeal should be made alike to the spiritual, the intellectual and the sensuous, to the graceful and the utilitarian, to the physical and the biological. Diversification which plays in different guises only on the same chords in our nature is no diversification at all, and cannot nourish the whole man. Again, reasonably small and homogeneous social units do not need to be buttressed by excessive organization or by local authorities acting in the capacity of godparents, palliatives which are only necessary when the size of cities and of over-specialized industrial undertakings has outgrown their capacity to cater for the real needs of real human families, and of real human individuals. Of all this, however, much more in subsequent chapters.

The conditions I have postulated for the growth of happy and united families are fulfilled to a marked degree on the farm. On the farm, the growing child has ample opportunities to go about with his father: he will be associated directly both with living things and mechanical devices, and will be able to help in a number of useful and interesting tasks. The farmhouse and the smallholder's cottage home rank high as schooling places for the family. This is proved beyond dispute in terms other than those of farming by the exceptionally large number of successful professional and business men who were brought up on farms. In the past, the tendency was, no doubt, for farming parents to overwork their children, especially on the smaller farms and market gardens. As C. H. Gardiner says: 'they were put to work in the morning before they went to school, and they started on the ground again immediately after tea'. Gardiner is unable to tell us whether the gardening or the schooling aroused the most *interest* in the young people. He does tell us, however — he is writing of the Evesham district of market gardens — that the 'fighting spirit', the ability to arise superior to difficulties, carried the small men triumphantly through the Depression. Work which is not unadulterated drudgery begets character: there is no escape from this fact. On the basis of the Peckham experience, Pearce and Crocker observe: 'Going out to work should play a most important part in the unfolding of adolescence, for association with adults in responsible work is itself an educative factor of primary importance.' I shall draw further on the findings of the Peckham experiment when I come to insist upon the value of apprenticeship in the next chapter.

Even excessive occupational work for young people is better than no occupational work at all. Today, moreover, the social conscience is aroused and the prospects on the land are no longer intolerably bleak. There need be little fear of children and adolescents being turned into slaves. For that matter there is now much less danger that either the parent, the foreman or the small proprietor will drive his workers in any undertaking in the way that small men often drove their families and employees in the early and blackest days of the Industrial Revolution. This is fundamental to my gradually unfolding argument, and to any plans aiming at the organization of society on smaller and better integrated units. The pendulum has swung back, for the years between the wars were marked by the fact that parents tended to spoil their children and relieve them – or deprive them – of all real and responsible work. In our criticism of the past, of which we are the sorely harassed heirs, we may easily blind our eyes to the possibility that arrangements which were then predominantly abused might well, under the more enlightened conditions of today, be predominantly good.

To return to the farm: I state with conviction from my own experience as a director of agricultural research with a wide and intimate knowledge of farm life, that the experience young persons gain from being intimately connected with the daily happenings – biological and physical – on a farm, affords, as near as can be, perfect conditions for training in the sciences and for a career in research. This is germane to my general argument, since integration rather than segregation must now be the trend of scientific advance. The farm is a school of integration: hence its unique biological and sociological significance. The home life and surroundings of the farm worker are similar in many important respects to those of the farmer. The children have elbow room: they associate freely with their father; they and their mother alike know what he does; they walk out over the fields on errands; more often than not they help with the harvest. At home they may work in the garden and tend the poultry. 'Gentlemen' and their estates are likely, soon, to be but memories, but with them will disappear a number of callings which gave admirable scope for the rearing of robust families. Gardeners, grooms, estate handymen, woodmen, gamekeepers and men of varied crafts were all supported by the great estates.

In the old days, too, the fishing village offered a splendid example of the close mingling between the home and the work of the father. The children spent much time in and about the boats, and the women were a party to everything that was afoot. Perhaps all is not lost in these days of the steam trawler and the mechanization of the fishing industry. Something of the old tradition probably still exists. The homes are near the sea and are really part of the activities of the ports — but just how much has been lost we may never know or realize until it is too late. Twenty or more years ago, and even now to a considerable extent, those working in the coal mines lived not only in small but in wonderfully homogeneous communities. Family and community life was a striking feature of the colliery towns and villages, and this in spite of the drabness of the surroundings. There was interest in the work and pride in achievement.

Family businesses have much to recommend them when they are placed in healthy and congenial surroundings. The parents share responsibility and the children have opportunities to help them. This is particularly true of the village shop, the local builder, the blacksmith, the small petrol station and garage and kindred undertakings. A virile agriculture, developing in all directions, adds decisively to the trade of local trade communities and, incidentally, gives valuable employment to competent master men in an ever widening range of skilled and specialized work. There can be no more profound mistake than to think that what happens in agriculture effects only the fields and the shippons. Looked at in the light of family life and the healthy employment of rural districts, a flourishing agriculture benefits greater numbers of auxiliary undertakings than on the farms themselves.

I now feel that I am in a position to complete my definition of human progress. I hope that, if only by implication, I have given good grounds for the view that human progress is something that goes far beyond a world of glittering achievements in architecture, the arts and literature and far beyond the dogmas and discoveries of science. It goes far beyond the masterpieces of ingenuity and skill in engineering and manufacture; far beyond well ordered cities and institutions; it goes beyond amenities and working conditions, and far beyond the social freedoms and securities. These are rather the luxuries and ornaments of progress and, in their nature, the outward and visible signs of the quality and direction of progress at any given time. They are not the terms in which progress can be defined, nor do they represent those aspects of progress that are the most deeply felt.

Life, as life, is an expanding adventure, therefore, human progress must be of the nature of an expanding adventure. Experiment is the essence of progress. Although man is a social species, individuals are the nerve centres and driving force of progress, so that, in the last resort, human progress can only be maintained at the highest pitch of intensity and in the most favourable direction by the fellowship of individuals living full and worthy lives, and under conditions favourable to human effort. Again, since spiritual values *are* human values, mere expansion without increasing the relative numbers living truly happy lives of spiritual gaiety would not be human progress. And where there is spiritual gaiety, as contrasted with mere spiritual contentment, there will also be a heightened acuteness and artistic perception. Human progress is not to be estimated by the achievements, no matter how illuminating or how helpful of the few: it can only be estimated in terms of the lives of the many. Human progress must, therefore, be defined in two-fold terms. Firstly, in terms of man's expanding comprehension of his own potentialities and limitations, in his expanding comprehension of all his human needs, and in his expanding comprehension of his ever expanding environment, together with a growing willingness to match his expanding actions to his expanding comprehension. Secondly, in terms of the increasing proportion of individuals who live full and worthy lives under conditions increasingly favourable to comprehension and to wise endeavour born of that comprehension, and under conditions which foster spiritual gaiety. Progress in one direction without progress in the other cannot be dignified by the term human progress. As often as not it is inhuman progress. Human progress in short is more a matter of men singing in the fields and whistling in the streets than of motor-cars and electric devices; more a matter of window-boxes and pleasing buildings in the working-class flats and the middle-class suburbs than of the creations and the thoughts, as such, of men of genius; more a matter of the judgment of the people than of the decisions of statesmen.

CHAPTER 6

HAND AND EYE, HEAD AND HEART

The object of education should be to co-ordinate all the functions of man. Nature's own method of integration should become a principle and a habit

---

'Without unceasing practice nothing can be done.'

WM. BLAKE

'And overcrowding, in education as in housing, means illhealth and turns the school into an intellectual slum.'

SIR RICHARD LIVINGSTONE

'. . . the heart is as full of mysteries which only genius can reveal as is the world of nature.'

HERBERT GRIERSON

THE AGE of perpetual motion dawned with the railway: this has been the forebear of what is to be an age of full employment, and an age of protracted formal education. If my interpretation of biology as applied to man has been just, it follows that education will have fallen short of its essential human purpose unless it operates as a discipline for the smooth and effective functioning of all the organs and attributes of which the individual is possessed. Not only must the intellect and the powers of conscious reasoning be educated and exercised, but equally the subconscious, the instincts, the senses, the emotions, the muscles; and all must be co-ordinated. In a word, the business of education is to draw out to their full extent all the potentialities of hand and eye, head and heart, and to integrate these manifold capabilities into one beautifully functioning whole — into the wholeness and oneness which alone declare a living creature to be organically and functionally a perfectly developed representative of its species.

109

The more protracted the formal education, the greater the possibilities of lethal consequences undermining all that may be good in the systems adopted; so that it is more than ever necessary to take wide views of the purposes, means and modes of educating. We should do well to be honest — even brutally honest — with ourselves.

Because we have to be consciously taught how to read and write, and consciously taught how to manoeuvre in an expanding assault of words, it is easy to be led into thinking that education is only an affair of the head. We should realize the possibility that in proportion as we load the brain with an increasing weight of paper facts and book knowledge, so in equal — or maybe greater — degree we must develop hand, eye and heart. How otherwise are we to sustain and mellow what can so easily become a dangerous and even explosive cargo?

Emile Cammaerts insists that: 'Knowledge is an instrument which may be beneficial or harmful. It all depends on the quality of the person who yields it.' A more pungent rendering might, however, be more to the point; can we fairly say: 'The greatest fools, or the most dangerous fools, are the well educated fools?' I believe, at least, that we must all admit that education in its care of the head has, to date, scandalously and flagrantly neglected the other faculties. Despite all the new educational legislation, as far as I can judge, far too much relative emphasis is still put on the head — and on the intellect at that: hand, eye and heart are still forgotten and come off poorly in comparison; that means *co-ordination* is forgotten.

It is necessary to give explicit meaning to three words — *teaching, training* and *conditioning*: they are the keystones of any broad and all-embracing system of education.

Teaching: This consists in the imparting of knowledge through the spoken and written word, perhaps with the aid of diagrams, graphs, symbols, charts, slides, films and the like. No more is expected of the student than to listen, look, take notes, answer questions, write essays, read set books and so forth. Teaching directs itself to the intellect and is responsible for those baneful 'preps' to which far too many tiring and boring hours are devoted. It calls for a retentive memory to respond to teaching — the more neatly pigeon-holed the better.

110

A retentive memory of itself and as a dominant attainment is at best a questionable advantage: it is doubtful if it should be allowed, as such, to exert a dominant influence at school, college, university or in afterlife. Teaching, then, in the last resort, is wholly a matter of words — of language. Teaching as teaching is frequently tantamount to the use of words without adequate context. Whitehead says that: 'the success of language in conveying information is vastly overrated, especially in learned circles. Not only is language highly elliptical, but also nothing can supply the defect of firsthand experience of types cognate to the things explicitly mentioned. The general truth of Hume's doctrine of the necessity of firsthand impression is inexorable.' Much teaching is conducted without the support of any supplementary training even in the subjects taught: in some subjects to do so would be difficult, but in few, if any, impossible. An excessively high proportion of school, college and university hours are devoted to teaching as here defined — classes and lectures — and despite improvements, teaching is likely to dominate curricula and the examination system for many more dreary years.

Training: Training is of two types, passive or active. In both, broadly speaking, the aim is to acquire a technique. In both the methods of procedure must be explained or demonstrated, and a more acute responsiveness will be demanded of the pupil than that called forth by the impersonal atmosphere of class and lecture-room. Passive training, which can be applied to the inner self, is a fine discipline and demands and encourages high powers of concentration. Every person, young and old, should be shown how to relax, and should practise that art. Passive methods should also be employed in the training of the subconscious, the instincts and the senses. The main distinction between teaching and training is that whereas teaching is wholly a matter of words and memory, words are only incidental to training — for which a retentive factual memory is not essential.

In the more usual sense of the word action is essential in training: active training encourages co-ordination between hand, eye and head, and to that extent is an advance on teaching. Active training is to perform an operation, to conduct and experiment, to manipulate pieces, to make something, to watch and preferably to handle animals and plants, to collect, to take part in exercises, drill, gymnastics, to play games, all under tutelage. Training invites and involves close personal co-operation between the student and the trainer. Character and human wholeness are necessary in the person who would aspire to train young people. A feeble person with no human understanding and little experience of life can do far more harm as a trainer than as a teacher. What is bad in teaching is bad in any teaching carried to excess, so that characterless teachers, if masters of their subjects, are relatively innocuous. I am sure that many grown men looking back on their school and college days realize that in so far as personal contacts are educative — and how profoundly educative they can be — they gained more of real value from the genius who presided over the carpenter's shop or the playing fields, than from any of their form masters. Training affords admirable opportunities for developing the team spirit, while groups of students can be set to make something together or to act co-operatively in other ways. Never has the need for the team spirit been as great as it is today. Team training under the direction of a man of fine character will appeal to the heart, as, indeed, will most good training. Thus training should be regarded as the core of our educational system, influencing alike hand and eye, head and heart.

Training stands to teaching as does digestion to swallowing. The great educational value of science is that teaching has to be co-ordinated with training — laboratory work, field classes, excursions. Art as an education has a similar value. The teacher of art or science is also a trainer, so he should be a person of sterling and infectious character.

In drawing up curricula for general training, it must always be borne in mind that man is a creative animal and he must be trained in terms of his natural creativeness. Like sex, creativeness can easily be thwarted or perverted. Successful training must arouse and sustain interest, and this can best be done by playing upon the creative impulse. Indeed, it is by means of training that so much can be done to nourish healthy and socially valuable interests and prevent the development of morbid ones. Young people are profoundly interested in life and in real things, and in real workaday things at that: a large proportion of the time devoted to training should be given to work of an occupational character. The creative urge can be satisfied by using the imagination for constructive purposes, not only in the sort of imagining that produces works of art or advances knowledge, but in doing simple things. All true craftsmanship makes constant calls on creative imagination — on seeing further than the work of any particular minute or hour. The creative impulse is further strengthened by doing work that can be seen through to a finish — making a boat or growing a crop. Sound training should always aim at helping the potential man to train himself, to start wisely and well, for training should be lifelong. It is here that hobbies are of such importance: I would go as far as to say that if a boy leaves school before he has found a hobby, his education must have sadly missed its mark. It is easy to encourage a hobby in those who, left to themselves, would find one, but difficult when the driving idea has to be discovered and then carefully nourished. If we consider our educational system as a whole, we must admit, I believe, that hobbies in this stimulating sense have not ranked and do not yet rank high enough in the scale of values. Of all hobbies those of a semi-vocational character are the most enduring and the most fruitful. An ordinary healthy and balanced hobby should have something to do with a garden, or with animals, or something to do with a boat or gliding or, for the more high spirited, something involving physical adventure, such as climbing. All of these hobbies would bring the boy, and later the man, into close touch with nature in action and would tend towards the continued training of the whole man. Hobbies are of an importance today that is pathetic, for the tragedy (it is nothing less) of highly specialized industrialization and of the highly organized state is that the percentage of the population compelled to drudgery increases every year. Drudgery is work that makes no demands upon the creative imagination. Creative hobbies allied to proper holidays is one direction in which salvation lies. In my view no general training can be complete unless it takes the student out of doors, on to a farm or into the country, and much of it should be carried on outside the precincts of the school, college or university. Training is as much the affair of wise parents as of good schools. It can be superb at home and at its best during school holidays.

Conditioning: The distinction between training and conditioning is narrow but real, although in practice there will be overlapping. Training is a matter of more or less set instruction and guidance, at least until the individual can take care of his own training. Conditioning is an affair of example and insinuation; it is also a matter of creating favourable external conditions. It is by far the most subtle, and the most generally neglected, of the three keystones of education. Conditioning at its best would be conducted in such a way that the persons conditioned — no matter what their ages — would have no idea that anything was afoot, or that any special care was being taken of them. I should than define conditioning in general terms as the production of conditions within and without the individual that will favour the development and functioning of hand and eye, head and heart, and the co-ordination of these into a single well balanced whole. Conditioning aims indirectly at arousing and guiding interests, attitudes and aptitudes. There is also such a thing as conditioning a human being's reflexes, and of making the brain and instincts ready for experiences to come. Conditioning, or rather the means and modes of conditioning, are the province of psychology and physiology; they are also the province of accumulated common sense. The physiologists are probably substantially correct when, in effect, they claim that the most important conditioning age is from two to seven, but the scope for conditioning does not end at the age of seven nor even at the age of seventy.

This view finds its counterpart in the setting up of nursery schools which are held to be of great value by modern educationists. Thus Sir Richard Livingstone: 'First in time and high in importance is the nursery school, where in infant years the child learns to live in a community.' This free mingling of children should be all to the good, provided the numbers brought together are not too great and those who preside are to a woman of the sort who love and understand children and know how to 'mother' them. Nursery schools today are an absolute necessity in innumerable districts where so many mothers go out to work or have only a single child. They are highly desirable, too, because under some conditions, even with the best will in the world, children from different families cannot be brought together in healthy conditions except at school. Granted all this, I think it should be realized that there are dangers inherent in nursery schools. Our major aim should be to create conditions favourable to the good family life and to educate the rising generation in the skills of parenthood and in the gentle and subtle art of conditioning. Ideally schools for potential mothers rather than nursery schools might well prove to be the correct psychological answer to the claims made by the psychologists. The sharing of mothercraft between teachers and mothers can only be of ultimate value if the mothers as well as the children benefit. Both mothers and teachers must be willing to educate each other. Psychology is an infant science and is permeated by many and strange views, while parenthood is age-old and has its own natural lore and tradition — some of it no doubt erroneous. There is a woeful amount of crass ignorance in the bosom of many families, but I wonder if the science of parenthood in all its implications is in a very much better case. The nursery school, since it goes to the heart of family life, can only be justified if quite extraordinary steps are taken to ensure that every single one of such schools is run on the soundest possible lines and is in charge of a person of exceptional qualifications. It can only be justified, what is more, if the mothers and the homes are brought intimately into the ambit of the arrangements: the importance of this is tacitly accepted by the establishment of parent-teacher associations. The mother herself must benefit as a mother and not merely as a woman and a bread winner; she must not seek to shelve her own responsibilities or permit herself to be a party to anything in the nature of the institutionalization of family life. Today we must hope as well as plan, and our plans will be wise in proportion as our hopes are high. Can we not hope that, when the people of England are properly housed and when life in England once more becomes merry and simple, mothers will combine to organize their own 'nursery schools' in their own and in each other's homes? Are we planning with *that* hope and hopes of a similar character ever in our minds?

As adolescence is approached not only surroundings but companions exert an overwhelming influence on condition-

115

ing: at this stage a discerning uncle or aunt can often tactfully and helpfully intervene. Amongst adults, an old and wise friend, by taking appropriate action at a psychological moment, may do almost everything to recondition a person who has gone awry or who has fallen on bad times.

Although conditioning is to a great extent beyond the direct reach of formal education, yet schools, colleges and universities are falling short of their responsibilities unless this aspect of the trinity — teaching, training and conditioning — is given its proper and essential place. The provision of milk to school children is an important action taken by the educational authorities because it recognizes that food and diet are essential conditioning factors, and they remain so at all ages and in all walks of life. Conditioning presents fascinating research problems, and here there is the widest field open to every man and woman who draws a salary from university, college or school.

In a broad way it is realized that good teaching supported by little or no training and bad conditions can only lead to disastrous results — dissatisfied individuals who become an incubus to the family and a drag on the state. I think it is fair to claim that unless teaching is at all stages supported by the more humanizing influences of conditioning and training, operating in an atmosphere of considerable freedom, then the teaching is almost certain to be both didactic, an affair of 'inkhorn' terms, and bad — an education narrow and over-authoritative. In this view is implicit a pungent criticism of oversized classes in schools and overcrowded lecture theatres, laboratories and colleges at the universities.

Teaching, training and conditioning — these are the terms on which I shall continue my discussion. And let me repeat that they must be used to assist individuals first and foremost towards oneness and wholeness and to make them good coordinators of all their faculties and functions: without this, knowledge, is a positive danger, making the lives of individuals, and the stability of sovereign states, the playthings of every storm, for storms are inherent in nature and in human society.

Despite the recurrence of wars, education has been responsible for some abatement in the natural cruelty of men and some amelioration in the lives of men. It can, however, be said that civilization has become increasingly uneasy and the lives of men increasingly muddled — values at sixes and sevens, family and community life deteriorated, simple happiness on the ebb, artistic perception on the wane, vandalism and tawdriness in flood, chivalry and good manners in decline. And all this in spite of the rapid extension of formal education. We are compelled to accept the fact that education has failed — not because we have had too little, but because what we have has been conducted on the wrong lines. All that counts in the long run is human values and contented and worthy lives. It is to the everlasting discredit of education that those occupations in which success does not depend on the head alone are held in low estimate: the exaltation of paper and 'clerky' callings is pathetic and pathological.

I shall now consider our problem in greater detail and begin with the subconscious. Can we train what we please to call the subconscious to come more wholly, and at command to the aid of our conscious mind in solving different problems and reaching wise decisions? I think we can. If we could devise a reliable technique for doing it, and start the training early enough, then I believe that new and interesting prospects of self-development would open up to us. I have experimented in this myself: and though my attempts are only in an undertone, I believe they are informative. I have lived an active life in the field of research, practice and administration. My interests have been diverse: like every man in charge of a growing department, I have been actively concerned with new developments. Fated to live a large proportion of my working life in times of stress, I have had to make decisions and balance widely conflicting aims and interests. On these occasions I have felt acutely the need to react to the situation with my total experience in order to act wisely.

There is nothing new in the thesis implicit in my experiments with myself directed to finding a technique for calling to mind the whole of myself at need: its interest lies rather in the fact that my little discovery was personal, quite accidental and had nothing whatever to do with anything I had read. In effect I happened upon a mode of relaxation which stands somewhere half-way between those states which Aldous Huxley has described respectively as passive and dynamic relaxation. 'Passive relaxation', he says, 'is achieved in a state of complete repose, by a process of consciously letting go . . . Dynamic relaxation is that state of the body and mind which is associated with normal and natural functioning' — very rare today!

'Sleep over it' is sound advice, but my experience suggests that we can train ourselves to achieve a condition which is neither sleep nor wakefulness, and which is more fruitful than either sleep or full waking consciousness in bringing the subconscious to our aid. The plan I slowly evolved was to hold my intellect and imagination completely in check, and to allow my mind to be conscious only of my sensuous self; parallel with this was the heightening, by design, of my sensuous responsiveness. I aspired to put myself into a state of complete sensuous domination. It is exceedingly difficult and requires much experiment and training and consequently demands much more than passive relaxation. I am most successful when I relax on a couch in front of a wood fire. It takes me longer to attain to this condition of controlled relaxation than to go to sleep: to go to sleep is fatal — and all too easy. The method is sensuously to enjoy the heat from the fire, to feel every slight change as the wood alternately glows and bursts into flame: to watch idly the ever-changing patterns of flames and embers, and to sense every slight difference in the fragrance of the burning wood. A changing rhythm of heat, fragrance and pattern seems greatly to help, so I like a fire of different woods, or of woods of different vintages. The effort not to weave ideas and thoughts in sympathy with the changing play of the fire requires great discipline, and it is difficult just in proportion as one is harassed or overtired. But that sensuous domination is possible I have proved beyond any shadow of doubt. It is far more infuriating and devastating to be aroused from this state by the telephone, by a caller, or a barking dog, than to be abruptly woken from a comparatively easily won and lazy sleep. To arise naturally and at the appropriate moment from a successful and long continued period of this controlled relaxation is most exciting. The mind is ablaze; an act of integration has been performed; new lights will illuminate problems which will be seen whole and large, and the remarkable thing is that answers will be forthcoming to the very questions that had been agitating the tired conscious mind. The hard thinking of the past that has become absorbed into one's being is released and mingles with the thinking of the present. Anything I have said in this book that may be of some real significance has to a remarkable extent been the product of my successful and longer continued periods under sensuous domination. Looking back over my life it has always been the same; when I have been able to relax in this manner on critical occasions, my decisions have been comparatively reasonable and my actions, judged by results, not unsuccessful. Without the aid of this technique, on the other hand, my decisions have been uneasy or erring and my actions faltering or muddled.

Three conclusions of importance emerge. When I first indulged in controlled relaxation, I did not realize what I was doing, so I did not begin training myself nearly early enough in life. Worse than that, it was when I was most harassed and most tired — and therefore most in need of controlled relaxation — that I was too lazy or too heedless to make the attempt. My experience suggests that the training should be started early and the exercise continued regularly and rigorously throughout the whole of an active life. The more busy a man is, the more important it is that he finds time for sensuous domination. I feel quite certain that had I put myself under sterner discipline I should have realized more of my potentialities. I say all this because it bears so closely upon the problem of fatigue and the social significance of that all-pervading malady. The second conclusion is that if I, an amateur with little discipline and endeavour, have been able to train my subconscious to some extent, then surely with research into ways and means, and with properly disciplined exercises, it should be in our power to train the subconscious to digest and render useful to us at call much of our acquired knowledge and experiences. The third conclusion is this: in all probability the wisdom of the illiterate and the quasi-illiterate owes much to the fact that they are past masters in the art of sensuous domination, although they don't give it a name and they don't appreciate its significance. 'Sometimes I sits and thinks, and sometimes I just sits.'

This is an age of worry and hurry; if the wisdom of the

119

illiterates of an easier going generation is to be reincorporated into our traditional way of living — as I am sure that it should — then it would follow that in proportion as we acquire knowledge and consciously think over what we have studied, so we must also devote proportionate time to 'just sitting'. We must make an ideal of an age of relaxation.

We must be careful not to confuse sensuous domination with contemplation — 'the impassioned vision of the worth of things'. Contemplation is consciously turning things over in our minds, divorced alike from books, pen and paper. I am convinced that every curriculum should include training in contemplation, and lessons as to the 'how' of contemplation. Nowadays it is very difficult to be alone and too many minds are too empty to enjoy being alone. For contemplation I prefer being out of doors and in soothing surroundings; not amidst wild, or too exciting scenery, or out in a storm. By the sea when it is calm, in a wood when leaves have fallen, or in one's own garden, of which one knows every inch and every plant, so that outside interest is less likely to make a violent intrusion — these are suitable places for contemplation. A ride on a quiet and favourite pony on an oft trodden track I find favourable, for a pony has this great advantage as a companion: when you talk to him he will seem interested yet will not answer back.

An overloaded, fact-ridden curriculum is condemned by far-seeing educationists: to insist upon the folly of it is to emphasize the obvious. But little seems to be done about it; yet in this fact-hunting and technical age, the dangers of overloading are greater than ever. Is there, indeed, something lethal about the obvious? Has it a deadening effect upon the will, the capacity for taking action?

Where the defects in a system, whether of education or of any other social arrangements, are obvious, we must remember that the systems in force today have been of slow growth. Various evils, like faulty bricks, have been gradually built into the expanding structure. The result is that infant trends, be they defects or excellencies, are not soon enough recognized as having emerged into the world of action or of thought: when they are detected, they are not at first considered to be of any particular importance — they are not obvious. All social errors are cumulative and have a long tradition behind them. This is why defects, even when obvious, are so exceedingly difficult to put right. Indeed, the more patent the defect, the more difficult it is to rectify, because it will be more deeply entrenched than those which are less easily discerned. If errors of long standing cannot be countered by reasons and arguments which are as obvious as the errors themselves, and which have been long tried, then perhaps the only hope is to bring new and different arguments to bear upon the systems which are permeated with defects. If, for example, the ability to acquire the habits of controlled relaxation and of contemplation are essential adjuncts of true education, then indeed we have imperative reasons for shortening the hours devoted to acquiring facts, for drastically amending the examination system and adjusting curricula to permit more training and less teaching. Ample time must be given for the development and training of self-efficiency and self-sufficiency. The capacity for the synthesis and digestion of facts should on no account be permitted to lag behind the rapidity of acquisition.

General education should have three major aims. The first, to make a student of the pupil — a person imbued with an enthusiasm for true learning and with a delight in reaching conclusions for himself and in the exercise of *all* his faculties. The second, to inculcate the knowledge of how to learn and what to learn. The third, to help individuals to recognize embryo trends within themselves and within society before the bud becomes such a well established and overgrown plant that it cannot be trained, pruned or removed. Every trend must be assessed in terms of its potentialities for good or evil. The need for this has been forcibly stressed, though perhaps incidentally, by Lewis Einstein. We shall never successfully challenge the overloaded curriculum with the old arguments: we must use new arguments based on a new approach closer to the biological and psychological 'facts' of human nature, how human interests are aroused. A system that stifles interest is lethal. All said and done, the aim of teaching considered merely as a quest for facts should be to show us how to acquire and arrange facts, and how to turn to the best advantage the facts which we have acquired: *method,* in the widest possible meaning of that too narrowly used word, is what we all need to be taught. This is an old argument and blatantly platitudinous, but it is desperately important as applied both to general and specialized education.

This is an age of specialization. We are beginning to realize the dangers of this, but are they fully and deeply enough realized, particularly as applied to the courses of study given at the universities? There is need for a much clearer distinction between general education and specialized education than exists today: no students should be allowed to specialize unless or until his general education is receiving, or has received, adequate attention.

Unless the universities cater for general education to suit modern needs, it is idle, nay dangerous, everlastingly to increase the schools of specialized learning. The rapidly growing number of Departments of Fragmentation must be offset by the establishment of Departments of Integration. Science for far too long has been left to run its own unfettered course, absorbing to itself far too large a share of the funds at the disposal of the universities, and blissfully ignoring the other faculties of learning. The other faculties for their part, and not without justice, are almost contemptuous of science as at best affording a narrow basis for higher and all-round education; while science but little diluted is not of itself sufficient nourishment for the development of a cultured mind. All must agree that science has the merit of catering through laboratory work for the hand and the eye, as well as the head. The classics, history, literature and the 'arts' in general, however, have the altogether greater virtue – if taught with any feeling at all – of appealing directly to the heart as well as to the head. This is the fundamental difference between science and the arts, the practical consequence of which is that appreciation of the innerness of the classics, literature and history and of detailed knowledge of even fragments of these subjects is more character-forming than is detailed knowledge of fragments and science. The difference between science and the arts is accentuated by the fact that the disciplines of science are usually narrower than those of the arts. Culture and character can only be founded on discipline, but on disciplines which sharpen the feelings and reach to the heart rather than those which only give 'head-meanings'. My own

122

view is that far too much relative importance is attached to the much vaunted disciplines of science. The humanities demand and inculcate their own and far sterner disciplines, for their quest is values and the meaning of facts; the quest of science as taught and practised on a subject basis, is *only* the accumulation of facts and the formulation of hypotheses likely to help toward the accumulation of yet more facts. This raises a further and serious criticism of science as it is taught in the separate Fragmentation Departments. It is not the explicit business (enforced by either curricula or examinations) of any department or of any professor to enlighten the student as to the *innerness* of science, and as to the implications of the facts of one science on those of another, and still less of the implications of science on all branches of learning and human endeavour. This defect is to some extent the outcome of the rapid growth of science and the excessive fragmentation into specialized departments which has necessarily accompanied, just as it has accelerated, that growth. Thus biology as such has been drowned in all its fragments – botany, zoology, genetics, physiology and the rest. A student may study in the schools of fragments, but where is he to study biology? Yet biology, which is the study of life, has become increasingly important as a subject in its own right because the various departments into which it is now subdivided have brought such a wealth of new facts to light. The duty of a Department of Biology – and such a department should find a place in every university worthy of the name – would be to seize upon the implications of fragments of knowledge in widely different fields, and to integrate the findings of all those sciences which bear in any way upon the functions and functioning of living things, and to take and teach a broad philosophical view of all the manifestations of life and of all the processes which maintain life.

That the offspring of biology, to all intents and purposes, have banished their parents from the universities, is significant it is the natural outcome of the complete divorce of science from philosophy. Lord Cherwell tells us that nearly twenty-five years ago an attempt was made in Oxford to establish a joint school of natural science and philosophy, and more recently the idea has been revived. Lord Cherwell adds: 'Unless something of the sort is put in train, I fear philosophy will stagnate.' So much for philosophy: but surely science has lost as much, or even more, by the separation of the two subjects? Perhaps the chief need of every university today is a strong school of Natural Philosophy. I use natural in its proper sense, and the function of natural philosophy as a subject of study would be one of integration – the integration of science and philosophy. The establishment of such schools would recognize at long last that science without philosophy can only erect edifices on foundations of sand; philosophy without science can only build castles in the air. The course at Oxford on Philosophy, Politics and Economics is clearly a move in the direction of integration: I speak in ignorance, but I imagine that it may be weakened by too much dependence on reading alone: it is not sufficient simply to read in these subjects.

Schools of Natural Philosophy would go some way towards bridging the gap towards the humanities and science, but I do not think far enough to fill all the needs of a sound university education in accord with the times. I would insist as first prerequisite of a university education that every student was brought into close intellectual contact (and within the precincts of the university) with both the arts and sciences. This need is beginning to be recognized. At Cambridge during the long vacation a reading course for men taking science, a course of ten lectures, was given by members of the Faculty of English Literature. These lectures drew audiences of over 500, so it is evident that the experiment was appreciated by the science students. Excellent as an extension of such arrangements would be, I do not think they would go far enough: surely today no university should consider a student worthy of a degree who has not read both in a school of science and in a school of the arts. It is only by establishing Schools of Integration that this would be feasible and profitable. I hesitate to suggest appropriate Schools of Integration for the arts: but a Professor and School of Humanities would perhaps meet the case; then with Schools of Natural Philosophy, Natural Science (a school of integration to cover all the sciences) and Biology (in addition to, and quite separate from the various fragmented schools) it would be easy to arrange syllabuses that would be worthy of a modern university. Degrees could then be awarded on a surer foundation of sound scholarship and understanding than under present arrangements.

Let us suppose that an undergraduate is primarily interested in science: such a man would have to work about one-third of his time under the auspices of the School of Humanities, one-third under the auspices of the School of Natural Science and one-third in the school of a particular scientific subject which he preferred. An Arts man would have to spend one-third of his time respectively in the School of Humanities, the School of Natural Science (or Philosophy might be a better name), and in his chosen art subject. On this plan, no student would come down from a university with a degree without having acquired a liberal education at university level — hand and eye, head and heart, each would have received some attention.

I took Part I of the Natural Science Tripos at Cambridge — a so-called Honours Degree! I read chemistry, botany and geology. Because I was mildly interested in geology, I spent more than one-third of such time as I did not spend in riotous living in the School of Geology. I am quite certain that if I had spent one-third of my school hours in the School of Geology and one-third in a School of Natural Science and if I had just added the other one-third of school hours to my riotous living (i.e., done no chemistry or botany as such) I should have come down from Cambridge a far better scientist. Suppose, however, that I had passed my other one-third in the School of Humanities, I should have lost nothing as a potential scientist (after all universities can only direct potentialities) and I should have come down from Cambridge more nearly educated and with a degree really approximating to Honours standards. I am sure my experience stood for quite 75 per cent of my contemporaries reading Part I of the Natural Science Tripos. So far as I am able to judge, conditions are still materially the same at Cambridge today and at 99 per cent of the provincial universities[1]. As to Oxford I would not presume to express an opinion!

[1]In many of the provincial universities there have, of course, since this was written, been new courses and departments set up along the lines suggested by Stapledon. Biology and ecology still suffer everywhere from fragmentation.

'Nothing, not all the knowledge in the world, educates like the vision of greatness, and nothing can take its place,' says Sir Richard Livingstone. It is only by integration of the arts with the sciences, within the arts and within the sciences, that visions of true greatness can be conjured up. Thus (to talk only in terms of science) biology broadly and philosophically taught would open to the students visions of greatness far in excess of what either botany or zoology separately expounded as self-contained subjects could possibly hope to achieve — for greatness is wholeness.

The universities are overcrowded, the members of the faculties are overworked; there is not enough space for new experiments; we have not the time nor perhaps the breadth of vision and outlook to anticipate fearlessly the results of the revolution in thought which we of this generation are witnessing. We seem too harassed and tired to undertake the actions which would strengthen the springs of learning and culture so that they can stand up to the stresses to which they are now increasingly subjected. Great courage is demanded of the universities to alter fundamentally their points of view, their curricula, their means and modes, and in ways which would reach back decisively to the schools and colleges. Sooner or later, however, the situation will have to be squarely faced, for in the long run fragmentation in education and research as in everything else is bound at last to drive us toward integration. Unless the universities are prepared to stand by and watch themselves develop into nothing more than glorified technical colleges — and that would be the herald of a wholly technical and utterly uncultured age — then drastic reforms, even more drastic than I have indicated, are essential.

I suspect that the first step should be drastically to reduce the number of students at the universities and to increase the period spent in taking a degree. Implicit in this arrangement would be to demand higher standards from all concerned and to abolish the so-called pass degree.

What I have insisted upon here as the general responsibilities of the universities is a necessary prelude to what I shall now have to say about craftsmanship and apprenticeship.

CHAPTER 7

INSTINCT: MEMORY AND CRAFTMANSHIP

We train our instincts every day but without design and without realizing what we are doing. We have given command to the intellect and neglect the great achievements of the post which were the result of training and conditioning

---

'But words plainly force and over-rule the understanding, and throw all into confusion, and lead men away into numberless controversies and idle fancies.'

FRANCIS BACON

WE CAN train our instincts. We are doing it every day but without design and only in an undertone. Unfortunately we have, as it were, given complete command to the intellect. Our instincts, uneducated and perverted, are not serving our human purposes to any well defined ends: indeed we are only grudgingly or unwillingly accepting their aid.

If it were possible to study the influences of training and conditioning only – or of these coupled with a bear minimum of teaching – it would provide the best way to achieve a sound basis for the education of the emotions and instincts. This would, in short, mean studying illiterates: not tribes wholly illiterate, but the illiterate amongst a civilized population, large numbers of which are literate. This could hardly be done in our country, though we still have a few grand old people amongst us who can neither read nor write. Today all that could be done would be to study the less literate – those whose reading is like that of my mother's cook who read only the Bible and the *News of the World.*

The quasi-illiterate have always greatly interested me and I have had numbers of dear and firm friends amongst them. I am old enough, too, to recall my boyhood friends among the truly illiterate. Maybe I was exceptionally fortunate in those early days and perhaps I am biased by my close boyhood friendship with my father's coachman, who could neither read nor write. Yet it was this man who first introduced me to gardening and taught me how to handle garden tools: he was highly self-disciplined and courageous; his memory was faultless and everything he did, he did well. A man of stature if ever there was one, he seemed to love everything and everybody surrounding him. He created this wonderful character in spite of having to battle with very poor health.

Let's be quite honest and appreciate at its proper worth the full range of material on which modern education first cast its net. In the illiterate class were to be found exceptionally large numbers of men and women of sterling character. Their heads were self-taught, save for a bare minimum of tutorial words casually directed toward them by parents and taskmasters. Their hands and eyes were practised and their judgments accurate. They had cultivated human capacities of the highest value to themselves and to their community. They may not have been persons of the highest possible human stature – if indeed characteristics like self-reliance, independence, loyalty, pride in work well done, untiring perseverance, kindness of heart, enjoyment in the sheer act of living, philosophical contentment and a deep appreciation of the simple realities of life including simple beauty are held to contribute to the stature of man. In the country districts the number of fine illiterates was large. In those far-off days I had no experience of towns, but I have no reason to suppose that there were not similar men and women in them, too. They certainly proved what training and conditioning alone can accomplish.

During February, 1946, I spent many hours watching two accomplished woodmen felling trees in my garden. They were brothers, countrymen to the core, and had worked together in the woods for years. One, aged about 45, had never been to London, and for the other Reading was 'too large'. Both were intelligent and had sound and decided views about the times: neither were well read or highly educated in the fact-laden sense. The interest lies in their method of going about the job. Everything was done to a plan, which, as far as I could gather, was never once discussed. At each felling the two men seemed to work as one unit; there never seemed to be the least doubt about the right mode of attack — rope or no rope, preliminary loppings of branches or not — hardly a word was said from start to finish, nor was any argument necessary when they decided which tree should come next. Mine was not straight-forward forest felling: if no damage was to be done to the standing trees, to fruit or fence, each tree had to be dropped almost to an inch — and so fell each tree. The masterpiece was a redwood of fine proportions, about 40 years old. All the trees impeding this giant's allotted inch had been felled, but still no attack was made on the redwood. No, the correct fall could only be made certain with the right strength of wind from the right direction so the redwood stood for 10 days. Then in a flash, one morning, those two men, impelled by some uncanny power of discernment, and without argument or discussion, knew that the moment had come — a fleeting moment it had been, they told me afterwards — and in three minutes the heavily branched redwood had crashed 'twixt cherry and oak' exactly to plan. There was a right way and, I expect, only one right way, to have felled all those trees without damage to standing limb or bough — a correct plan of attack and a correct technique for each tree. Those two men, conditioned and trained for years in a world of trees, axes, sledge-hammers, wedges and cross-saws, instinctively and immediately sized up the whole position and dealt with it unhurriedly, unerringly, and in a manner to match the unfail-ing precision of a homing pigeon. Is *instinctively* the right word? Not very far wrong, I think: or shall we say that with men so trained and conditioned, intellect, instinct and senses work differently and more harmoniously than where intellect has been promoted to the position of senior partner; work differently, more rapidly and with less fuss and with a pre-cision that would put the senior partner unaided to shame? Precision is the hallmark of instinct: so I shall suggest that these skilled woodmen were skilled just because of long years of experience and practice, and with little interference from conscious reasoning and unhampered by a wealth of scientific facts about the properties of timbers and the mechanics of motion, strains and stresses. They had conditioned and trained their vocational instincts.

The training of 'vocational instincts', although it is thorough among the majority of those engaged in agriculture and forestry, is by no means confined to countrymen. A few years ago I had the pleasure of watching day by day three highly skilled men erecting a large and massive Dutch barn. The foreman, like my woodman, had not been schooled in the laws of mechanics; he and his mates, again like my woodman, were highly intelligent, but I do not think they brought any greater degree of minute-by-minute conscious reasoning to their aid than did the woodmen. There was the same certainty and precision, the same absence of talk or argument. The way those three men got the massive girders in place and brought every piece of it to fit demanded rapid decision almost second by second a slip or a mistake would have meant almost certain disaster to men and metal. Watching the men at work led me to suppose that disaster was not even a remote possibility — no more likely, shall we say, than if a rider plunged his horse into a slow-moving stream it would not make the opposite bank. The working of instinct is suggested in both cases. The erectors of the barn were committed to a rigid specification and to the handling of matched pieces, yet in the actual erection they were not directly dominated by any machine. For years they had been practised in the taking of quick decisions in a restricted vocational field, decisions that involved lightning co-operation between hand, eye and head. Do not both woodmen and barn men afford valuable hints as to how vocational instincts operate and can be trained?

Let us now see what we can learn from higher types of vocational skill: for example, the sort of man who was near to being the life blood of the old estate, a man skilled with many tools, as well as being an artist at all kinds of joinery, could often build a wall, lay bricks or work in metal. Mercifully such men are still to be found in country districts and I have had close dealings with two such master craftsmen. One was a key man in my day at the Welsh Plant Breeding Station, the other, later on, at the Grassland Improvement Station.

Here in general we have a class of men with no great knowledge of mathematics, little or no formal knowledge of stresses and strains, with no head for elaborate specifications and plans, but with an eye for a job and an uncanny instinct for quantities. Men who seem to carry everything in their heads, and who have the same sort of warm and affectionate feeling for the materials in which they work and sympathetic understanding of their properties as a good groom or stockman develops for the animals under his charge. It is sufficient with such men to discuss what you want on the spot; it may be anything from an idea about something needed for a field experiment, or a special building for a special purpose, though it may be something quite different from anything the man has made before. Always, the minimum of explanation suffices, but excellent suggestions will be offered as to design and materials. You decide to proceed: little or nothing is put on paper; the craftsman turns it all over in his head, perhaps makes a few — very few — simple calculations, and you are informed as to the quantities of the different materials needed. In a surprisingly short time all will be finished; well finished, in good proportion, substantial and pleasing to the eye — for the lines will be right — a work of art by an artist who takes a humble pride in his creations. It is remarkable what a good all-round master craftsman of this type will manage by himself; heavy timbers will be moved into place, joints and fixings effected without boy or mate holding at the other end: help from other men about the place is seldom accepted.

Mostly the master craftsmen of this school have been self-trained. They may have been apprenticed, but most likely to a man of few words. It will have been chiefly by watching, by helping and practising that they win their technical skill and broad understanding. I remember once asking one of these men how he had acquired his abilities: without a moment's hesitation the answer came: 'Watching my old dad.' An answer of great significance for educationists — watching rather than listening, action rather than words, is the key to training.

The countryman, when of good stock and still living the life of yeoman or peasant, is a superb watcher: hence his honest and well grounded mistrust of words. The well educated yeoman or peasant, a man with a reasonably good armour of paper facts, remains as ever a good watcher with a still deeply ingrained belief in the efficacy of watching as the best method of training. Since he has been trained by watching, he is usually a reluctant teacher. During the war I had many interesting tussles with farmers and skilled farm workers on the training of land girls and part-time workers. My entreaties for a little more trouble in showing recruits how to do things were invariably sagaciously countered by remarks such as: 'Best leave them: those any good will pick it up.' In this attitude there is a germ of downright hard truth. The hard truth is that self-training, and for that matter self-teaching, are arduous, but extraordinarily efficacious, and, above all, character forming.

Watching! It must be watching acutely with a view to action and practice: then in practice feeling sensitively every slight difference in resistance and friction, seeing vividly every changing shape as the work proceeds, and afterwards remembering all those differences and comparing them, subconsciously perhaps, with the different materials used, the different tools. It is some such sequence as this which trains and strengthens a sensuous memory of great power – a memory filled with images of sight, sound and feel. The master craftsman who will have acquired his skill from practice and watching will not have been overloaded with empirical knowledge and paper facts – for these destroy the memory as a tool of creative action: a craftsman sees his work through from start to finish and works with a sense of the finished product in mind. The normal skilled peasant or landsman has an extraordinarily good sensuous memory and my woodmen and barn men were assuredly of this type. I have myself gardened from childhood and I have quite a remarkable visual memory of all the gardens I have tilled and of the precise operations and results in different gardens. My gardening experience has been of the illiterate type; I learned by watching and not by reading. Thinking again of my father's coachman, I know that the skilled illiterates had amazing sensuous memories: that man could not have done half the things he did without being thus equipped.

What is the stuff and substance of a sensuous memory? It partakes of a wonderfully efficient weaving of intellect, instinct and senses, the sum of all of which are, as it were, rapidly integrated by the subconscious, so that the possessor of a vivid sensuous memory responds almost instantaneously with the whole of his being to any situation. The mind is an active mirror of all the experiences of life: it is uniquely dynamic. Faced with any problem great or small, trivial or involving life and death, the whole of the accumulated knowledge and experience of years, stored as an intricate sensuous memory, crystallizes into spontaneous action; the individual reacts seemingly subconsciously, surely, immediately, suitably. The man brought up on an expensive diet of book learning and paper facts reacts more haltingly, baulked by a conscious striving to pick up threads of knowledge, baulked even more by a conscious desire to look up notes or to check up on reference books: to take, in short, some conscious and definite action to assist in the sizing up of the *elements* which make up an immediate problem. The highly educated and fact-laden man may have (he will not necessarily have) a wider field of knowledge and experience upon which he *could* draw than the less educated and less fact-replete but better trained man, but it does not follow that he will have instantaneously at his service as much integrated knowledge-experience when he needs it. Nor does it follow that the fact-man will have at his day by day disposal more wisdom to assist him in the mundane business of living a good and useful life. On both counts the odds are in favour of the really well trained sensuous man. I do not for a moment suppose that intellect and conscious reasoning rummaging among facts have not a part to play in the achievements of the sensuous man, but in this case they are not the master factors at work. It is certainly within the power of the man with highest intelligence and who is a veritable encyclopaedia of facts to respond to the whole of his vast knowledge and experiences. It depends upon how he has trained himself and his attitude to facts. Indeed, I would define genius as the ability to respond unerringly, in a flash, with the sum of personal knowledge and experience. Genius thrives better among the less educated and fact-ridden than among the highly educated. When geniuses arise among the highly educated and master their surroundings, they tend to shake the world: those amongst the humbler classes merely hold the world together. Geniuses among the higher order often win immortal fame, those of the lower win moral contentment and contribute to the stability of the nation.

The point is really this: Is there any reason whatsoever why the ordinary well educated and fact-stowed man should not combine within himself all the virtues of such learning and also all the virtues of what we may fittingly describe as the true peasant's mode of thought and action? I would reply, no reason at all. It is purely a matter of balanced education. With a properly balanced education it should be within our power not only to add to the number of manifest geniuses, but to add greatly to the effectiveness of the majority of men. If my diagnosis is basically correct, then apprenticeship to an appropriate craft should be made an integral part of our formal system of education. Just because this is a technical age with the machine and the brain (the brains of relatively few men) dominating our lives, apprenticeship becomes essential if we wish to benefit from well-tuned instincts and senses. To consider one example: new scientific devices have reduced the dangers of the sea, but these devices will defeat their own ends if implicit reliance upon them undermines the old capacities for instinctive and instantaneous adjustment to emergencies. In proportion as scientific apparatus takes over the function of instinct and sensuous memory, so it is essential to find methods of training and vitalizing these faculties in man. We should avoid the risk of developing one side of our potentialities at the cost of side-tracking or submerging another side. In order to secure maximum safety at sea, for instance, the sailor's aptitude for sensing danger should be trained in addition to dependence upon instruments.

Can we train our senses? To some extent we do so every day, but not advisedly with the aim of integrating all our faculties. The senses of the average man are certainly not as acute as they have been in past times. It is probable that the monotony of rationed diet during the war and the scarcity of flowers has built up habits of indifference to the taste and quality of food: to this we must add the immense amount of food that is frozen and canned and processed in innumerable ways — often treated with additives to make it seem as if it were fresh and natural. All this has tended to weaken man's capacity for co-ordinating form, colour, sense and taste in one satisfying and harmonious reaction. The range of sense response in the individual varies as much as the brain of individuals; the range is immense. Eating and preparing food

134

should be an art and a craft; its refinement is therefore dependent upon sensuous experience, as in any other craft. Handling food should kindle the imagination as much as handling the soil, plants and animals kindles the imagination of farmers and gardeners. The senses are sleeping partners in the creation of sensuous memories and are privy to instinctive decisions.

In the choice of vocation we should take especial account of work which calls forth a wide range of sense-response. It is here that the importance of apprenticeship lies as a part of formal education.

CHAPTER 8

APPRENTICESHIPS:
SPECIALISTS AND EXPERTS

We must now reorganize our methods of education in terms of our new biological knowledge

'The earlier a man realises that there is a craft and an art which will help him to improve his natural gifts in a regular way, the more fortunate he may be called. Whatever he may receive from outside — nothing can impair his inborn individuality. I call the highest genius the man who can absorb everything, who is able to make everything his own, without at the same time jeopardising in the feast his real and fundamental destiny which is commonly called his character — on the contrary, carrying it to the highest peak, fulfilling all his potentialities to the last degree.'

Written by GOETHE *on 17th March, 1832 — five days before he died.*

'And the last and greatest insult you can offer the human race is to regard it as a herd of cattle to be driven to your selected pasture.'

W. MACNEILE DIXON

IN LAYING stress on apprenticeship as a formal part of education we are at once confronted by an acute problem and yet another antithesis.

Apprenticeship will serve its purpose only if craftsmanship continues to be largely an affair of the instincts and the sensuous memory. Will this still be inherent in craftsmanship, if the craftsmen themselves are taught rather than trained, and if their book and fact-winning education is carried to far greater lengths than that to which the old-time craftsmen were subjected?

The difficulty is real but not insuperable. We may be encouraged by the fact that first-class training in experimental science, followed by a sustained occupational pursuit, does help in the development of instinct and sensuous memory, though it is not as efficacious as the old-time training in craftsmanship. Craftsmanship need not be ruined by modern trends; it is only a matter of assessing these trends and adjusting teaching and training appropriately and in time. The danger of ruin will be least where the craftsman attains most closely to the ideal of doing a whole job for himself or, alternatively, of being actively associated at all stages with a particular enterprise. He must not become a cog engaged in the unimaginative task of making another cog.

This is an age of cogs, and the next best thing to seeing through to a finish alone and unaided, or with the assistance of somebody constantly under one's eye, is to be engaged upon work which is not isolated from all the other work aimed at the same goal, as, for example, building a house or producing milk. These are the essentials to be kept in mind when choosing the occupations which will be of the greatest value if, and when, apprenticeship is made a part of formal education — occupations valuable in themselves as training and containing the type of craftsman who naturally, spontaneously and without effort radiate the right atmosphere, fostering the desire for purposeful action. To *act* correctly and spontaneously must be the main object of training.

In selecting our occupations deference must also be paid to all the complicated biological and human antitheses we have discussed: equally we should have in mind the influence of occupational training on developing a taste for, and skill in, the right sort of hobbies: this in turn enriches the value of leisure and the longer holidays that must be anticipated in the future. We have four main classes — and many sub-classes — of individuals to consider in relation to occupation.

In the first place there is a sharp distinction to be drawn between those who are called upon to make day-by-day or even hour-by-hour decisions in the course of their work, and those who. practically speaking, are not expected to make any worthwhile decisions for themselves at all. In the second place there is a broad distinction to be made between those like research chemists, historians and stenographers, the results of whose work is expressed in work-patterns (the research chemist must explain and describe his achievements), and those whose achievements are manifested without words. The distinctions are not, of course, absolute and are always a matter of degree: to talk and think in terms of those who work with their brains and those with their hands is stultifying to all the individuals so designated. That is why I prefer to discriminate between the word-pattern and the action-pattern occupations. 'Head' and 'hand' or 'brain' and 'manual' are not satisfactory as categories, nor for that matter is the normal classification of the various professions, businesses, trades and services. The actual tasks performed in any major undertaking are now so manifold that the traditional designations tend to obscure the real issues. *What really matters is the quality and quantity of the decisions that have to be taken by individual workers.* A statistical statement classifying the working population on this basis should be possible. It would, I am convinced, be of greater social value than any body of statistics that has ever yet graced Blue Book or White Paper. With this knowledge before us we should have significant data upon which to found an educational system: we should be able to decide the sort of training, leisure, hobbies and holidays that are essential for the different classes (plus or minus) of decision takers.

Everyone knows that the percentage of the population who in their daily work would stand in the lower 'quantity-quality' classes is overwhelming and probably constitutes the greatest evil in the social structure of modern civilization. The percentage of low 'quantity-quality' workers is no doubt as high in the black-coated as in the shirt-sleeve and overall occupations: indeed it is certainly higher if one acknowledges the extent to which office routine has now been mechanized and the retail trade dominated by proprietary articles. Thus we have the peculiar position, so well brought out by Dr. Fritz Marbach, that any distinction between the lower middle class and the upper working class is wholly artificial: it is a delusion of social snobbery itself dependent upon a blind acceptance of meaningless social values. The irony of the situation lies in the fact that decision is inherent in so many of the action pattern occupations that are looked down upon.

From the point of view of developing human potential and maturing character, the occupations associated with agriculture cannot be bettered. Agriculture is a school of integration. It is at once a science, an art and a craft. No matter what a particular man does on a particular farm — let him be expert ploughman or expert stockman, he will perform more than one type of manual action most days and during every week. He will be forever taking decisions and will be in close contact with the activities of the farm as a whole. The best specialist agricultural craftsmen are always deeply interested in all that goes on. From the angle of apprenticeship, therefore, there is no need for the pupil to have worked on every job on the farm since close association with one side of the enterprise would probably serve the aim of training.

To depreciate the machine is now futile: whether we like it or not the machine age has come upon us with a vengeance, and it should be a part of training to make us all spanner-minded and spanner-handed. On the modern farm machinery is used for a great variety of purposes and is not employed for the turning out of parts, but in such a way that the man is master of the machine. Constant adjustments and constant decisions are called for in relation to ever-changing conditions and differing uses. This is true in respect of ploughs, drills, cultivators, threshing machines, grinding mills and so on. Much farm machinery is now intricate and complicated and calls for skill and finesse in servicing and operation. Both the good farmer and the competent farm craftsman of today are spanner-handed and minded, and the mechanization of the farm is probably only in its infancy. Mechanization on the farm is not deadening in its influence on those working on the machinery — or it only becomes so when the workers have no interest in the end in view. The good worker uses machinery as a hand craftsman uses a saw or a lathe — to assist him to do something that he could not do so well and perhaps so quickly without those aids. Like the hand craftsman working in wood, the ploughman will see gradually unfolding before him the final result of his skills. If he has been properly trained, his visual memory of past ploughing and past crops carries him along with enthusiasm toward the end of his labours. He has an ideal of what it should be like that has been shaped by past experience. Ploughing, cultivating, harrowing, preparing seedbeds and sowing the seeds is one continual process and the methods to be adopted for each depend not only upon the circumstances but also on the degree of skill with which the preceding operations have been conducted.

There is nothing wrong with machinery as such: it is our attitude of mind towards it that is wrong. The function of machinery ought not to be regarded as a means of getting a job done with the least trouble, as quickly and as cheaply as possible, without respect for the worker's dignity or the quality of the product. This is not yet the case in most agriculture: and the very conditions under which farming must be undertaken demand such skill and such forward seeing and thinking that it is hard to see how the machine can make life on the land intolerable and meaningless, that is to say how it can undermine the essential wholeness of farm work. (The social consequences on rural society of new methods of production is another matter — I mean the deliberate restriction of production to a few highly mechanized farms and the further starving of the countryside of true country people.) The relation of farming to machinery, and of machinery to farming, is an important additional reason for choosing agriculture as the best of all occupations in which to serve a period of apprenticeship.

Because the majority of people are town born and town educated, it is of great importance that apprenticeship, for them at least, should be served in the country, at sea or in the air. Forestry, shipping, rural building spring to mind, always remembering that seeing through to a finish must be the major aim.

We must now consider certain fundamental aspects of the training of specialists and experts. Specialization in industry makes far too many workers who are not called upon to make decisions and who are committed to drudgery and to working hours that savour of slavery: in order to render the lives of these people tolerable and in accord with the full range of human potentialities, we may be compelled to recast our whole industrial pattern and our whole attitude towards gadgets. Perhaps we could avoid this by organizing our social life in such a way that full employment was balanced everywhere by ample leisure and holidays spent *fully* — spent in the interests of the full, useful, good life. This will be at the core of our discussion when we come to final grips with the great and intensely exciting subject of holidays.

There is a considerable gulf between the word-pattern and the action-pattern experts and specialists. The action-pattern experts are concerned with the actual making and running of the various machines, processes and procedures – they are the expert operatives. We speak today, and rightly, of expert herdsmen, ploughmen, fitters, mechanics and a host of others. The skills of the planning-cum-advising experts are very different in character. The numbers of these two classes should bear a proper relation to one another, and this in respect of each major industry. Further, the type of education suitable to the two classes should be different. I should not be surprised to find that the number of operative experts is not proportional to the number in the word-pattern class; such is undeniably the case in agriculture. If this is true, to what extent is the blame to be laid on educational trends?

I will hazard a broad generalization: where the head is to take almost complete charge (and a potentially good book-and-paper brain can usually be recognized early), it is of the utmost importance not to hurry forward the teaching. Intensive book-and-word teaching should start relatively late – late probably in direct proportion to the potential of the brain power. The word-pattern expert should start his formal learning late and then it must be continued long. The action-pattern expert should start his specialized training relatively young, probably at an age of such tenderness that the modern educationist would be horrified. The exact age would be a function of the trade and skill required, and also a function of the different temperaments of the individuals. Fourteen or even younger I have little doubt would usually be the right age. Generally speaking, the rule for training an expert herdsman, shepherd or ploughman is to 'catch him young': that there are remarkable exceptions to this rule does not seem to me to invalidate it. It should be a good working rule, not a dogma. The Peckham Experiment comes to my aid in explaining why I lay such stress on this: 'We have been very impressed with the differences we have observed in the physique and balance of development of boys who go to work at 14, as compared with those who remain at school until they are 16, 17 or 18.

141

In the former there is an all-round, robust functional development, often in spite of adverse industrial conditions, while those who continue at school seem overgrown. . . .' By forcing the brain too soon we risk inviting precocity and overburdening the young and delicate tissues, with the frequent result that all the high promise comes to nothing. But by deferring sensuous memory training too long, we lose the most formative years for acquiring craftsmanlike skills and hold the would-be operative expert too long in what, to a boy with potential skill, is a boring and uncongenial life. The best riders and the best games players are usually those who start young and the same is certainly true of the best craftsmen. It is not easy to acquire the sensitive and delicate habits of manual skill late in life. The human hand is as wonderful in its dexterities as the human brain is wonderful in its flights: indeed, the brain the hand and the eye are intimately related in man. In the cerebral hemispheres of the brain and in the hands we are almost incomparably different from other animals. The important thing is to recognize this in education and make sure that brain and hand are trained together.

Here is a fundamental human issue and there can be little doubt that any future age which is to be truly cultured and progressive will be the one that first applies means and methods of correctly characterizing the potentialities of individuals at a sufficiently tender age, and then adopts methods of overall education appropriate to the individual and to the work of the world. Such a civilization will not make the fatal mistake of rigidly fixing by law the school-leaving age. Apprenticeship will begin young where it should begin young, but the system of continuation training and of adult education will be highly diversified. Those who in their own and in society's interest are apprenticed young will be given ample facilities for evening classes and for periods of weeks or perhaps months together at continuation schools or colleges and later at centres of adult education. In this there will have to be the closest co-operation between industry and the educational authorities — a direction in which, fortunately, we are moving already. A rigid and too old school-leaving age is very nice in theory and sounds very idealistic, but it is all wrong in practice: if persisted in, it will damn all that is good in current educational trends.

Our 'Great Age' will set immense store by apprenticeship. If it is good and right and proper in the interests of human wholeness that those who by temperament and talent are best fitted for the vocations of hand, eye and action – and who will have been apprenticed at an early age – should spend long periods in the aggregate at centres of continuation and adult education, so it would be an equally good thing if those whose brain training will take many years – specialization will demand even longer courses of study – are compelled to spend during their school and university careers at least three or four months in the year apprenticed in a hand-eye-action capacity to an appropriate industry. Education of the higher and highest orders and vocational training for the high and highest vocational professions is woefully one-sided at present and ties those concerned to books and special studies to an exaggerated degree. Those destined to become word-pattern specialists tend to move among a restricted circle of fellow humans with interests and modes of thought similar to their own. In the light of general experience of life they live narrowly. The more intellectual and the more specialized a student, the more he needs the different type of discipline and experience which he could derive from periods of apprenticeship. A good deal of the misunderstanding and even hostility that exists between different levels of industry and different economic classes arises from this inhuman and absurd segregation of the two types: it breeds snobbery and ignorance; it is deplorable on social, political and human grounds, and it has its roots in our unreformed system of education. If apprenticeship were to become a part of prescribed education and a form of compulsory national service, then no professional or specialized training whatsoever should be regarded as affording grounds for exemption.

I am not concerned with the details of vocational and general education, but I must again emphasize that there should be very little difference in the means and modes of training for pure and applied science, and I must again insist that the technical scientist should become fully conversant with the practice and organization of the industry which he will serve. The scientist, be he pure or technical, needs to have

143

a broad-based general education: a wide and appreciative understanding of literature and history is, in particular, a sound foundation on which to graft an intensive scientific training.

We must realize that the complexities, opportunities and difficulties, for which the machine and material progress have been responsible, demand a system of education as complex as the times it must serve. We have to aim at higher specialization, and as a set-off to that, we must also aim at a wider based and more comprehensive grounding. Today no one should be considered well-educated unless he has acquired an informed and *philosophical* outlook towards literature, history, science, art and craftsmanship. Hence the crucial necessity for chairs of integration, as well as of fragmentation, at our universities.

Adult education will have to cater for two distinct needs: the one vocational, the other general. In the vocational field it will be necessary to teach the theory behind practice to those early apprenticed to hand-eye vocations, and also to provide refresher courses to those engaged in the higher callings. It should also be the function of the vocational classes to cater for those essential hobbies to which we have referred. The character of the general teaching and training given in continuation classes and by adult education on balance will, however, be of even greater importance than that appertaining to vocational training.

Although all this is bordering upon platitudinous, I will not apologize and I will go on insisting on it. I am adamant that apprenticeship should be made a part of prescribed education. I am convinced that both classes in further training and in further general education will fail sadly in their purpose unless highly diversified, and unless well and philosophically trained specialists share the responsibilities of teaching and training with well and philosophically trained integrators. The lead must come from the universities: I shall have little faith with all that is afoot in the world of education unless the universities recast their curricula and create many more chairs of integration.

Democracy can only flounder if it is afraid of highly differential methods of teaching and training. Fundamental biological laws must be recognized and it is highly immoral,

144

unscientific and anti-social to ignore the wide range of sharply contrasting capabilities inherent in individuals. The more diversified our system of education, the more geniuses we shall develop and the fewer dissatisfied and downright neurotic students will leave school and university to be a drag upon themselves and society. Education will be doing at least one part of its job properly when as much thought and attention are given to the training and general education of an expert stockman as to that of a specialist in biochemistry, and when both are held in equal honour. We must esteem equally the man who keeps an intricate machine in perfect running order and the man who invented it and regard both as at least of equal importance to the man responsible for marketing it.

CHAPTER 9

WORK, HOBBIES AND HOLIDAYS

The mass outlook and mass psychology of urban industrialism is contrary to the principles of biological growth. What methods are open to us to arrest this lethal trend in our conditions?

'For then only will men begin to know their strength when instead of great numbers doing all the same things, one shall take charge of one thing and another of another.'

FRANCIS BACON

MAN today is far too urbanly domesticated. In the case of the vast majority of men in this and other highly industrialized countries, the mass outlook and mass psychology of the cities and their factories dominate everything from politics and education, through recreation and leisure to what we eat and think. All this transgresses against fundamental biological laws and has led to dire consequences in many directions, consequences that will become increasingly lethal unless we are able to achieve a better balance between the urban: industrial and rural: agricultural. There are two ways open to us: the first to rearrange completely the geographical orientation of agriculture and industry; this would also mean some people could work, if necessary to their health and well-being, partly in agriculture and partly in factories. To do this, however, would be a slow business and we should have to move warily and experimentally to begin with: this reform has become so long overdue that it might now be too drastic to be practical; if we did it now it would certainly be necessary to pave the way by a well conceived plan of overall conditioning, training and teaching in order to prepare a generation of people who would be eager for change and who would be physically and psychologically equipped to benefit by it: otherwise large numbers of people would not be able to adjust themselves to new surroundings.

146

The second way is to give people the necessary contacts with the country and a sympathetic understanding of the ways of nature and of country activities through the medium of proper holidays spent in rural surroundings and by the pursuit of hobbies of an out-of-door and vocational character. In any case the first plan could never be put into effect until the second was well under way and proving successful.

Today, however, the great majority of urban dwellers are not even educated — and certainly not conditioned or trained — so that they can derive any lasting benefit from a proper country holiday: to be prepared for that they must spend part of their education in the country every year. Yet every child born into modern industrial towns needs to add new and acute experiences of biological phenomena to its stock of environmental influences as a counterblast to the narrow and predominantly material content of its everyday environment. We are now approaching what should be the great era of holidays with pay with no basic plans made and, what is infinitely worse, with no guiding principles to assist us in the formulation of plans.

The very people who would be the least responsive to an entirely new and wholly vitalizing environment are those whose psychological need for it is the greatest: they represent probably the majority of the urban-industrial population. This makes preparation for a new and balanced society both more urgent and more difficult: those most in need and whose psychological condition is most desperate must be expected to offer the most resistance to change. They are found chiefly among the lower quantity-quality decision-making classes, but by no manner of means wholly there: some of the highest politicians and businessmen are inevitably of this kind since they spend the greater part of their lives in cities and offices.

Amongst the most pathetic lessons of the war was the revelation of the extent to which large numbers of adults evacuated from the cities had completely lost any feeling for the country and nature; on this they had sunk below the fully human. The pathos was increased and the lesson accentuated by the rapidity with which so many of the children developed a warm sensibility and responsiveness to country things. Yet children born today in the towns cannot enjoy our great heritage of English literature because its background amid the countryside is quite outside their experience. With industrial towns we have sacrificed a great part of our traditional poetry.

A revelation such as this constitutes an open challenge to our system of education and affords a damning commentary on our social and industrial organization. The challenge cannot be ignored and we must look for the grave errors which palpably have been inherent in all our policies for progress.

So far we have been at pains to diagnose the major errors — which in the simplest terms are that education has paid all too little heed to action and too much heed to book-learning. To put it brutally, book-learning unsupported by a liberal conditioning and training is of little or no use to the majority of mankind. It has been an appalling mistake on the part of education to take no interest in holidays: to prepare children for their holidays is a major function of education, and I do not only mean school holidays, but holidays throughout life — for many of them will become workers whose working life will be sheer drudgery. To educate the young without regard to the dismal lives that society is preparing for them when they leave school is almost criminal. It is for the life of society as a whole that most children should be prepared — not for a career in a university. Action should be the keynote of general education for the generality of people. The master aim of education should be to awaken the desire for action and then to direct action into fruitful channels. Fruitful channels are those where action demands minute-by-minute and hour-by-hour decisions, not necessarily great decisions but real decisions, not actions dictated by a machine, fixed regulations or a mentor. These are not actions at all — they are simply mindless activity. Holidays and leisure should both to a very large extent be affairs of action and decision-taking for those whose lives are subjected to mechanical activities. It is also the function of holidays and leisure to compensate liberally for those elements in the environment that are missing in working hours: this is the time when those faculties must be awakened which our money-winning vocations allow to slumber. It is, then, the paramount duty of education to cater equally for holidays, leisure, vocation and culture. Our great mistake has been to suppose that culture, a word that consequently has become self-conscious, affected and overloaded, can be relied upon to make amends for all the defects in our civilization. No, it cannot: action comes first; the urge, the ability to act, these lie latent in every breast; a passive culture is no substitute for an active creative life, and to the extent that we behave as if it were, we declare to the world our own decadence. We must direct the biological urge to creative action into the right channels: then we must develop skills in the right actions; then we shall be able to claim that we are really a progressive and creative nation. At present this is more a verbal claim than a real fact.

Let education attend to all these things and we shall have gone more than half-way to real culture, and we shall form roots upon which to graft the more sensitive tissues that proclaim a well nurtured and vital cultural people. To put the cart before the horse is preposterous — and futile. It has well-nigh proved fatal in education, so we have lying before us an extraordinarily difficult task — more difficult than even those who advocate reforms on the right lines have yet realized. We have got to unharness a stubborn horse that has grown to like his false position and then induce him to lead and not to push.

It is my firm belief that in holidays we have the greatest of all hopes and our best educational weapon — holidays and hobbies, that is the magic recipe. What in the name of fortune is the good of machinery unless holidays can be longer and what in the name of fortune is the good of long holidays unless they are potent instruments in the making of full, useful, good lives, and what in the name of fortune is the good of book-learning and idle dreaming about culture unless the majority of men are living full, useful, good and culturally active lives in their own sphere?

Men there are who can profitably spend holidays around the museums, picture galleries, libraries, theatres and concert halls. But culture does not consist of that alone for any man: unrelated to creative action it is dangerous pedantry. Action is, I say, the fundamental need of man, and since the will to act has not been trained and harmonized with the emotions, the action-impulse has become dangerously perverted. Result — men flock in their millions to the cinema to watch, quite impartially, the images of men doing ridiculous, sensible or beautiful things; they flock in their thousands to the stadiums, courses and arenas to watch the modern equivalent of gladiators perform prodigies of skill. In the realm of sport and athletics more performers and much smaller audiences are needed. In that respect with a few highly trained and dedicated professionals providing distraction for millions, we are heading for the character of the Roman mob at the Colosseum.

I am persuaded that at present the lack of training and conditioning for holidays is a much more serious matter than the lack of facilities: if the training and conditioning were right and started early enough in the education of the child, a new kind of people would demand the facilities which we are in no hurry to provide on an adequate scale. Here, as in every direction, there is grave danger of panic action masking the really fundamental problem: such actions may postpone or even render impossible the right action that would lead to a lasting solution.

My thesis is now, I hope, clear and patent: the country and hobbies provide the two surest, but by no means the only, means of counterbalancing the lethal factors inherent in the crowded urban life of today. The immediate problem is, therefore, how to set about educating the urban population to make the wisest use of their holidays. The first essential is to take all children into the country young enough and often enough; the second, to give to both primary and secondary education wherever it is a sufficiently strong biological and country bias; the third, to train young people to act rather than to watch, and that in most cases means hobbies.

A broad understanding of biological principles and of life in action is a necessary equipment for every adolescent and is the soundest basis upon which to build real interests in the country, in simple things and in real life — not life reflected on the television and cinema screens. To the vast majority of action-pattern workers such knowledge would tend to be more character forming and be more likely to put to useful purpose — holiday purpose, one would hope — than much of what now clogs the school curricula. It is of little use, however, to attempt to teach biology without the aid of land and domesticated animals. Every city and town school should have a garden as something useful in itself and as a stepping stone to a more widened experience that should be gradually opened up. At present we can only feel our way and try and move in the right directions. A good start would be for teachers with a country background to teach biology to illustrate country lore. The next stage would be to set up camp boarding schools in truly rural surroundings where the pupils would be sent in groups for periods during each year. This may seem an exceedingly extravagant procedure, since it would involve duplication of schools and teachers. The school buildings could, however, be used for other educational purposes, for vocation classes and for vocational training, and the same teaching staff could be made available, on a rota basis, for all these purposes. The war proved some of the advantages to be gained from camp schools. This is the foundation on which to build.

A large proportion of the staff at camp should be men and women with a rural background and with an inborn love of the country and plants and animals. Attitude of mind is what chiefly matters: without the right approach, formal qualifications may conceal a total inability to teach, train or condition the young. Large and well kept gardens should be an essential part of every camp school, and small domesticated animals must be kept. Well equipped workshops with carefully selected mechanical devices should also form an important part of the equipment: dynamos and internal combustion engines would be seen in action, the one driving a saw or lathe, the other a small garden tractor. The pupils would work in the gardens and shops, help tend the animals and by visiting and working on farms and taking country walks would acquire new and real interests. When they grew up the country would not be a foreign language to them; to wander in small groups or to do things alone would not be a bore — they would have already been conditioned and trained to spend their holidays in action, participating in country life, not amongst masses of people merely idling or watching organized distractions.

The building of central schools in rural districts and grouping a number of one-time small village schools together — although no doubt attractive from many points of view — I believe, is a retrograde step: it will do nothing to ruralize the urban and it savours strongly of urbanizing the rural. A great deal of money is involved and, probably, this expenditure can only delay attempts to ruralize the urban which is our primary need.

Those who agree with me about this are certain to experience many disappointments: we must be content with small beginnings. I would myself be content for the time being with a few superbly staffed and admirably sited camp schools for the reception of groups of town children for periods of four to six weeks together. The cities and towns themselves should, however, cater more generously for a rural and action-pattern education. Parks should be on a more generous scale and altogether less sophisticated: our indigenous trees and the commoner and most frequently enjoyed wild plants ought to be given a home. From the street-girdled school, to the 'natural' park, to the camp school, to the wide country should be the sequence.

This is a sequence that adult education must do everything to encourage until it seems inevitable and a shameful thing that it does not spread over all the country: conurbations must be turned into conruralizations if life in Britain is to be tolerable for the mass of the people and if they are to remain human as we have traditionally understood that word. Are we to plan an urban captivity for our children's children? Long years will inevitably elapse before we have thousands of camp schools, though when we think of the many functions they could fulfil all the year round, it is disheartening to contemplate any delay in initiating on a grand scale such a sane and, in the long run, economic excursion into the fruitful fields of integration. In the meantime, however, adult education is gaining strength: since the overwhelming majority of those who make use of adult education are townsmen, I consider it of the first importance that centres of adult education should be established in glorious rural surroundings. They should have associated with them well run and beautiful gardens and a well equipped and well managed farm. I would hope that as much time could be devoted to the affairs of the countryside, to food, health, agriculture, forestry and a broad biological outlook as to current 'affairs', literature, history, science and art.

Education is a ladder which gets progressively steeper rung

by rung, but there is no going back. It is a lifelong process, always preparing for the next step. The individual needs to learn how to prepare himself and society and the state to lend a helping hand at all stages.

If action were to become the senior partner in education, young people would have far more opportunities for sorting out their bents, and the teachers would have far greater scope for giving help and advice as to vocation and hobbies. Training of this kind would reveal the strongest of country bents in large numbers of town children: it would be highly desirable to deflect such children to country vocations. Of course many people young and old are congenitally incapable of much response, but will have strong bents in other directions; perhaps towards mechanical things, crafts, books, music or the arts. Hence the importance of having shops in camp schools: because rural affairs are to be the bias, other aspects of training must not be neglected.

Army experience has shown that large numbers of men become most interested when required to take a responsible part in carrying out operations. To arouse interest should at all times be the primary aim of education — it is impossible to say this too often. The right procedure for this should be to graft all the final subtleties on a sure foundation built of training sight, touch and hearing in action. Great difficulties will arise and there will always be unavoidable conflicts in aims, but the primary importance of action must not be lost sight of.

When we pass beyond the stage of the periods at the camp schools, we come to national apprenticeships. National apprenticeship needs to have three main aims in view: first, to continue the general training; second, to provide vocational training, and, third, to provide training in hobbies. Rural apprenticeship should not be overstressed in the case of those with no sensibility at all for the country; they must be apprenticed to industries in accord with their bents. I am going to insist, however, that some rural training is necessary for everybody, and if this cannot be given at camp schools or during the camp school period, then some proportion of the actual apprenticeship should be rural. When Bacon wrote the words quoted at the head of this chapter, he could not have foreseen

153

that specialization in any field, and least of all in industry, would have stretched to the present lengths, nor that such specialization in effect would have led to multitudes of people doing, if not precisely the same things, things of the same general character, things which have the same psychological influence. The result is that Bacon's dictum, if not taken too narrowly, is of greater importance than ever today. It applies with as much force to holidays and hobbies as to vocational work, and perhaps with even greater force. It is very difficult for teaching to discriminate widely between individuals; it is much more easy to do so in training. Discrimination should be the hallmark of good training. The capacity for discerning selection is the outstanding attribute which distinguishes man from the other species. Yet it is now fashionable to express horror at the adoption of preferential methods in education. Indeed, in all directions — dress, food, type of holiday — freedom to choose seems to be frowned upon and made ever more difficult. This is a-biological and pregnant with lethal consequences if regimentation is carried too far. Selection of individuals, except on the basis of artificial standards, may open the door to favouritism, but to refuse to apply discernment for the fear that somebody will favour somebody else is the height of democratic cowardice and, humorously enough, will do nothing to banish favouritism from human affairs.

'They are happy men', says Bacon, 'whose natures sort with their vocation.' Men who are thus fortunate make their vocations their hobbies and therein lies their happiness, but such fortunate people must beware of making their vocations also their holidays. Specialization, it is generally said, makes for happiness and makes for the full, useful life: I consider this a very unsafe generalization. It is true of those specialists and experts who deal with tangible things, see a cycle of work through to a finish and exercise personal initiative. Expert farmers, expert handcraftsmen, expert scientists, expert professional sportsmen — including those who train others — are amongst the happiest of men, men who, in the main, live full, useful lives. I find it impossible to believe, however, that the same sort of satisfaction can be obtained by being an expert in the making or finishing of a mere part of something, and probably something the expert part-maker will never see.

154

Here is the danger of all this high-placed, high-powered modern insistence on efficiency. What is meant by efficiency is a dutiful bow to economic laws! Efficiency is invariably judged in output a man-hour, output a ton of raw material, output a unit of working capital, output a unit of factory space, output a unit of mechanical energy and suchlike wholly sub-human standards, and they are standards which defeat their own aims because they discourage initiative to an amazing extent in an ever increasing number of individuals. The initiative lies in the design of the machines and the organization of the work, while the tendency is to commit more and more people to tasks which, though requiring accuracy, are almost incredibly restricted in scope and involve the maximum repetition of limited movements. This is a terrible price to pay in the cramping of human potentialities for cheaper commodities and in sufficient quantities to satisfy the demand. This urge for quantity and cheapness forever restricts the range of design in nearly every commodity. When all this is carried to its logical consequences it spells the end of craftsmanship, the end of any pretence to artistic perception, and, in fact, the end of the truly human and civilized person as we have always aimed at creating him. Yet this is what is happening in an ever increasing number of industries. This dehumanization of man is not countered by simply paying him higher wages: in fact higher wages may increase the spiral of dehumanization by simply increasing the demand for standardized goods and mechanical entertainments. The root of the problem is far more basic. Cannot the industries themselves do more to keep the hobby spirit alive and to give all their employees some scope for the exercise of genuine initiative and craftsmanship?

That to be a Jack of all trades is to be a master of none seems, nowadays, to be accpeted as a profound truth. This dogma has got such a hold on industrial thought that Astor and Rowntree, in their study *Mixed Farming and Muddled Thinking,* with quite sublime assurance go almost as far as to base a whole agricultural policy on the elimination of 'Jack'! This displays an astounding ignorance of our leading farmers and of the best of our farm craftsmen. The first-class farmer or the first-class farm craftsman is a specialist in a surprisingly large number of intricate action-pattern and/or word-pattern aspects of his industry; and because he is a multi-specialist he is most certainly the better specialist in each of those things in which he is expert.

The 'Jack' dogma is all bunkum and is perhaps the most fatal of all the fatal outcomes of the dominance of economic and specialist doctrine as affecting all our affairs. To take an example, if I had to have a major abdominal operation for a presumed to be particular reason, I should feel much safer in the hands of a first-class all-round abdominal surgeon than in the hands of a man who spent all his operational time tinkering only or chiefly with one organ. I am sure I am not alone in this feeling.

The first necessity then is to re-establish Jack in his rightful place as a man of perfection and honour instead of a back number of no account. Then perhaps industry would seek ways and means of making Jacks and Jills instead of male and female automatons. If Jacks and Jills are no longer trained, then industry is simply organizing itself on the basis of preconceived ideas. It would be nice to think that every factory in the normal course of events would provide shops in which employees of all grades were given opportunities of doing work that involved complex operations which could be seen through to a finish. Shops, too, where operatives, if they so desired, could pursue hobbies of a vocational kind, or at least of a kind related to their vocations and which called upon initiative. Astor and Rowntree hope to bring what is worst in our industrial methods to the aid of agriculture: I would prefer to bring what is best in agricultural methods to the aid of industry and industrial workers. Astor and Rowntree put their all on economic efficiency: I put my all on human efficiency, in the widest sense of drawing out potentialities.

Irony is always over the hedge or under the bush or the bench. The irony here is that in the long run industry based on human efficiency would be more economic than that advisedly based on economic efficiency: on the human base would stand the maximum number of happy and contented people and of people with initiative ready to respond imaginatively to altered techniques and able to contribute to the evolution of improved industrial methods and organization.

Museums, picture galleries, art schools and colleges of technology all serve creative ends because they are designed to have an educational and creative value. Yet open spaces — grievously limited as they are at present in scope and area — are inherently of incalculable potency: properly utilized they would probably constitute the greatest of all assets to our oversized commercial and industrial towns. I can see no incompatibility whatsoever in open spaces being made to serve equally the vital needs of recreation, rest, comparative solitude, contemplation, education, culture and utility and all in beautiful surroundings savouring strongly of the naturalness and simplicity of the country. It is all a matter of layout and design and of the motives that prompt the 'landscape gardeners'. A new age and new ideas call for new schools in all directions, and this is an age that calls imperatively for a new and integrated school of architecture, landscape gardening and civics with simplicity for its coat of arms. Oh no! the planners with all their first-rate intentions and designs, have not yet inaugurated such a school. They give themselves away, as they have sadly given themselves away in their lack of appreciation of the significance and potentialities of open spaces. Take the one organic link between town and country — gardening: gardening in private gardens and gardening communally undertaken by townspeople, for its cultural and educational value. True enough, there is a half-hearted recognition of the claims of allotment holders, but in the County of London Plan it is suggested that the allotments 'could be in small areas interspersed among the houses'. I am certain that such a plan is born of outmoded ideas relative to gardens and gardening. We need something quite different and altogether more generous. Of all dreadful words 'allotment' and 'tenement' are among the very worst and have become associated in our minds with some of the worst features of our national life: they engender visions of squalor and ineptitude. The first thing to be done is to banish the offending words from the English language. So here and now I decree that 'allotment' and 'tenement' shall be expunged from our vocabulary. In future we shall talk about a garden instead of an allotment. What a world of difference: one word conjures up visions of dreariness, disused builders' sites, insecurity of tenure and formal untidiness; the

158

other suggests gaiety, security of tenure, beauty and informal tidiness. A block of allotments is henceforth to be described as a garden paddock. Here we introduce a worthy and joy-laden word of some 300 years' standing. A word dear to the Londoner as it is to every Englishman, a word which to liter-ally millions of town dwellers brings back happy memories of the Epsom Downs and all the thrills of expectation as the favourites and outsiders — gallant and beautiful horses all— are led into *the Paddock*. I put all my money on 'paddock' and it shall now become a household word in every city, denoting everything that is to be seemly, satisfying and sooth-ing and within the walls of the cities themselves. I will not have it that I am labouring this question, for words are either preg-nant with creative impulse or lethal and soul destroying. Pad-dock, as such, is a good and descriptive word; its basal mean-ing is an enclosure and by common usage it has come to imply an enclosure within an enclosure, which suits well our pur-pose. If we respect the historical background of the word, it is not necessarily implied (save by context) that an enclosure, designated 'paddock', needs must open on to a stable or be of the nature of a pasture. To the names reminiscent of the country gracing the London Directory — names like Kensing-ton Gardens and Lincoln's Inn Fields — we will forthwith add Islington Paddocks. How nice it would be to think that our dreary commercialized century had at least created Islington Paddocks as a counterblast to its innumerable vandalisms.

What will be the character of Islington Paddocks and their functional purpose? Islington Garden Paddock will be our old enemy, a block of allotments, in an entirely new dress, a dress even more sumptuous and elegant than anything that has yet been designed by the untiring and anxious fairy godmother of the allotment movement — the National Allotment Society.

We will start with this assumption: that England is in fact being sensibly replanned, the cities, the towns and the country-side alike; the basic principle behind this great enterprise is the harmonious integration of the urban-rural. In consequence high priority will be given to open spaces, and particularly high priority *within* those garden spaces to garden paddocks. This *high priority* will cover both suitability of site and ample elbow room.

159

Wherever possible gently undulating ground is best for garden paddocks, as this gives additional scope to the landscape gardener. Needless to say, some effort would be made to select an area where the soil was neither of a heart- nor back-breaking character. A large paddock would provide for well arranged groups of gardens (alias allotments). Each group should consist of a number of gardens: a good-sized demonstration garden, which should include greenhouses and frames, fruit, vegetables and flowers; a botanical garden; playing lawns for children; ample lawns for rest, meditation and contemplation; a central pavilion; appropriate storehouses for the individual garden holders — and these could probably be most tidily provided in terms of a single house (with lock-ups) to each block of gardens.

The master aim in the layout should be fourfold: (1) to avoid formality and achieve simplicity; (2) to ensure a high degree of privacy to each group of gardens; (3) to break up the rest lawns in such a way that people could collect in large or small groups, according to taste, while with well arranged paths and seats scope could be given to those who wanted to wander off alone; (4) to make the whole paddock gay with flowers and shrubs.

Successful planning would depend upon the judicious use of even slight undulations, and the clever employment of small trees, hedges, clumps of flowering shrubs. A particular paddock would not be open to the public at large: it would be the 'property' of a particular district. At first it might be necessary to restrict entry only to the garden holders and to their families, and, under supervision, to the pupils at the nearby schools which would be using the demonstration and botanical gardens in connection with their routine curricula.

With these safeguards, and postulating good layout, individual garden holders would on balance achieve no less privacy than on present-day allotments, and they would be given countless advantages. There is only one way to garden privately in a town and that is behind an eight-foot wall — even then the recluse would be under observation from some window or other. This much is quite certain, a garden holder in a paddock would work under conditions of far greater privacy than an allotment holder working in one of the small blocks 'interspersed among the houses'. He would have escaped into a tranquil paddock away from the houses *and the town* which is the whole point of open spaces.

I have only painted the background on a large canvas, much remains to be filled in. The idea of bringing the local health centre and garden paddock together in one unit would probably make a strong appeal to some. There are arguments for and against; I will leave the problem in the hands of my new Research School of Integration: that school would also do well to consider the pros and cons of bringing poultry and other small animals into the garden paddock scheme.

I cannot resist a little homily on difficulties: planners plead guilty to paying no mean deference to difficulties. There is no escaping from the fact that shirking difficulties is at the core of most of our troubles, yet by compromising – in order momentarily to escape a colossal expenditure of money and a gigantic undertaking – we only increase our difficulties on a compound interest scale of magnitude and in the end we are committed to an even greater expenditure of money and an even more gigantic undertaking. It is either that or we do nothing and cut our losses, losses which have to be counted sometimes in real wealth, sometimes in deteriorating human character, health and happiness, and usually in both. The urban-rural mess that we are now in is the legacy of protracted years of doing nothing about it, then of more protracted years of shirking the difficulties and half-heartedly 'doing a bit'. We are now a nation in half a mind to plan for the future – instead of just for tomorrow which is worse than useless. In planning for the future we have to ask ourselves squarely if we mean to make the most densely populated areas of our big towns places really fit to live in: do we intend to create towns that really human persons a couple of generations hence *will be willing to live in?* Or do we mean to cut our losses in terms of real wealth crumbled to dust to preserve paper wealth in the pockets of speculators and shareholders? If so, we are responsible for denying human lives their birthright. If we start our fine plans for the future by shirking this question, which is basically the question of open spaces where they are most needed, we shall only add to the very mess we are planning to clean up. The problem, however, goes very much deeper than the expense and magnitude of the task of converting concrete bricks and mortar into gay garden paddocks and parks, for in the last resort to do this is merely a matter of *must* and *will;* the war abundantly proved the power of these two forces when they are well and truly mobilized. Every single plan we make — let it be urban, industrial, to do with roads, railways or airfields; or rural, to do with agriculture, forestry or fishing or housing — should be ultimately determined by the fact that our land space is exceedingly limited in relation to the size and needs of our population. Therefore the question of priorities in respect of land usage stands at the core of our domestic policies.

Without priorities all is confusion, and if the priorities are sadly wrong the end is the strangulation of our national life — quite possibly strangulation amid plenty.

It stands to reason that we cannot even begin correctly to scale priorities until we have drawn up, with as great accuracy as possible, a balance sheet against the one obdurate constant that enters into our calculations — the size of our island. At the moment the data for showing up such a balance sheet are far too scattered; indeed, it is most unlikely that some of the most important particulars have anywhere been tabulated, so the probability is that the gaps far outweigh the known facts. I submit therefore that the present phase of our planning efforts resembles nothing as much as an artist pertinaciously attempting to paint a masterpiece on a canvas which changes hourly in shape and size. We have to grasp that all planning is futile and indeed dangerous until we have discovered ways and means of nailing down our canvas and marking it out into appropriately and variously sized squares, each to be allocated to different subjects, the details to be filled in for each square separately by master craftsmen trained in their special crafts.

In drawing up our balance sheet the sort of data we require are on the one side the present-day acreage and productivity of our farming and forest-bearing lands, together with an estimate of the full potentialities of such lands. On the other side we need particulars of the non-farming and non-forest lands, with acreage at present devoted to each usage, and a well considered estimate of the increases or decreases in acreage which are considered to be necessary in the national interest. This spatialization, so to speak, of the data of our national life needs to be exceedingly detailed. Railroads, roads, airfields, factory and industrial needs, all types of housing, open spaces (themselves duly classified), disused sites and all types of wasteland and sterilized land cover the canvas of our country, and this is the only space that we have to manoeuvre on when we plan. Statistics of national productivity, housing, agriculture, etc., which ignore space, time and the ratio of employment in given areas, are far too abstract and do not give us the information needed to plan a balanced and wholesome national life. In terms of present world trends and pressures and our altered position in the world's economy I would predict that the calls likely to be made on our land surface by those concerned with planning for non-agricultural and non-forestry purposes could only be met at the price of too high a sacrifice from farming land. Whether this in fact will be the case is the fundamental issue determining a sane domestic policy. In facing this issue coldly, I would implore those who will have to make the final decisions (assuming that the issue will be squarely faced which judging by precedents is unlikely) to pay due regard to the necessity of a harmonious integration of the urban-rural, and therefore to the transcendent importance of a virile countryside and a thriving and progressive agriculture.

I am unable to present my balance sheet statistically: but I am fortunate in having had the opportunity of forming a comprehensive visual picture of our island, and to me it is obvious that we have not a yard of land to spare and that we cannot afford to unbalance a single inch. I would implore the planners to realize that the thoughtless unbalancing of land wastes more of our precious space than perhaps any other single error or crime that can be perpetrated against what should be our most treasured possession. I shall have more to say about this presently when discussing the new towns.

Unless there is a new attitude to 'difficulties' and to 'space', it is nothing but an academic exercise planning for the future of our country: there will never be a new age in which our progeny will be grateful that we were their ancestors. They will have no option but to curse and despise us for the un-livable-in environment we are bequeathing them, because we

163

could never transcend our own immediate commercial interests, or what we ignorantly supposed were our commercial interests.

A radical change in our planning must be inspired by a new vision of what can be done with space. Commercial principles are excellent in their place, but their place is not as a ruling principle in the Cabinet of a great country. Let us assume then that businessmen have been 'put in their proper place' and it is possible to plan the layout of our country for the benefit of the country as a whole – on the human principle. Then land will no longer be the profiteers' commodity *par excellence:* land, the most precious thing that we possess sold like the masterpieces of the great painters to the highest bidder!

What if open spaces covered one-third of the town space! Looked at from the point of view of land surface, I believe that there is only one way of preventing spill and spread from big towns and keeping them within their city walls and that is by the generous provision and wise use of open space, well distributed within the walls. I believe, moreover, that in the long run, and particularly when we consider the unbalancing influence of spill and spew, that farming land would actually be saved from paying forfeit, rather than the reverse, if the most strenuous efforts were made to provide the cities with open space far in excess of anything the planners consider feasible or perhaps even desirable. Until our towns are worth living in we shall never solve the problems of the countryside. As the Luton report so admirably says, 'Social policies of the next ten years *must be socially optimistic policies.*' But in these and kindred matters planning for the next ten years will not achieve much and simply displays the smallness of mind and imagination of contemporary authority. We should think and plan in at least 50-year units and hearten up our courage and optimism proportionately. Defeatism is at the core of our social life today. What if the cost of saving our way of life and our civilization is stupendous? Let us remember the money we have squandered to no purpose or to bad purposes – and I am not thinking of wars, but rather of money lavished in the past in a 'socially optimistic spirit', but, as results have proved, to ends that are not socially beneficial. Money, for example, that has been lavished on our absurd educational system — examination-ridden, wordy and pedantic, producing rather the windy-minded debater who takes up the time of the House of Commons than the practical, mature and experienced human being. Money, wealth and endeavour wisely directed to the betterment of the race can never be wasted: so here I am back at the difficulties again and I am going to make three further points to help combat the national outlook of defeatism.

I am not a town planner: whether I am deemed to be but an idle dreamer or a man with workable ideas, it is of England as a *whole* that I always try to think in formulating my ideas, and not those specific interests which have too much power in the control of national affairs. No doubt (apart altogether from defeatist 'difficulties') the town planners may say that to meet such schemes as mine would make transport too difficult and require scattering houses, shops and business premises, all that makes up a town, over too wide an area. If, however, open space, and its *functional potential,* were to be made priority number one, the planners would think yet again about the problem of making absolutely the best use of both building sites and of the space actually built upon. There is still scope for economy in these directions and there is high promise in the increasing realization of the fact that living and working conditions are a plaything of design as well as of cubic feet: what is lost in feet may be compensated for in design.

My second point is that if and when the population of the country as a whole diminishes (as some day surely it must) the open spaces will prove neither a menace nor an eyesore. A future generation will not be faced with the alternative of removing them or leaving them to become ever more telling witnesses to our folly. Behind all sane planning should be the determination not to bequeath intolerable legacies to those who follow after us. The true function and most noble aspiration of an ancestor is to be wise in the estimation of the generations that will follow. So behold yet another baffling antithesis that social man is peremptorily commanded to resolve: politics — ancestorhood. No student of our times can deny that we live in an age remarkable for nothing so much as the exaggerated ascendancy of politics. And this brings me to the last of my three points.

M

We will take a hypothetical case. As a result of the difficulties and opposition from influential pressure groups (political reaction) we will assume that it has been decided to increase the open spaces of London by no more than the acreage of the London County Plan. To find alternative sites for dispossessed houses, factories, etc., would mean sterilizing farming land somewhere: the whole undertaking would cost a considerable sum of money. But if at a later date it was decided by a new and enlightened generation that the open space in the city must be trebled, the cost of this operation — and the amount of additional agricultural land that would be sterilized — would be far more than three times the cost of the original operation. Anyone who has had experience of the consequences of continually breaking up balanced units and attempting to restore them elsewhere or replace them with something else will not need to have this proved to him. In other words, if the original planning and action had been sufficiently far-sighted to provide the right amount of open space at the outset, then it is certain that the savings effected by one overall operation would have made it unnecessary to sterilize as much farming land as is required by two piecemeal operations: similarly all expenditure would be correspondingly reduced.

The actual amount of real wealth and money saved by a bold and comprehensive plan may be variously computed, but there can be no question that piecemeal planning such as I have cited is ruinous.

The moral to be drawn is that on which I have insisted again and again: that we should not be in too great a hurry; that we should first conduct the maximum amount of well integrated research into all the human factors affecting a project before launching out upon it. Here is another merit in planning rather in terms of 50 years than 5 or 10 years — time is given for research and for revision and re-revision of plans before a final and comprehensive and all-embracing enterprise is begun. The urban-rural mess in this country — not to mention the traffic strangulation in our great cities alone — has assumed such menacing proportions that mistakes will be fatal. As the mess builds up, pressure for hasty and perhaps spectacular actions of a temporary kind will increase, especially when the Press find this good news value: yet delay, if it represents time strenuously spent in research, will yield golden rewards. The first essential is to experiment in a comparatively small way: even as things are today it would be possible to set a few first-rate garden paddocks in many of our great cities, and it would be profitable to do so in the larger parks. This is the only way to gain experience in design and in organization and to test popular reaction. One cannot enter in projects of this kind with geometrically fixed ideas that one assumes can be applied to all places at all times in the same way. All creative plans grow slowly under the influence of general principles: although the vision behind every garden paddocks should be exactly alike. It is the curse of modern planning to try to make everything the same from one end of the country to the other as quickly as possible. This rational approach arises from man's brain and has no relationship with the working of nature and it sterilizes nature in man.

Planning runs the gravest risk of becoming only restrictive and intensely irritating, unless it is boldly conceived and is based upon a sagacious anticipation of trends founded upon long and well integrated research: a shorter working week will create a keener demand for holiday camps and holiday facilities in this country — and there will be massive trouble when these cannot be provided by the Government of the day. It will take the blame for its predecessors' mistakes. The British Commonwealth, for example, might be held together in part by extensive inter-Commonwealth travel holiday organizations within it. Planning as a science is new and has much data still to collect and much evidence still to sift. A period of slow motion forced upon us by lack of materials and shortages may be a blessing in disguise: a sudden burst of prosperity and extensive and nation-wide building and planning might be fatal to our future prosperity and happiness. In the modern world development moves at a prodigious rate and no one has yet sufficiently taken into account the consequences of changing man's environment so rapidly. We need time for more discussion, to explore in greater detail all the factors involved. This is the sense in which we require both a conservative and a socialistic (if by that is meant taking into account the community as a whole) approach, which is to imply this is too serious a matter to be a plaything of politics.

In the forefront of the factors involved is the difficult problem of keeping a balanced use of land: this brings me to the question of the new towns and to the closely related question of the downright spoliation and waste of land.

Any action that is taken in a town to provide open space is bound to react on farming land: somewhere forfeit will have to be paid in whole or in part in terms of broad acres to provide, or help to provide, alternate sites for buildings that will have been demolished. Similarly, every generous act of planning within a town's boundaries that makes demands on space will inevitably have repercussions on the countryside. This aspect of planning cannot be too strongly emphasized, for it is exceedingly far reaching. The truth is that any action taken in London, Manchester or Birmingham might, in its ultimate effect, influence land usage in a particular locality as far away as, say, Cornwall or Dumfriesshire. When great projects are afoot, then, like an insidious disease, the unbalancing of land will run rife right through the country. Since our land surface is so limited and so precious and since we dare not squander farming land, the planners have had imposed upon them two fundamental duties. The first is to determine the average relationship of land absolutely sterilized to that unbalanced since the era of spill and spread began, and then to establish a reasonable factor as a rigid datum line to stick to in all future planning. Balance-unbalance is at the core of economic and seemly land usage. The problems are difficult because they are not black and white but a matter of degree. Unbalance has, however, dominated the scene during recent decades, and in all probability has exercised just as adverse an effect on the food-producing potential of our island as the loss of land to agriculture. Piecemeal operations are the greatest of all enemies to balance, so that it is essential when inroads have to be made on farming land that the whole operation should be treated with foresight by means of a comprehensive plan from the first.

It is fashionable among planners to pay high-sounding lip service to the sanctity of first-class farming land, but are they seriously considering the best means of avoiding inroads on such land? For example, in the case of building a new airfield

or a new town, if alternative sites were available, one on
something not much better than heath land and the other on
well farmed and well laid out farming land which might cost
ten to twenty times less to develop, could we be sure that the
temptation to sacrifice the farming land would be resisted? I
certainly am not. The Slough Trading Estates and London
Airport were built on some of the finest market garden land
in England.

It is of the highest importance that milk, vegetables and
fruit should be delivered to the consumers absolutely fresh;
of what value then would all this fine, flat land have been to
London — as it once was — before the greedy, profiteering
sprawl began? In building our new towns are we going to continue the same mistakes? It is only too likely while urban-
minded planners consider that all the food we need can be
imported in deep-freeze or refrigeration transport. Yet if good
living and security of food supplies means anything at all to
modern politicians, then it would be the height of folly to
build a new town on an oasis of fine farm land surrounded by
poor land — whereas the converse would be wisdom.

A Minister of Town and Country Planning has stated pub-
licly that the intention in building the new towns is to experiment.[1] If the Government really means business in this matter
of experimenting, then there may dawn a wholly new and
vastly exhilarating relationship between Government and
people. Dare one look forward to the day when elections
will be won on the basis of action-patterns, and not on word-
patterns, slogans and high promises? The party with the best
record for conducting wise and fearless experiments will be
voted to power. The day is not yet, but the quality and degree of objectivity of the experimenting put into the new
towns may well influence the trends of political and social
thinking for generations to come. Experimenting is the zest
of life and the only sure way of progress.

I feel this so strongly that I have never voted for any party
in an election, because in my lifetime I do not consider any
party has ever offered itself to the electorate advocating a
programme of objective experiment. Modern politics are
doctrinaire and rigid.

[1] See Appendix III

With this expression of lack of faith in the political parties I will now optimistically offer a few suggestions for experiments in connection with the new towns which it seems to me any political party could undertake without perjuring its prejudices.

What D. H. Lawrence has so well described as the spirit of place should be encouraged to waft a healthy fragrance over every town. The first essential then is to provide within the city walls the ingredients of a healthy spirit. It follows from all I have said that the new towns should be used first to test, town against town, what can be done with different allocations of open space, adopting a range per town from about 7 acres per 1,000 to 20 acres per 1,000. In due time the influence of these different allocations would manifest itself in 'spirit'. Secondly, there would be scope for first-rate experiments in planning the functional use of open space, and testing different proportionate areas for different functions. Thirdly, attention would be given to detail and opportunity would be afforded for testing a wide range of designs and layouts for garden paddocks. At one town at least the experiment should be tried of bringing together health centre and garden paddock within one park. Since the towns will grow up in rural surroundings, there should be the highest incentive and great scope for experiment aimed at giving to open spaces of all types a less formal and more countrified aspect.

These suggestions for experiments follow automatically from my thesis of integration and are therefore of the nature of repetitions — worthy repetitions, however, in a great cause.

It is not for me to make suggestions as to design and orientation of *other* cultural centres which will create a healthy and characteristic town spirit, but the need for experiment is certain to be as great as for open spaces.

I hope that great attention will be given to the question of market places — and to all facilities for helping the farmer and the consumer to make easy contact with each other. Planning of facilities can undoubtedly go a long way towards providing the inhabitants of reasonably sized towns with really fresh vegetables and other farm produce.

If in very truth it is intended that the new towns should serve as functional laboratories, then I am certain that each town, as such, will be the gainer, and the gain to the country as a whole will be incalculable. The question is: Does the Government know what constitutes an experiment? Or is experiment just another vote-catching word that goes no further than a public speech and is unrelated to an action-pattern?

At present there is still a large leave-over of land wastage due to the breakneck military necessities of the war. Wealth is wealth and space is limited. Research is needed into the question of how to return all this blistered, scarred and concrete-ridden land to the best usage, possibly as the nucleus of a new town, or a new village; as a site for a camp boarding-school; as a factory site or to restore the balance of the surrounding agricultural land. There are manifold possible uses. It is to be supposed that the Ministry of Town and Country Planning is engaged upon a comprehensive survey of all this waste land and that it is in the hands of well qualified integrators. The land in question is in blocks of all sizes, varying from large disused airfields and camps to mere observation posts, but on all areas, large and small alike, concrete — the worst weed known to agriculture — continues to flourish and partially or completely to sterilize far more ground than that upon which its obdurate roots have gained so firm a foothold. Manifestly, too, research and purposeful action have to be devoted to all the land that has been sterilized or partially sterilized by surface dredging for coal and iron ore, and by kindred operations.

A great deal of space is wasted in towns as well as in the country, and often in quite small towns. With good and compact planning a great deal can be done for the urban populations without making undue inroads on farming land. But I repeat that we cannot be certain of our facts until the necessary surveys have been conducted and the balance sheet drawn up. Let Priority Number One be for adequate open spaces in the towns, then all true countrymen will join with all sane townsmen in rejoicing and gladly accept any reasonable sacrifices that have to be made.

My aim is no less than to indicate an idea, to initiate a movement, to give a new and long-felt bias to education. If there is a grain of sense in my major thesis, we can anticipate an ever-increasing interest in natural things and a consequent demand for more biological factors in the urban environment.

CHAPTER 11

INTEGRATION: INDUSTRIALIZING
THE RURAL

Before the industrial revolution industry existed in rural areas and people were not segregated into two classes, industrial and rural. Nothing can now stop industry flowing back into rural areas. But unless it is balanced and planned the results will be lethal

---

'For *dispersed* this *Wen* must be, mind, by *some means or other*! This must happen at last. Houses equal to those of ten market towns cannot be added yearly without a dreadful dispersion at last. . . . They (the people) have been drawn here by unnatural causes. They must and they will be scattered.'

WILLIAM COBBETT

IN ORDER to effect a closer union between town and country, urgent though the need is, we must be content at first to walk warily and slowly. It is in the towns where the start has to be made: final success or failure will inevitably be decided by the quality of those who are brought into the country. Only families which are ready and eager for the change will be competent to play their part in this great drama of urban-rural integration: a drama which, to be great indeed, must be the product of faith, science, artistic perception, education, practical acumen – and time.

Before turning to the country aspect I must therefore discuss the town at considerable length. At every stage there are decisions to be made and we shall have to draw heavily on our unique human endowment – judgment.

There is nothing original about the idea of bringing industry into the country. The originality was when factories and the machine superseded rural craftsmanship and deprived country people of the opportunity for employment in industries. Things have come to such a pass now that to withhold from industrial workers the opportunities for establishing themselves in rural areas would be to perpetuate the folly that rigidly divided the occupations of town and country under

173

the obsession of a dominant idea. There are only two courses left to us: one negative and fatal, the other positive, difficult and creative. The tide has turned and it is the urban which in recent years has been flowing unchecked over the rural. Nothing can stop this. The only issue is whether we shall have the courage and imagination to regulate the flow — that much is vaguely intended — and regulate it in such a way that we shall create a harmonious mingling of the urban-industrial and the rural-agricultural interests in homogeneous communities. The end of the age of segregation must be the age of integration: the alternative is to continue the segregating impulse which, though relatively new in history, has become a habit of thought, a tradition, with conservative support. If we surrender uncritically to this negative tradition then we set up new towns, housing estates and factories in the country with no regard to the inter-relation of the industrial and rural populations. This accentuates the evils of segregation and ends in a haphazard intermingling of people scowling at each other across their fences, as untrusting and unsympathetic as different races suddenly confronting each other or the protagonists of hostile ideologies. No, our modern plans first and foremost must be human plans. We must revert to the *true* English tradition and create a setting favourable for the fruition of that tradition under the entirely altered conditions of our generation and of those which will follow.

The question then is no longer one of 'yes' or 'no', but solely and only of 'how'? Triumphantly to meet 'how?' demands the acceptance of three postulates and the successful solution of a number of problems. Here are the postulates: First, that the real wages — skill for skill, responsibility for responsibility and honesty for honesty — applicable alike to the rural worker and the industrial worker, should be on all fours to the last penny. When the real wages of industry and agriculture are under discussion, we hear much about the perquisites of the agricultural worker, as if the industrial worker to a man was entirely without perquisites or facilities to help him in augmenting his effective income — an untenable assumption. A single example: the rents for allotments are not high and the industrial worker comes into his garden to exercise entirely different muscles and aptitudes from those he has used during his working hours — not so the farm worker when he steps into his garden at the end of a long day in the fields. The backyard hen is capable of laying just as many eggs as her cottage garden cousin. True, the farm worker may obtain some food from the farm, but the fact remains that rural perquisites are in large part won at the expense of the worker's toil.

Second, that the living conditions of each class of worker should satisfy their special needs. Their precise requirements are unlikely to be the same in every respect. Third, that there should not be a serious disparity between the working hours of the two classes. Work on the farm calls for considerable flexibility in hours per day, while the care of livestock makes exacting demands on time. It is essential that farm workers should work overtime ungrudgingly at certain seasons of the year and it is frequently unavoidable for stockmen to avoid awkward hours. Adequate pay for overtime and for work of special responsibility is not a sufficient counterweight for long hours: those in different employments will always be comparing pay and working conditions. The only effective set-off to long hours is a keen interest in the work itself and a lively appreciation of its value. This appreciation must be shared responsibly between the employer, the employee and the nation. It is here that the status of agriculture assumes its greatest significance. If agriculture is held in the national estimation at its proper worth, and if the farm workers and craftsmen are everywhere given their due, not only in wages but in social respect, then such disparity in working hours as is unavoidable will not become a chronic deterrent to raising a sufficient and efficient labour force for our farm. Under present conditions farm labour will dwindle more and more as industry comes out into the country. Justice must be done to one of the hardest working and most essential bodies of men and women who well and truly serve the country. Holiday periods on the farm should be longer — though this is, admittedly, exceedingly difficult on small farms, where perhaps no more than one man is employed and where the farmer and his wife work from dawn to dusk, and often by lamplight as well. This is an urgent question and a solution on a community basis must be sought.

To bring industry into the country, except as a small experiment under unusually favourable circumstances, before the above requirements have been met, in my view, would be a fatal mistake — is already a fatal mistake — and seriously jeopardizes the prospects of achieving the desired organic integration. The greatest danger as I see it is in respect of houses.

The needs of the countryman are greatly influenced by the character of his work: abundance of water and drying facilities in his home are essential. Both the farmhouse — which is much more than a normal dwelling — and the cottage must be dry and convenient as well as structurally sound. The National Farm Survey for England and Wales[1] reveals that 58 per cent of the farmhouses and 50 per cent of the cottages are in 'good condition' and 47 per cent of the holdings with farmhouses have a piped supply of water to the house. No information is given about the piped supply of water to the cottages. About 27 per cent of the farmhouses have electricity, but the number of cottages must be much smaller. If then we consider structural soundness, convenience and facilities (water, electricity and drying arrangements) we should be safe in concluding that far less than half of the farmhouses are satisfactory while the proportion of cottages would be even less. This is certainly not a healthy state of affairs in an industry in which men and women have to work out of doors in all weathers. Those serving agriculture are dependent upon facilities provided in the home itself to a far greater extent than workers in most other industries.

This unsatisfactory state of affairs must be looked at in terms of the housing standards being provided for the urban workers. When the worker is confronted with the choice of a good urban house and a poor rural one he will usually choose the occupation which gives him the good house irrespective of

[1] This survey was published in 1942. The last one was published in 1946. The information contained in it differs hardly at all from that quoted above. The reason why there is no information about the amenities in farm workers cottages is perhaps revealed in the Minister of Agriculture's preface when he says 'Most of this information has now served its immediate purpose — that of increased production.' It is obvious that there have been great improvements since 1946: very few farmhouses are now without electricity: but it is still difficult to get statistics about farm cottages.
See also Appendix V.

his personal preferences. He has his family to consider. I do not see how the agricultural industry can thrive and expand if it cannot attract the best workers by offering them good houses. This means that before new industries are brought into a country area, it must be established that the rural housing is first-rate or else all the working population will flee to the new industries and the new housing estates. If this rule is not kept we shall introduce discontent and unhappiness into the countryside instead of a new harmonious community.

I was not thinking of new towns but of more intimate rural-urban integration in villages and hamlets. New towns are new towns and I am in favour of them, as I hope I have shown, if they are properly sited in relation to their size: but wherever they are built they will create an acute rural problem. Being English, we are not likely to forbid entry into the new towns from the surrounding countryside by regulation. No town has, however, ever yet sprung up, or ever will spring up, without exerting its magnetic concentric attraction. Everything compatible with freedom should be done to control this influence, which means that it must be done by counter-measures, not by edict. The most important of these measures is that the rural housing within the ambit of attraction is abundantly adequate both in quality and quantity. If this is not so, then dire mischief will be done to the surrounding countryside, a mischief which will react back on the towns themselves in the reduction of the fresh farm produce readily available. My three postulates apply in their totality to the influence of the new towns, as to all industrial towns, because the effect of these towns is felt by agriculture over a very wide area, even when the factories are contained within the town boundaries and are in no sense integrated with the countryside.

I revert now to the country proper, including those small country towns which authority does not intend to enlarge out of all recognition.

Country space, as I said, can no longer be regarded as the prerogative of country folk. Modern means of transporting speech (radio, newspapers), energy, people and raw materials have completely broken down any case that ever existed for the exaggerated segregation of agriculture and industry. Those, and there are many, who would go to any lengths to keep the urban world out of the rural, should deeply ponder the reasons on which they have taken their stand, reasons which may turn out to be unjustified fears, selfishness or prejudices. To those who revel in the seclusion of their broad acres I would say this — and they know it: The greatest farming problem for many years to come will be skilled labour: there is only one way of increasing the skilled labour force and that is to increase the population in rural areas. If our plans are well and truly laid, if we proceed slowly, step by step and on the basis of courageous judgment, then many of the most intelligent children of families settled in rural areas will prefer working on farms to working in factories. If this is to happen we must choose with great care the particular villages and small towns to which to bring factories, as far as possible choosing the families to be transported, and settling upon the correct size of industrial unit appropriate to each separate town and village. We are planning for the future and the fruits of our wise planning will be garnered in later generations.

We must remember that work on the land is altering rapidly in character, that it is becoming increasingly mechanized and increasingly specialized: the skills on the farm are becoming increasingly diversified. Labour and housing are the two great agricultural bugbears. With sensible selection it should be possible to ease the rural housing situation. The aim should be for one overall plan to include factories, houses for the workers and where necessary for the rural population as well and all amenities for town and village that modern taste and interest demand. Herein lies the undeniable advantage of methodical procedure and working on the basis of town by town and village by village. This concentration of endeavour should effect an economy all round. Farmers and countrymen do not perhaps sufficiently realize that greater wealth and greater diversification of interests are the crying needs of most country districts, and these are the very needs that properly thought out integration would go far to meet.

Far too many good countrymen are obsessed with the idea that urban people are a race apart and are a positive menace and danger to the countryside. This is to take an exceedingly poor view of human nature and to display a total lack of faith,

178

both in the influence of the country and in the influence that lies latent in countrymen, if only they would exert themselves. Two facts, I think, should lead to a juster appreciation of the potentialities latent in the urban masses, and it is with the unfolding of potentialities and not with the past that we are all of us now so deeply concerned. Under the conditions of the last fifty years it is impossible to expect great numbers of townspeople either to understand or to value the country. They have been taught, trained and conditioned in conditions utterly remote from country lore, and unfavourable to an awakening of interest in country happenings. The holidays of great numbers of urban workers are simply impelled by the need for change and escape. There has been no grand exploration of new ways of life. The noise and hurry of urban life do not encourage dreaming. Holidays abroad may be awakening a spark in those urban workers who can afford them, and fortunately their number is increasing. These holidays are, alas! still much too short, much too hurried and involve far too much bustle, organization and tearing about. The widening interest in camping is perhaps the most helpful sign.

Yet we must not overlook the fact that amongst townsmen there are great numbers of real country-lovers, as good countrymen at heart as any that trudge the lanes and fields. *The way of faith is to hold to the fact that there is nothing congenitally wrong with the people but everything wrong with their environments.* But environments can be changed. There will be a heavy responsibility laid upon countrymen, for upon their hospitality and cordiality to the newcomer everything will depend. For better or for worse the destiny of the new England will be settled in the pubs, on the village greens, in the village halls; in these centres the new social pattern of rural England will be laid down without conscious striving. Planners can make a setting favourable to invigoration and growth, but if the growth is to be healthy and creative it must be in the English tradition — simple and spontaneous. Rural life in England has lost much of its vitality and spontaneity just because its interests have been allowed to become too limited. Today agriculture and the pursuits of agriculture dominate the attenuated scene. This was not so in the old days when, in effect, every small town and village had its thriving little industries. *Vitality is a direct result of a homogeneous population representing a reasonably wide range of occupations*; mono-culture is always destructive whether in man or crops. The problem, indeed the whole problem, is how to arrange matters so that one group of vocational workers is not swamped by another and to bring all groups together in happy and helpful relationships.

At the core of the complex practical problems are two simple issues: the type of industry suitable to particular rural localities and the size of the industrial unit appropriate to each town and village. In my view no possible harm can be done if the right decisions are taken *and balance is preserved.* Let me quote Thomas Sharp: 'The comparative failure of most land settlement schemes is to quite a considerable degree due to this evil of occupational unbalance. People have been set down in concentrated agricultural colonies, where every worker was either a smallholder or a co-operator in some scheme of inten-sive cultivation, where not even a shopkeeper or an innkeeper varied the occupationally standardized character of the colony.' Wise integration would tolerate nothing of that sort for its aim is to break down vocational barriers everywhere, in town and country alike, and particularly in regard to housing and social relations. It is beginning to be realized that housing and social relations are a function of each other: consider the evils of unbalanced suburbs and ribbon development – and the failure of families living in immense blocks of urban flats to develop any community spirit. Such families have no com-mon meeting-place – not even a fence to chat over or window overlooking somebody else's kitchen.

No one writes with greater understanding of the village and with more sympathetic feeling towards the needs of country people than C. H. Gardiner: I consider his views should carry great weight. He writes: 'I see no reason what ever why light industries should not be admitted to the village and the countryside. . . . My observations of several evacuated light industries leads me to the conclusion that such innovations are in fact a benefit to the villages that have received them.' Later he makes this significant point: 'Not every village boy or girl wants to go on the land or on the farm: but they ought not on that account to be forced into a town.' In short, bring industry into the country and it will benefit everybody. We shall have the healthy position that in one and the same family and living under the same roof will be young people employed both on the land and in the factory.[1]

Dr. C. S. Orwin has also argued in favour of bringing industry into the country and has supported his arguments with a massive weight of evidence. In a penetrating passage he writes: 'The country districts need repopulating if life and labour in them is to prosper, but this can be achieved only by accepting the evolution of industrial organization as something inevitable, while taking steps at the same time consciously and deliberately to break down the segregation of town and country people by which so much of it is characterized.' Dr. Orwin has reached the same conclusions as I have, though our agreement is not founded on the same point of view, or on the same basis. I am a little afraid of Dr. Orwin's treatment because he has such a partiality for large units: 'largeness' is a matter of degree and it is always influenced by particular circumstances and cases, but with what he says about village units I have no quarrel. I do not take as favourable a view of the vitality of country towns in general as Orwin: I am convinced that more of them are in a moribund condition that he appears to think. So in my view it is just as important to bring industry into country towns of all sizes as it is to bring it into villages. We cannot do justice to the villages unless we also consider the towns.

The intricacy of modern industry has made it extraordinarily flexible. The war has shown that it is capable of wide dispersion. Different parts can be made in different places. The parts of parts can be assembled in one place and the whole assembled somewhere else. With modern transport the range of possibilities is immense and offers hopeful prospects for setting up small working units, so small in some cases as to correspond to workshops rather than factories.

It requires no great flight of imagination to imagine a concentric system by means of which industry may be brought into all the villages. The larger parts will be made in factories in the country towns, the smaller parts, requiring less intricate machinery and perhaps more craftsmanship, in the villages.

[1]See Appendix V.

The headquarters of the industry and presumably the final assembling would continue to be based on a large industrial town. I am only pointing out here that the scope for bringing industry into the village under modern conditions and with modern techniques makes possible a new industrial revolution which can restore many of the social and psychological deprivations of the earlier revolutions, and for that reason alone, as an act of justice, it must be done: otherwise the Industrial Revolution, considered in terms of its historic intention to benefit mankind, will be left unfinished.

As I sense what is happening, the approach to the problem of new towns is wholly urban — to alleviate the congestion of the massive industrial centres. Yet, as I have argued, there is an urgent country issue also at stake: the countryside needs new towns and new villages for its own sake, not merely to solve an urban problem. Fortunately the two needs are compatible: it would be a quite unnecessary calamity to solve one at the expense of the other. And yet it is only too likely to happen.

Let it be agreed that a small number of quite large new towns are necessary, and that there is a case for siting some of them reasonably near to the parental industrial towns. The danger is that the 'necessity' is likely to be pushed altogether too far. If we take into account — which is the greatest 'necessity' of all — our limited land space, then it is obvious that we must make the maximum use of what are known as our rural backwaters.[1] These are the areas — and they add up to large areas — in our little island which are not pulling their weight in housing our people, or contributing to the vitality of the countryside. The building of towns and villages in backwaters should receive urgent consideration. Again, if industry is to be brought to small towns and villages, it may well be that the over-concentration in the great cities can be relieved by building fewer large towns and more small ones. The big town plan unduly prescribes the choice of site: it can hardly fail directly or indirectly to do harm to agriculture. On the other hand new moderate-sized country towns and villages, properly sited in our backwaters, as well as serving the interests of industry would be of inestimable value both to agriculture and

[1] See Appendices III, IV and V.

the countryside. The scope for experimenting with new towns is far greater, in my view, than any Ministry realizes. After all this is the age of light industries, electricity and motor transport, rather than of railways, factory chimneys and heavy industries: so backwaters as such are now to be regarded only as survivals from a less mobile age.

The backwater is invariably agriculturally effete. With modern techniques, however, few of them are devoid of agricultural potentialities. The work of the War Agricultural Committees showed that many backwaters, particularly on the heavy clays, could be raised to a condition of high farming. But this level of fertility is bound to fall again unless communities blended of different vocations are brought into these areas. In many backwaters capable of high farming – and a number of them no great distance from our large industrial centres – there is no adequate housing even for farmers and farm workers and there is not even the nucleus of a community. I am not thinking of either hill or marginal land, nor of remote country cut off by physical barriers: I have in mind land which today is easily accessible and presents normal agricultural problems. Such backwaters, I insist, now present a special problem in themselves, but it is a political and social problem. Their rehabilitation should be brought to the forefront of our plans for the dispersal of industry and the urban population, as well as for agricultural rejuvenation.

This brings us to long-term planning: no doubt it would be more expensive at first to establish balanced communities in attractive towns and villages in backwaters than elsewhere, but to do this would certainly in the long run yield the higher reward. We must ask ourselves fairly and squarely if under any circumstances we can afford the doubtful luxury of backwaters. In the aggregate the acreage is surprisingly large: once more I will bring Dr. Orwin to my aid. He says: 'In the four counties of Devon, Berkshire, Huntingdon and Westmorland, non-industrial counties representative of different parts of England, there are 772 parishes with populations not exceeding 2,000. Of these only 10 per cent exceed 1,000, while 45 per cent, nearly half of them, have only 300 people or fewer. The great problem of the countryside is how to make life more abundant to the rank and file of dwellers in these little places.'[1] To which I add the postscript — bring more people in and in so doing also make 'life more abundant' for those who will have come from the overcrowded cities. In this, as in all matters affecting integration, there remains much detailed research to be undertaken before we can draw up balance sheets and take a comprehensive view of the whole urban-rural situation — before, in fact, we are entitled to formulate an *ad hoc* plan for any particular region, locality or town whatsoever.

It is clear to any sensible person who has had to direct an even moderately sized staff that there are very real limits to the numbers that can be brought together in a single working unit in order to combine maximum efficiency, enthusiasm and devotion to the work in hand. I have definite ideas as to the correct size of a research institution, but am not entitled to express an opinion on the correct size of an industrial unit. I do, however, know that within pretty wide limits the smaller the units the better, and particularly so if quality is important. It does not seem to have occurred to modern industrial man that happiness and efficiency are functions of each other, and the new scope for the dispersal of industry has made it possible to organize production in a manner that corresponds far more closely to the conditions that encourage happier human relationships. Unfortunately the prestige attaching to 'empire' building and controlling large units leads ambitious men to sacrifice happy and efficient organization to their personal advantages. It is a lamentable principle to reckon a man's salary according to the number of people he has under his command. It is simply one more example of mass and quantitative values taking the place of personal judgment and discrimination.

I do not think it matters what particular industries are brought into the country provided they do not bring with them smoke fumes, dirt, grime or untidiness. The consideration which should carry weight is the practical one of flexibility of size in relation to concentric orientation.

There is much sentimental and antiquated nonsense talked about the industries appropriate to rural areas. Some would only permit handicraftsmanship, others would only allow the

[1] See Appendices III and IV.

processing of the products of the local soil. I have yet to be persuaded of any fundamental difference between making shoes in a village and milling wheat, even in the unlikely event of the wheat having been grown locally. Shoes are largely the product of somebody's agriculture. Of course, co-operation between several local activities — as in the sugar beet crop — is an advantage where it is possible. But it is not essential to bringing industry into the countryside.

It is increasingly difficult in these days of plastics and synthetic materials to draw hard and fast lines between industries whose raw materials are of plant and animal or of mineral origin, while in our small island we can ill afford the luxury of growing industrial crops — a reasonable bow to timber is about as far as we can go. It is all to the good that industries with an agricultural flavour — like the blanket industry, for example — are still located in medium-sized country towns, even if their raw materials are no longer the product of our own land. Scatter and multi-proprietorship in an indirect way nourish the idea of quality and are a healthy counter to undue standardization. The tendency to vast amalgamations known as monopoly capitalism whatever economic and competitive advantages they may have, leads to other consequences that are dire in the extreme and should be arrested before it is too late. How much longer shall we have innumerable country breweries? Yet the standardization of alcoholic liquors by a few giant combines would be a crime against the artistic satisfaction of thirst and tend to reduce man's appetites to mere automatism. If only industry at large would realize that what is true of wines, spirits and beers is true of every commodity that man needs, or thinks he needs, then the ruralization of industry into small units would become inevitable. By no other means, as is so conclusively and tantalizingly vindicated by the vineyards of France, will it be possible to produce those varied and subtle shades in the quality and appearance of the everyday foods, utensils and gadgets that the average Englishman is still — though only just — capable of appreciating. With a rise in the standard of living this sort of appreciation should increase, yet standards of living appear to rise because industry increasingly goes in for the quantitative rather than qualitative: thus the object of the exercise is cancelled out. Money —

and nothing worthwhile to spend it on — seems to be the be-all and end-all of much of what we are doing. Is everything that makes man distinctively human to be sacrificed to some supposedly inevitable economic trend? I should not be surprised if some industrialist with the courage to turn his back on this trend and all the advice given by economists is the one to make the greatest fortune. Quality, largely based on artistic appropriateness, is the crying need of our age: quality is the product of individualism and individualism is the product of small units. This thesis (*pace* Dr. Orwin) applies as much to farming as it does to wine, knives and forks, or women's frocks and hats.

I now, and finally, come to the question of 'size of unit'. This is intimately connected with the further questions of precise situation and architectural appropriateness. My most intimate contacts with rural England and Wales have been on the fields and farms, and although I have always taken a keen interest in the villages and towns, I have never had the opportunity of doing detailed survey work there on my own account. I must rely on general impressions. This may turn out to be an advantage, because accurate data obtained from a limited number of districts can be dangerous in formulating plans for the country as a whole. My view is that it would be premature to dogmatize about size of units before reliable evidence has been collected from every country town and village within our shores. This evidence, moreover, would have to be set against the agreed needs of the industrial towns, for all planning that ultimately affects rural England is up in the air until we know the number of millions of people and the number of factories and other buildings which should be removed bodily as it were from the congested areas. I shall therefore confine myself to general principles, which is in keeping with the temper of the book — a book concerned deeply with principles and only incidentally with details.

The elements which influence size of unit are many and conflicting. From the point of view of balance of vocations, it is obvious that the numbers engaged in each vocation should bear a just relationship to each other. When a rural village gives hospitality to an industrial unit what, I wonder, in the first instance, would be the correct ratio 'new industrial' to 'old-time rural'? Such evidence as is available would suggest that the purely agricultural contributes excessively to the population of most true villages. We must, though, remember that if we bring an industrial unit into a village, this will have the effect of increasing the general services necessary, and so will indirectly add further numbers to the non-agricultural population. Although the agricultural population predominates in so many villages, in nearly all cases that population is, nevertheless, not large enough to service the farms in the neighbourhood. Clearly, also, whatever ratio is considered ideal, the greater the agricultural population, the greater the new industrial population in direct proportion that can be allowed without unbalancing the village. Thus any substantial increase in the truly rural population would greatly add to the scope of bringing industry into the villages, while still maintaining the essential balance of interests.

This is a point that is likely to bring home the essential value of agriculture to the town dweller, especially the town dweller of the next and succeeding generations, for these will be the people who will have tasted the influence of the ruralization of the urban: it will influence them in a strong and personal way. So far so good, but now we come up against an exceedingly stubborn problem: what is the ideal size of a village and what should it be at some future period? Looking ahead it is evident that size will prove to be the ultimate limiting factor to the amount of industry that can be brought into a village. As the years go by and the new villages settle down into homogeneous communities free from 'caste consciousness', with the industrial workers themselves living a rural life, keenly interested in their gardens, and perhaps on occasions helping on the farms, then the ratios between the different vocations will perhaps lose something of their original significance. It might then be safe to increase the industrial population.

Size, then, is the decisive consideration, because at all costs we must maintain the village character. It is, I am convinced, far more serious to make our villages into towns, than to increase the size of smallish towns. A village should be sufficiently large to provide within itself all the elements that make

187

possible a vigorous, simple and well balanced social life. This will entail providing all the amenities that will encourage the intermingling of all castes and classes in a free and natural way. There should be a sufficient number of families to support a good village school in the village. A central school serving a large number of villages tends to become too urban. In short, a village is nothing unless it is a definite and dearly loved place with a spirit peculiar to itself. The traditional distinction between a village and a town is, I think, to be found in these terms. In a village everything is shared between all: one village green, one pub, one hall, one church, one grocer, one butcher and so on, all the inhabitants personally known to each other. In a town there is duplication and much splitting into sectional communities. Today the distinction is not absolute: chapels share religious worship with the church, one pub seldom suffices and there is duplication and segregation in other directions; so we have to be content with the loose definition that replication and segregation are the hallmarks of the town, while integration and unification are the distinctive features of the village. The best we can now say is that a village should not exceed a size that makes integration and unification impossible. We must give the village tradition the chance to continue its evolution and regain its vitality in sympathy with the altered conditions of our time. This is to some extent an act of faith and it is difficult at times not to feel despairing about it — the economist and the planner are so often utterly obtuse to all values that directly effect the subtler influences on human happiness, though these influences are the most important in human life. At the same time growth and change are the only hope of the survival of the village. It might well be, if the old tradition of integration and unification came to permeate the new and better village communities, that larger populations than we now think possible could live and prosper under that principle. The future alone can show.

The size and population of a village have to be considered in terms of the character of the parish. Dr. Sharp, his mind chiefly on education, regards a village of 450 to 500 as satisfactory for a parish with a population of about 650; and I think that it would be agreed that a minimum of this order would be necessary for the multi-vocational unit we have in mind. Maximum size presents equal difficulties, since it is essential to foster that spirit of place and traditional unity that makes a village so much more than a name. I would tentatively suggest something of the nature 600-700, though possibly, in favourable settings, with a good balance, this number could be slightly increased. Now the question arises, would villages with a range of population 400-700 permit of sufficiently large units of industry to satisfy industrial needs without giving too strong a bias to the non-agricultural section of the community? It would be essential not to set the percentage too high at first. Let us take 15 per cent as the initial quota for the new industrial population and see how matters would stand. We should have to allow for children who had not arrived at the age of employment and for mothers who were unable or unwilling to work part- or whole-time in the factory. Against that we should have to set both men and women who would be drawn towards the factory. If we take all these points into consideration, I imagine that in a village with a population of 500 there would be about 30 whole-time workers immediately available. The crucial point at issue is, then, the feasibility of profitable enterprise based, initially, on units of about this size. These considerations are fundamental to my thesis of integration and call for deep research in many directions. My own opinion is that with the introduction of the right sort of industry, good dispersal and concentric planning, these numbers should prove adequate.

Apart from the limitations of numbers imposed by a sound percentage quota, I do not think it would be an advantage to bring outside industries into villages with a population below 450. In such villages—until they are enlarged—we should have to redouble our efforts to extend those trades and vocations which serve the needs of the village itself and the immediate countryside. There are many villages with these small populations: both from the point of view of agriculture (under-housed and under-manned as it is) and the industrial-urban (congested as it is) there can be nothing more important than to increase the size of the best and the most usefully sited of these villages. The building of new villages in the backwaters and the doubling or more than doubling the size of others, with the treble aim of providing for industry and agriculture in an integrated and unified pattern, would be an exciting social and architectural experiment and one that would rival in value the building of new towns. At the centre of the whole idea of integration is the absolute necessity to resist segregating the industrial and the rural. It would be a fatal mistake, as well as an unpardonable crime against artistic perception, to dump down the industrial factory or workshop and cottages as a tidy little annexe with features peculiar to themselves and foreign to the surroundings. No, all new additions *must* and *will* be made an integral part of the village and blend harmoniously with the character and tradition of the village.

This harmony does not rule out controlled spread—provided it is controlled. Controlled spread is often an attractive feature of a village when it blends with the general character of the village. Not all beautiful villages are built on the village green pattern. I do not think that size of unit as such need present serious architectural difficulties. On page 70 of Thomas Sharp's *The Anatomy of the Village* there is a photograph 'A Rural Factory: Mill at Aylsham, Norfolk'. This is worth studying. It is a superb setting for a village factory. Why on earth shouldn't a modern architect produce a modern factory to fit the scene as well as this mill does and many other mills too? It is not really the architects who are not worth their salt: it is the British people. Architects and people must now unite in a passionate endeavour to pick up the threads of the British tradition and set about the long overdue, dangerous and fascinating task of increasing the number and size of our villages in a manner worthy of the craftsmen of bygone centuries, and of the restful beauty that is England. In this task the heaviest responsibility is thrown upon every man Jack of us and most heavily of all upon those who in Parliament and in county, rural district and parish councils, exercise or abuse the will of England and who have it in their power to nourish or wound her spirit.

The whole question of our local government is involved in these changes, for it will have to play a vital part. Two things would appear to be essential: the first, to ensure the most intimate organic connection between regional and ultra-local bodies—without such a truly organic relationship my idea of concentric planning would be impossible. The second, to in-

190

crease the powers, status and responsibility of the parish councils, for if factories are to be brought into villages and all is to be well and truly arranged, the parish will become a unit of the first importance. The artistic integration—or seemly integration—of industry into rural life can only be achieved in detail if it is the ultimate care of those on the spot. The greatest danger of the over-centralization of power is that directives can only be given in terms of explicit regulations. All human cases are in the last resort a matter of the particular and personal. Rules and regulations can never take the place of the personal judgments required by those with intimate knowledge of the situation: that usually means the ultra-local authority. Here is another unavoidable antithesis, regulations: local knowledge.

At the best the methodical industrialization of the rural must be a slow process. I think we should best proceed on the basis of a first, second and third plan. The first would be to ruralize the urban and prepare for the second: this, incidentally, would give time to complete the neccessary rural surveys and perhaps for experimental extensions in a few carefully selected villages. The second plan would be to cater for a specified number of people from the congested urban areas, and to do so on the basis of a definite building programme in the villages to be completed in a specified number of years. The population of the rural areas in England and Wales is about 8 million[1] : this is totally inadequate, so we

[1] Statistics of this kind are a very rough guide to the ecological adequacy of what is happening. The number of people living under rural administration has risen to 10 million since the 1940's and yet there may well be far fewer people living in true rural conditions. On the other hand if more care were taken for ruralising the urban, many people living in towns would have far more satisfying lives and would not need to empty the centre of cities and move to the outskirts which spread out and out in shapeless waves. Urban regeneration is essential to rural conservation. We know that the farm worker and other rural workers are falling every year in number: so much that it is anticipated there will be as many farmers as farmworkers before long: we know that the countryside is being infiltrated by commuters and retired people. These people select the choicest spots in which to live and thereafter they are not so choice. Many rural settlements grow so rapidly they are little more than barracks, we see more and more of these from the train window. There is no trace of a community design: the only thing one can say is that the mini-manor house and the matchbox bungalow are not so common. A huge number of regulations exist to control rural and urban growth, but the final result is petty fogging because there is no overall plan. The new town does at least have the advantage of being on a big enough scale for a design to be imposed on it. We also need well designed new hamlets and villages. But the old piecemeal development under population and economic pressure goes on. So there really is a problem, as Stapledon says, of providing rural accommodation for a new rural population in new villages and hamlets to stop the spread of the rural twilight.

191

shall assume an increase of 4 million for which our second plan will have to cater. In order to allow for maximum size of industrial unit, we shall assume that 20 per cent of the new total will be 'industrial-urban' largely brought in from the cities. We should than have to provide additional village accommodation for:

New industrial-urban	2,400,000
New Rural	1,600,235

I realize that this is no mean target, but on the credit side must be placed the fact that the second plan would not be initiated in bricks and mortar or their equivalent for at least another 15-25 years, and by then it should be in the natural order of things to make rapid progress with all creative undertakings. On the debit side we have to place the following facts: (*a*) That there is much leeway to be made up in the proper housing of the existing rural population; (*b*) No doubt many villages and some whole districts will be considered unsuited to any form of industrialization at this stage; (*c*) Some villages will be too near the maximum size for the introduction of an industrial unit, while in others any addition permissible may be essential for agriculture; (*d*) There will be villages where physical obstacles debar all question of any extension. These debits will have to be set off by the building of new villages and by increasing the industrial quota in certain selected villages where the conditions are exceptionally favourable.

The most problematical point of all may be bringing some 7–8 per cent of the urban population from congested areas into rural areas. True enough the effects of the ruralization of the urban would not have gone very deep at the beginning of the second plan, and the span of a generation may not have elapsed during the interval between initiating the first and second plans. The dual campaign would, however, have been launched and publicized, interest would have been created and tidings of new things would be in the air, while the rural intake up to 2,400,000 would necessarily be spread over a great many years. Moreover, as we have already pointed out, there are at present an appreciable number of urban workers ready and anxious for the change, given only good housing conditions and the sort of work for which they are fitted and accustomed.

In order to round off my second plan I must now consider the country towns: I am thinking in the main of those with populations of less than 15,000. In this group we have many most attractive and well-proportioned towns, including some of England's greatest treasures, but we also have a large number devoid alike of beauty and seemliness. In 1931 the population of such towns in England and Wales was 4,473,204. To mention at random a few of these towns: towards the upper limits of population we have Aylesbury, Barnstaple, Basingstoke, Lewes, Trowbridge and Truro. Those with middle populations are typified by Cirencester, Devizes and Monmouth. Lower in the scale—2,000-3,000—we have, Faringdon, Ledbury, South Molton, Thame, Wincanton and Welshpool. Populations of less than 2,000 are represented by Machynlleth, Presteigne, Moretonhampstead and Moreton-in-Marsh. In my view there is the greatest possible scope for the semi-industrialization or further industrialization of towns of this sort. Most of the larger towns are already industrialized to varying extents, but is there a single one of them that would not greatly benefit by an increase in industrial potential? It is when we come down in the scale that I am convinced the need is greatest. There are numbers of towns of the 6,000 order that are semi-moribund and not pulling their weight in any particular way. True, they may lack facilities, but today such a state of affairs can be rectified anywhere. In the case of all moribund towns it is vicious circles that have to be broken. Lower still in the scale we come to towns, often with little or no industrialization, and frequently with a deal of waste space, all too many of them not remarkable for vitality, enterprise or beauty, and, of course, lacking in facilities.

It is just as essential to devote care to the siting and architectural design of the additions to the county towns as to the villages. Just as much attention would also have to be given to open spaces and garden paddocks as in the great cities. The small towns have afforded the most glaring examples of what not to do—to build suburban annexes having the minimum of organic or structural relationship with the parent town.

The concentric siting of industry in the country districts as a whole would demand a substantial contribution from the country towns. The percentage basis of new-industrial to old population would allow much larger factory units than could be established in the villages. Taking those towns with populations of less than 15,000, I believe it would be a gain on all counts if the numbers were increased by 25 per cent—this would relieve the congestion on the industrial towns by over a million. This would give a total contribution from what I have called the country proper of no less than 3,500,000. And this takes no account of the large new towns under immediate construction or contemplation by the Government, nor of new country towns which I consider to be urgently needed and which would be a part of my second plan.

My third plan would only be initiated when the second was completed in respect of both villages and country towns—and this would not be for fifty years or so hence. We should then move into the era of rural organic integration: the new age whose principles we have been laying down. There would be no scope left for the further extension of existing villages and country towns. Anything that then proved to be necessary would have to be met by further new villages and country towns.

All the figures that I have brought forward are tentative and have no claim to final accuracy. I have used them as a basis for illustrating what would seem to me to be appropriate, reasonable and possible in re-creating our country with a new vision in which a new age makes explicit the principles applied in the past. I am not speaking in a political sense when I say that our actions must be radically based on conservative principles. I hope that I have indicated directions in which research is urgently necessary. To me it is evident that the rural can contribute in a substantial way to the alleviation of congested urban pressure: if all is properly done without harm to the spirit of England we can once more design a land and townscape on the canvas of our country which will not disgust vital and artistically minded people and bring to an end the barbarism of the does-it-pay principle which alone seems to have guided our destiny for too long. Of course it pays: what does not pay is the single-minded purpose of the old-fashioned commercial economist. People will want to pull down what is ugly whether it pays or not.

My actual figures can of course be scaled up and down in

the light of change or of more exact evidence. My aim, to use an appalling phrase—but one well in accord with the jargon of a one-eyed age—is nothing less than gradually and methodically to rehumanize millions of inherently innocent, simple and lovable members of the race. In the last resort the aim is inspired by the desire for beauty, restfulness, and loving-kindness inherent in all of us, a desire which is fundamentally stronger than that for material comfort and social security. To plan simply for so-called 'welfare' will get us nowhere; to plan to rehumanize ourselves will truly open the gates to happiness and prosperity. Time! Time, we always have time on our side, time so patient and fruitful, provided we would husband and replenish her gifts instead of stealing them for the benefit of a very momentary present.

CHAPTER 12

RÉSUMÉ OF PRINCIPLES

Principles are the materials of statesmanship. Integration is the most necessary principle in our time in order to counterbalance an age of segregation. Life itself provides the clues to the art of integration. In practical terms 'integrity' demands certain conditions of education and work. These conditions are still found in agriculture but are disappearing in the nation as a whole

---

THE PROBLEMS that face the present generation are so numerous and so insistent that it seems almost impossible to take long views, yet long views have probably never been so necessary. Long views depend upon abiding by principles.

Statesmanship and craftsmanship are closely akin: no design can be worthily accomplished unless the materials used are worthy. The materials of statesmanship are fundamental principles, and only designs made with these threads can be strong, stable and durable. Principles are more than scientific techniques. To understand and apply in action the principle of integration requires high imagination and a sense of purpose. Like any other craft, statesmanship cannot be learnt from a book and applied mechanically.

I have always insisted that broad biological principles are essential to understanding the affairs of men: they are a clue to creativeness. My own reflections on these principles have led me to some definite conclusions, as this book should have made clear by now. If progress means anything at all, then the way-going of man is due for a long period of integration to counteract the long and unbridled period of segregation. Integration means closer adherence to the laws of biology, rather than blind allegiance to the findings and discoveries of the physical sciences. Thus agriculture and the countryside assume paramount importance in any social design that can have reasonable hope of achieving both glory and stability. I go so far as to believe that agriculture should take a prominent place in national policy for its own intrinsic sake as well as for its economic contribution. A nation needs a thriving and purposeful agriculture with a large and adventurous agricultural-rural population, just as it needs fresh air and wholesome food. The land and the affairs of the land are a necessary and vital part of national life and an essential complement to the physical environment of the cities and factories. Agriculture and the land should play a leading part in all systems of formal education: the country and its pursuits should contribute a giant's share in well spent holidays. That is the major thesis I have expounded and more follows from it than I have the energy and perhaps the wit to pursue: in any case, once the general principles have been grasped, it is the duty of everyone who believes in their validity to discover by trial and error how to apply them in particular cases.

So I shall make no apology for once again emphasizing some of the major points, because it is essential that the fundamental principles should be clearly and constantly borne in mind.

Great stress has been laid on the value of training and upon the necessity of a national scheme of apprenticeship as a part of formal education; this led me to insist upon the importance of hobbies and holidays with a strong biological bias. It is of the first importance to arouse and train active and creative interests. When interests have once been aroused, young and old alike should be given ample opportunity to follow them in their own ways. The calibre of a teacher-trainer would then be estimated by the enthusiasm with which his pupils and students devoted themselves to worthwhile interests: he would not be graded simply by his success in getting pupils through examinations. Early apprenticeship is advocated for certain vocations: as much harm can be done to individuals with these vocational bents by continuing their orthodox schooling too long, as good can be done to others by greatly extending the period devoted to postgraduate studies.

The significance of action and decision have been discussed in detail together with the healthy effects of seeing work through to a finish. These disciplines in their influence on human capacity and character have been at the core of our

o

argument in favour of apprenticeship and hobbies in rural pursuits. Nearly all the tasks of the country entail skill and decision, while intimate contact with the problems and work of the land begets a looking-ahead, planning-for-tomorrow attitude of mind. The machinery used in connection with the land is both intricate and simple. The land apprentice will work with machines on a wide range of performance, with his own bare hands: he will associate with a fine class of man —and with animals. His jobs will be varied, and he will experience in a real and intimate way the vagaries of our delightful English climate: this will help to weather and mature him.

The present trend in the organization of industry tends to give master consideration to the amount and cheapness of production with scant regard to quality: this trend is almost regarded as a necessity with the need for mass-production and standardized articles. Quality may be variously defined, but artistic merit must always be regarded as an essential characteristic. In foodstuffs, appearance, taste and fragrance are the artistic content and quality is lacking without them: they contribute to effective nutritive values; a bored palate can hardly favour digestion. In any event a discriminating appreciation of food adds zest to life and helps to keep our senses alert. Men in our Puritan and stoical country may think this is cissy, but on the Continent it is accepted as an essential part of the cultivated life. Industrialism has brought upon us this sensual poverty and we must enrich ourselves again before it is too late. Let other industrializing countries take heed of what has happened to us, who were once a great civilized race.

This matter of artistic perception goes very deep: the artistic object appeals to us because of its integrity. It is timeless: the satisfaction it gives extends far beyond its immediate and limited usefulness. What is true of drama and novel is equally true of the most mundane of man's creations. All alike are great in proportion as they do justice to what is at all times true of what we recognize as the essence of being human. Although enormous numbers of the everyday products of industry are of exceedingly restricted use, there is not one that could not be fashioned to give at least a rudimentary artistic satisfaction.

On this account I have pleaded for workshops to be set up in factories so that the employees can have the chance—as a hobby—to make and design the very things which at work they only make in part and to which they contribute nothing in design. The strength of hand craftsmanship is that he who makes also designs—and he sees through to a finish. A good scheme of apprenticeship would never lose sight of the importance of design—which is now to a large extent segregated from real experience of working with materials and confined to speculations on the drawing-board, often with ludicrous results so far as the 'integrity' of the product is concerned.

A good scheme of apprenticeship would never lose sight of the importance of design in relation to every other factor: perhaps one of the great—but secondary—advantages of national apprenticeship would be that in times of slump in any industry the workers would be given opportunities to devote their time to apprenticeship and be more concerned with quality and design than with monotonous mass production. Bad times are a challenge and I have seen some of the finest ideas in agriculture come out of near bankruptcy when a pioneer farmer with imagination and resolution refused to be beaten. Now for a point to which I have not yet drawn attention: the vigorous rural life which I anticipate in the future, and a larger rural and country-town population, will of itself be extremely important, because the views and the will of country people should count for more than is possible at present. One man, one vote and urban-minded politicians give the preponderance of outlook to town and suburban thinking.

The countryman is prone to hold strong views, but they are not usually so politically flavoured as are those of the townsman. He is, I think, more concerned with the merits of particular cases than he is with the politics that distort the real issues. He is seldom rabid in his political opinions. I have been particularly struck with this when discussing the thorny problem of nationalization of the land with numerous farmers and landworkers. They have not shown an inclination to discuss and consider the matter in relation to political parties or political platforms or, indeed, against the background of any preconceived political prejudices. The country has a mellowing influence on all who serve it and on all who are brought into intimate connection with its affairs. The country therefor should be helped to influence the broad educational policy of the nation. The country is a school of equal value in juvenile and adult education: a school alike for the hand and eye, the head and the heart, with splendid facilities for teaching, training and conditioning. The opportunities that lie latent in our parishes and shires should be realized by social reformers, by 'progressives' of all shades of thought and by educationists, and turned to maximum national advantage before it is too late. In that one sentence I have, I think, epitomized my whole contention.

POSTSCRIPT TO A DREAM

It is only arousing enthusiasm and imagination of the mass of the people that this great revolution of integration will succeed. But there are grounds for optimism since such a turning-point in history can alone provide permanent satisfaction to the full nature of man

I GLANCE back over my pages wistfully. Have I only been dreaming idle dreams? Here we are in a world distraught with immediate life and death problems pouring on us from all directions: distracted statesmen devote all their energies to hectic efforts to find immediate solutions and seem committed beyond recall to crossing these dangerous rapids with no better foothold to support them than ill-balanced and slippery stepping-stones cast under their feet by political pressure groups and partisans of conflicting economic tenets, usually, it would seem, with devilish intent. The stream of progress seems to carry us forward with the intention of drowning us all. How, then, are the human problems of the world to be faced with cool deliberation, without the prejudices born of ages, without mistrust, and without distorted memories at all points undermining reason and sapping the heart springs of good intentions? I answer unhesitatingly, by daring to dream dreams.

This is an extraordinary age: with all its suspicions and uncertainties, it is not devoid of hope: grounds for optimism are not lacking. Grounds for optimism, indeed! And where are they to be found? Not in the papers, when we read about the international tangle and the inability of the Great Powers to get together. Those of us who believe that food and agriculture are at the core of a better world cannot feel very hopeful after reading Karl Brandt's deeply penetrating book on the reconstruction of world agriculture. Too heavy a responsibility falls on the United States of America too soon. More time must elapse before the virile and conflicting interests in that all-powerful creditor country can be expected to stand behind a policy sufficiently farsighted and drastic to set the wheels of international trade and interchange everywhere in motion again. Great Britain today has the will—the will perhaps as never before—but no longer the power of her own resources, to revitalize and redirect the flow of international trade. Russia has her own ends to serve and is minded first and foremost to serve those ends as *she* sees them.

The grounds for optimism then do not spring from the actions that statesmen are willing to take at present, but in the stronger desires of the masses of people of the world to improve their lot. No matter whether the cry is for greater political freedom, higher standards of material comfort, greater security of better education, in all cases the cry is the echo of a terrific urge to attain to something better.

Out of all the conflicting desires in due time the true values upon which alone human progress can be built will emerge, and will sink deep into the mass consciousness of mankind. This will lead to a more philosophical understanding of values: then both nations and individual men will have a higher incentive to give and take; they will become endowed with a greater patience and a deeper tolerance.

Human societies cannot recover rapidly: true harmony amongst men of all nations, all creeds, all colours and all tenets, can only be slowly won. Yet there are real grounds for optimism, for, despite the political discords and social upheavals of the day, men realize, even if half despairingly, that such harmony is attainable and the urge to achieve it runs high in the breasts of millions of individuals.

It is significant that in this country so much has been written, and from so many different angles, about agriculture and the inner meaning of rural life and rural values. Action has not followed: there has, as yet, been no pronounced movement from the towns to the countryside, from the urban to the rural. This is because, at present, all is flux, and ideas rampant.

The modern zest for planning is an obvious, if at present over-material, manifestation of the urge for the better ordering of the affairs of man, for a more even sharing of the bounty of nature and of the products of man's ingenuity. It represents a quest for values. Man is no longer willing to rest content and that is itself the surest of all grounds for optimism.

At this moment we have probably not yet reached the zenith of strife, discord and uncertainty; but these are born of the same urge that will sooner or later carry us to tranquillity and to a world of greater harmony and of more equitable arrangements between nation and nation and man and man than anything man has known before.

I am optimistic enough to feel to the very marrow of my being that the present era of disharmony and sore trial, end when it will, is the prelude to a golden age of real human understanding and progress. Otherwise I would not have been able to write this book—a dream, perhaps, but a dream of conviction. My mind in retrospect dwells on the rural scene in England and Wales that I have known so well and I am at once thrilled and appalled—thrilled at the almost incredible change in farming enterprise for which the war years have been responsible; appalled at the horrors that have been perpetrated through lack of social plans and human values. Nevertheless, to put one's mind back to the dereliction of 1939 and then forward to the end of the war is to see a new England, the making of which has given new life and new zest to the farming community. The thrill of reclamation with its sumptuous crops where before grew only scrub and weeds is something that goes to the heart of the true countryman. Enterprise, as the war proved, is strangely infectious. On every score it was a bad strategical error, an ill appreciation of true values, to have slackened in the food production drive as the war began to draw to its close. When the force of a great momentum has been allowed to decline, it is exceedingly difficult to regain power and work up again to maximum acceleration. So much was learned during the war, that by 1945 it would not have been beyond the capacity of our sorely tried farmers and of the War Agricultural Executive Committees to have redoubled their efforts and carried both reclamation and good farming yet further afield. Much as the war taught us about the high farming of our little island, the greatest lesson of all, well learned by both the best farmers and the agricultural scientists, has been how very much we

still have to learn! At the height of the food production campaign I felt this acutely; for I flatter myself I was second to
none in my ardent desire, inspired by understanding the
urgency of the need, to grow the last ounce of food compatible with good husbandry from our own soil. My problem,
since at that time I was in charge of a considerable acreage of
derelict land, was to conduct two incompatible enterprises at
one and the same time with an inadequate labour force. My
instinct said *food*: my reason was inclined to say *investigation*. The dilemma, which was in the realm of values, was
almost heartbreaking. Looking back, I think, in some moods
at all events, that I may have allowed my instinct too much
scope. But who can say? At least I initiated enough investigation—I will not say research, that was impossible during the
war—to keep my dreams alive, for I taught myself that despite the magnitude of our war effort, we still had a long way
to go before we could aspire to the full agricultural potential
of our little island.

What appals one about rural England is the horrors that
have sprung up without rhyme or reason in the most absurd
and unlikely places.

Surprisingly enough, however, and infinitely heartening, is
the fact that taking England and Wales as a whole and despite
everything, the rural character still remains, bruised, yes, but
virile, still capable of vigorous growth and fine achievements
and still capable of redeeming all that is bad, narrow and un-
satisfying in our urban and industrial life. Our unremitting
search must be for right values, our unremitting aim must be
to educate and plan against a background of correct values.
Correct values are hardy perenials indigenous to our soil, difficult totally to eradicate, but all too prone to become mon-
strosities growing under conditions completely foreign to
their simple needs so that they are unrecognizable.

False values reigning as half gods or false gods can only lead
to chaos. True values are divine and can sweep aside all difficulties, all suspicions, and with surprising rapidity rectify all
the errors and malpractices of the past. If this era of turmoil
represents a search for true values—as I think it does—then all
will be well. If, on the other hand, it represents the final domination of false values, then the human chapter is nearing its end.

upon acquired habits, acquired knowledge and acquired discernment, all of which need to be constantly practised and extended to be fully developed. Good taste and discrimination acquired in one sphere usually tend to foster those graces in other spheres. Since every human being must eat and drink, it follows that the kitchen and the dining-table are the nurseries of culture and of a truly cultured people. Good living is not the prerogative of any one class, as is so clearly shown by France, but France is not a country of wine and vineyards for nothing: she has understood where lies both the cradle and the nursery of culture. William Cobbett, as is wont, goes to the heart of the matter and as it affects all men alike, when he says: 'Let anyone who has eaten none but baker's bread for a good while taste bread home baked, mixed with milk instead of with water, and he will find what the difference is.' He will! and I expect that today most men in this country (though few would care to say so at *home*) would heartily agree with Cobbett's dictum that 'every woman, high or low, ought to know how to make bread'.

Complete control over the food of a people is a dangerous weapon to place in the hands of any Government. Civilization depends as much on the scope afforded for exercising preference and discernment as upon full stomachs, so it is just as important to redouble our efforts towards the production and distribution of a wide range quality foods as of food grossly considered. Food could and should be made the easiest and most pervading means of levelling upwards rather than downwards, and of encouraging individual aptitudes and appetites. ('The individual—stupendous and beautiful paradox —is at once infinitesimal dust and the cause of all things'— C. V. Wedgwood). To place a wide range of quality food and drinks on the market at the cheapest possible fair price is an obligation of every Government: to aim at this constitutes official recognition of the supreme importance of giving to the individual of all classes the opportunity to exercise discrimination. With food, as with every need or desire, it is quite impossible to attempt an arbitrary definition of where 'luxury' begins. We can, however, assert with some assurance that unless quality and opportunities for developing good taste and refined judgment are given full rein in all directions, then these virtues will come to be held of small account and individual men will be dominated increasingly by superimposed and necessarily arbitrary and drab standards and decreasingly by their own finer feelings and perceptions.

The mischief arises from the fact that many of the choice luxury foods and alcohols are not only scarce but expensive to produce and are therefore associated with privilege. This is, however, only half the story. Those who can afford the most expensive luxuries in food and alcohol are privileged not so much because they can acquire what is best, but rather in virtue of making it possible for the superlative craftsman, upon whose skill the quintessence of quality depends, to continue in the arts which have been developed and handed down through the centuries. We shall do well to remember that supreme quality in all things is a gift from the centuries and not from science, is the reward of high skill and intense devotion and not the ability just to follow dry prescription or blue-print. When as William Morris has said, 'there is a conscious sensuous pleasure in the work itself, it is done by artists'. In the case of food and alcohols to a very special degree literally centuries of dogged peasant perseverance, backed by love of place and love of perfection, have been both the price and the reward of achievement. Nothing of the first excellence can be produced except against a background of experience built up inch by inch and handed on from generation to generation with an ever-growing sense of pride and love. What Stephen Gwynne has said of the *vignerons* of Gevry-Chambertin, men who thought 'of themselves as belonging to a craft apart, and were very conscious that they . . . were an aristocracy of their craft' is equally true of those who have been responsible for the finest indigenous cheeses of our country, and for the production of the breeds of cattle and sheep that have made possible our 'sirloins' and 'saddles'. These arts are hazardous and exceedingly exacting. Writing in 1934 Stephen Gwynne tells us that the peasant *vigneron*, although he may glory in the charge of choice vineyard, 'also may find it costly. His sons begin to look about for an occupation that will bring in more net cash in return for shorter hours.' Will it be realized in time, can it be realized in time, that excellences are the supreme care of individuals and that

207

the individuals concerned are far more priceless because of the skills *qua* skills which they husband and cherish than because of the articles they actually produce?

If we are heading—and it seems that we are heading there fast—in the direction of a factory wine replacing vintage wine, factory cheese and butter totally replacing the best farmhouse 'vintage' and in all directions blended and standardized products replacing those that are place and skill bound, has anybody tried to balance the debit and credit account in terms not of monetary gains or losses to particular groups of persons, but in terms of ultimate human values, as affecting vast numbers of human beings and perhaps the whole human race?

My own feeling is that if, because of social pressure upon a population that has become unprincipled—fear of loss of privilege or of dire economic catastrophe and other direct or obscure reactions—we are no longer able or willing to aspire to the production of supreme excellences in food or alcohol, then that is the first nail in the coffin of all excellences—the beginning of the end of striving after perfection, the beginning of the end of all art, the beginning of the end of a truly cultured civilization, the beginning of the end of the human race. In fact all one's dreams of a well-planned relation of town to country can come to nothing if it is not inspired by the idea of quality in life. Standards will sink to those of the grossest materialism, and this a highly standardized mass production can satisfy. Riches will be accounted simply in money.

Such spiritual poverty threatens us in the midst of riches procured by new industries and new techniques that I foresee a time when the emperors, kings, knights, and squires alike of wine, spirits and beers will all disappear together, drowned in standardized beverages—a strange application of the democratic principles of equality! For just as there must not be men who stand above the shoulders of others, neither must there be any such foods or goods. Alas! then for men of all classes, tastes and incomes, the pendulum has already begun to swing in this direction. It is not the instincts and feelings of men that are going to shape the future, but the mass market, the greed of industrialists with scientists as their servants, the usurpation by government of traditional and conservative principles.

I am not so naive as to argue that science has made no contribution to the excellences, but when we consider those articles and wares manufactured for the personal use and edification of individual men, we have to agree that there was an undertone of hard truth in William Morris's assertion 'that the great achievement of the nineteenth century was the making of machines which were wonders of invention, skill and patience, and which were used for the production of measureless quantities of worthless makeshifts'. The electric and gas cookers have simplified and perhaps cheapened the process of cooking, but can it with truth be said that they have widened the scope of that art? The tendency of the application of science is always towards standardization, which in the ultimate things of life (e.g. food, alcohol, clothes, the more simple equipment of the household and decoration) is the arch-enemy of perfection.

The great majority of processed foods are now standardized to a greater or less extent, while refrigeration has in the main had a similar influence on natural foods—meat and fruit. Even in normal times, for example, the number of varieties of apples imported into this country is limited and they do not arrive in a natural or perfect condition of ripeness. In the main the work of the scientists has been devoted not so much to quality or nutritive value in crops or animal products, as to matters connected with yielding ability and ease of handling. Thus great strides have been made in the methods of countering disease, in the standing ability and early maturity of cereal and other crops and in the productivity of both animals and crops under a variety of conditions. It is true that Sir Roland Biffin's pioneer breeding work with wheat was largely directed toward the baking quality of the grain (although in the interests of a standardized loaf) and that much successful research has been conducted to improve, by breeding and manuring the malting qualities of barley. Science has gone a long way to explain the processes involved in making wine, cheese, bread and butter, but done little to improve their intrinsic quality or widen the range of particular excellences obtainable in different brands, samples or vintages.

Already it is apparent, however, that it should be possible for the scientist to bring together in one variety of a particular plant or in one strain of a particular animal the capacity for high productiveness together with unusually high nutritive value and an exceptional coefficient of appeal. This will all be achieved when we have the fullest co-operation between the geneticist, the physiologist, the psychologist, the biochemist and epicurean. Teams of this sort are already beginning to come together, although up to the present insufficient weight has been given to the importance of the part that the epicurean has to play. We want our standards of appeal to be based not upon vulgar and uneducated reactions but upon a discriminating appreciation of the subtleties that alone proclaim real quality.

Nutritive value and appeal is of import for two entirely different but equally imperative reasons—acres and appetite. If it were to be proved that size, bulk and high yields per acre were not compatible with maximum production of nutrients and a sufficiently good coefficient of appeal, then the problems of agriculture and of the feeding of the peoples of the world would need to be re-examined and on a considerably broadened basis. It is premature to dogmatize on this aspect of the problem, but evidence is not lacking to suggest that in many instances bulk and yield per acre are not safe guides as to value-appeal per acre. Broadly speaking, it would be true to say that those cows which produce the highest yield of milk per (all-in-all) acre are not usually those which produce the highest percentage of butterfat in their milk, nor by any means necessarily the highest yield of butterfat per acre. When appetite is taken into consideration, and particularly the appetites of different individuals for different foods, it would not be surprising if concentration of appropriate value-appeal factors is actually more important than generous supplies of a mediocre product. Milk may well be a case in point, particularly if we also take heed of vitamin and mineral content.

In many crops there is a tendency for the more important nutrients to be concentrated towards the periphery of the edible product. It is the outer layers of the cereal grains that are the richest in protein. Thus of the ordinary oat varieties 'Potato' with a relatively small grain is exceptionally rich in protein, while the little Grey Oat (*Avena strigosa*) and the improved variety of this type, S.171, bred at Aberystwyth, both with exceptionally small grains, are not only exceedingly rich in protein but considerably above the average in lime and phospheric acid content. Thus the oats we have mentioned come far nearer the modern heavy grain producers in terms of important nutrients per acre than is fully realized, while on poor soils the advantage is often with those more modest varieties. This leaves out of consideration the value of concentration as such and of appeal. The 'Potato' oat is notorious for the excellence of its oatmeal, while an experimental batch of oatcakes prepared from the meal of S.171 gave cakes of a peculiar nutty and singularly pleasing flavour. Concentration is of great importance to the dairy farmer (and this has a parallel human significance) and particularly so now that he is so largely dependent upon relatively bulky home-grown foods. It is because of its high protein content and of the exceptional properties of its protein that the field bean, despite the fact of its rather fickle cropping capacity, is such an important crop on the dairy farm.

The apple affords another example of concentration of a desired nutrient towards the periphery: it has been shown that the concentration of ascorbic acid (vitamin C) increases from the core to the skin. It does not, of course, follow that maximum yield of periphery and maximum bulk per acre run parallel, so that we can see from the examples I have quoted every justification for being highly sceptical of any tacit assumption that yield per acre is necessarily a good guide as to yield of nutrients (and still less as to yield of appeal factors). Nor can size of edible product be necessarily taken as a safer criterion, yet crops have been evaluated primarily on the basis of gross yield tests, and size has been given far too much prominence in judging the quality of fruit and especially vegetables.

Gross appetite and differential and selective appetite for different foods, and for foods variously prepared, influence in a fundamental manner both the total amount and the precise amount of the different nutrients eaten. This is a fascinating subject, the elements of which, when more fully understood, are bound to have an all-pervading influence on a sane food and agricultural policy for the feeding of the peoples of the world. The subject is too large for detailed consideration here and I shall content myself with one broad generalization. Animals have the definite capacity to hunt out and choose for themselves eatables (if only in small quantities) that contain particular nutrients which they need. Man has similar instincts, but because he is given limited opportunities for exercising them, they become decidedly blurred and often, worst still, actually perverted. It is not only a question of seeking or choosing foods for the nutrients they contain, it is equally, and perhaps to an even greater extent in man, a matter of the acceptance value (a current term for appeal) of the various food forms in which the different nutrients may be presented to the individual. Thus a particular person might prefer to eat anything up to perhaps as much as twenty times as much of one eatable (acceptable but of low concentration of the desired nutrient) as of another, but one endowed with an unusually high concentration of the nutrient in question. A second person might prefer the more concentrated form, while a third person, except under the compulsion of extreme hunger, would be unwilling to taste it. Grave issues are at stake. A rigid drawing-up of diets based upon presenting the right quantities of all the necessary nutrients (assuming that we do in fact know *all* that is necessary and the right quantities of each) in a too limited number of separate eatables from which individuals may choose (at one and the same meal) is dangerous for two reasons: little or insufficient deference is paid to differences in individuals' acceptance coefficients, and no deference whatsoever is accorded to the training of the instinct of nutritional selectivity. Here, there is a striking example of the lethal that lies hidden in knowledge, and the dangers that man gratuitously takes if he disregards his instincts and backs his knowledge-acquiring ability the whole way.

The general principle I have briefly outlined adds emphasis to the need of offering to every individual the greatest possible range of eatables, both in respect of ultimate ingredients and the methods of presentation. This is the more important because it does not follow that the nutrients which an individual requires one day either quantitatively or qualitatively are the same as those he requires the next. Agriculturally the

212

principle is of no less importance, because it shows the danger of over-insistence on particular crops, or varieties of crops, or of particular animal produce, on the score either of concentration of nutritive ingredients alone or of economic production alone. As far as acres permit, *diversification of production should be everywhere the rule.* Both appeal and acceptance value of nutritive value are greatly influenced by the form in which a particular food is presented. This can be well illustated by reference to fruit and vegetables in relation to vitamin C content; wide differences are revealed by chemical analysis.

Lucky is the man who likes blackcurrants: he need not devote much time to satisfying his Vitamin C needs. The high place taken by sprouts is fortunate, for they have a long green and picking season, and, well cooked, appeal to most people. But, be it noted, like all green crops, sprouts lose vitamin potency if kept lying about—and most sprouts eaten are at the very least 24 hours old. They do not, however, lose potency with such devastating rapidity as spinach. If money were no object I should be content to take care of my vitamin C needs every day of the week with asparagus tips; others might prefer a greater weight of new potatoes. To eat enough apples especially the lower concentration dessert apples, one would need to have an exceptional liking (acceptance value) for this fruit, and no mean appetite if full justice had to be done to all the other essential nutrients. In practice most of us prefer to obtain our vitamin C by eating a variety of fruits and vegetables.

Marked divergences of vitamin content also reveal themselves between one variety and another of the same fruit or vegetable. For example the vitamin C potency is decidedly low in most varieties of plums, yet is relatively high in Rivers' Early Prolific, while the popular Victoria is even below the poor average for this fruit. Wide divergences also show themselves between different varieties of oranges.

This shows that varietal work is of vital importance. It needs to be undertaken in respect of all nutrients. Equally urgent is detailed work on the palatability, which is tantamount to acceptance value, of different varieties and of such matters as 'cookability' and 'canability'. Evidence is steadily

P   213

accumulating on all these points: in other words, the time is approaching when it will be possible, in respect of every crop and every animal product, to set the breeder in categorical terms the precise values, qualities and appeals, which he must try to unite in a single crop or animal eatable. The plant and animal breeders, for better or for worse, will be the magicians of the coming age.

Our ultimate aim should be the production of a wide diversification of crop and animal products, each the ultimate offspring of true breeding stocks. We need an extended range of perfect products within each nutritional group: the animal protein-rich, the vegetable protein-rich, those rich in the several vitamins, minerals and so forth. A 'perfect' product would be one exceedingly rich in the nutrient or nutrients for which it was primarily responsible, and would also have a uniformly high acceptance value. Within each group the aim should be to make available numerous products which, when compared with each other, exhibited the widest possible qualitative differences in (high-class) acceptance value.

In stating the breeding problems of the future in these terms, we are not overlooking the peremptory needs of high production (we are asking for production in terms of nutrients and acceptance values) and of adaptability to different conditions of soil and climate. Breeding is like laying bricks: we add to our structure little by little, all the time; it is gain that we seek, pure gain, not the gain of something valuable at the loss perhaps of something even more valuable. What we shall lose, or what we are likely to lose, is nothing more important than the outward and visible signs—certain show-table and show-ring characters—of long-continued selection and breeding, animated by the striving after erroneous or fortuitous standards.

A sane breeding programme aiming at using acres to the best advantage and the production of acceptable nutrients can only be envisaged and planned as an exceedingly long duration undertaking — continuity of endeavour and aim is an absolute prerequisite to success. This means, in the first place, that the breeder should only embark upon a project with material which prolonged research by a competent team of workers in the several appropriate fields has shown to contain within itself all the properties that would seem to make final success a possibility. When, in 1919, the Welsh Plant Breeding Station was founded, the first term of reference which I set myself and my colleagues was to find out not only which species of herbage plant it was most desirable to improve, and in which direction it was most desirable to improve them, but also which species—by virtue of the range of natural forms inherent in the aggregate make-up of each—appeared to afford the greatest scope for improvement.

In the main, this preliminary work was not for the geneticist: it was soon evident, for example, that white clover on all essential counts would offer a far more promising field for the plant breeder than Alsike clover. I am satisfied that, had the amount of work which was put into S.100 white clover been devoted to Alsike clover, the gain to British agriculture would have been incomparably less, though I am not for a moment suggesting that Alsike clover is not improvable within worthwhile limits.

The work required is so great that we cannot afford to dissipate our research energies on the rather remote possibility of achieving advances with difficult material, itself only of secondary value. The apple is a fruit of such widespread appeal and utility, and of such decided value as a late season and winter source of vitamin C, that it would seem that no trouble would be too great and no research programme too ambitious that aimed at producing a variety of the standard of appeal of the best Cox, with the vitamin content of the best Bramley, unless informed genetical and biochemical opinion considers that there exists a fundamental incompatibility in the way of achieving this desirable combination.

I mention this fruit merely as an example of the sort of considerations that should be borne in mind in dealing with our essential crop plants—decide first which species are the most important, and of these which the most improvable, and then spare no trouble and no expense to improve.

Before concluding with some remarks on animal products, I want to emphasize an essential point in the technique of breeding. It is this: our procedure should be based upon 'one thing at a time' or, in the words of that discerning practical breeder of dairy stock, George Odlum: 'It is easily discoverable that the shortest road to getting balance (fixity or true breeding) for superiority in several factors is at first to achieve balance in not more than two and perhaps only one.' We would draw up a list of the factors or qualities that we wish to embody in a single product. Thus in the case of the apple, our first aim might be to fix high vitamin content, but in choosing material for this end we would have to bear in mind the other desirable qualities and, as far as possible, not select high-vitamin varieties upon which to build if they were grossly lacking in, say, acceptance value and cropping properties. Each of these other qualities in due course should be dealt with separately, and one by one built into the high-vitamin content. Unless we proceed methodically in this precise and timetable manner, we are certain to drift into confusion of aims, to waste much money and energy and attach importance to features of no consequence: in short to make a complete muddle of our well intentioned endeavours—such indeed has been the case with much livestock breeding.

Of all our domestic animals the bovine more than any other would repay a comprehensive breeding programme. Milk is essential everywhere in the world: in this small country, if we are to produce enough milk and also a proper amount of beef, there is no escape from the fact that a large proportion of our beef animals will have to be the progeny of our dairy herds. I am fully aware of the potentialities of our hill and marginal lands for beef production and I am by no means ruling out the beef breeds. I am similarly alive to the fact that the cattle beast is of first-rate importance in maintaining the rougher and poor grazings in a condition suitable for sheep—an additional reason to attaching major importance to the bovine. In so far as milk is concerned we must remember that hill and marginal land have much to contribute in the rearing of the dairy breeds, and by agistment to the grazing of young dairy stock during the summer. It is therefore quite wrong to suppose that the future usefulness of our hill and marginal land depends solely or even primarily upon the full exploitation of the hardy beef breeds or upon beef production as such.

What manner of bovine do we need then as the chief representative of that species in this country? Can we produce in one and the same strain the several characteristics that we require? The first essential is to decide upon our needs and catalogue them more or less in the right order of importance. We will presuppose the necessity of a high measure of self-sufficiency on our farms. It can be justified on many grounds. First and foremost we would place high milk yield, though much depends upon the terms on which we define high milk yield. My own evaluation would be milk produced in relation to the life of the cow: this would postulate a cow capable of living to a reasonable age and incidentally capable of producing a number of calves. Milk yield to be justifiably regarded as 'high' should be high per overall acre of a wholly or reasonably self-sufficient farm. Our high-milking cow would therefore be sturdy, a good converter of a ration consisting of no mean proportion of bulky feeds and it must yield uniformly well in each lactation. If we accept these standards for the proper definition of high, we shall start on sure grounds. In selecting foundation animals for this factor of high milk yield, we shall automatically start with beasts of good constitution, with frames, organs and functional abilities capable of dealing with rations consisting of a goodly proportion of feeds produced on the farm where a particular herd lives. We would then, in effect, be starting with two factors, milk yield and constitution: in practice the breeder would proceed on two parallel lines to superimpose yield on constitution and to superimpose constitution on yield. After obtaining a high measure of equilibrium here, he might next attend, step by step, to the improvement of the quality of the milk: he would first tackle butterfat. With this equilibrium also established, he might turn to the potentialities of the vitamin content, and then to the potentialities of high calcium and other mineral content. Equilibrium established on all these points, attention could be turned to the potentialities for beef production of the male calves: here we must remember that sturdy animals have been a necessary postulate behind the whole breeding programme. The beef standards could not be set unduly high, since milk must come first, but with good feeding all the way reasonably beefy calves should grow through steerhood into beef of no mean quality to supplement the products of our beef breeds.

The aim is utility and real quality breeding (based, of course, on rigorous progeny testing) all the way, so that preconceived notions as to type and fancy points will not influence the selection or matings. Nevertheless, supreme utility based largely—as it must be— on constitution will be certain (although by accident rather than design) to fix a comely and presentable type. A comprehensive bovine breeding plan might result in the production of a new breed, or of authenticated strains within particular breeds or both; but the desired results are likely to be obtained in proportion as attention is paid to needs and animals as such rather than to breeds *per se.*

The crucial argument in support of an exceedingly long-term and an all-embracing bovine breeding policy is that we can only obtain the milk we need, and of the quality we deserve, by a high all-round production from each and all of the milk cows, and from each and all of the acres that contribute to their sustenance.

We live in dire time when the problems with which we are beset are not less momentous than those we had to solve when fighting for our lives in the war. In the war, priority was given to the solving of life or death problems—to solving them at any price. The same rating of priorities is necessary now and the same concentration of money and brains on the rapid solution of the most urgent. At present we cannot afford to dissipate research energy or our strictly limited resources in first-class research brains in unlimited directions: and for the life of me I cannot see the use of the Medical Research Council and the Agricultural Research and Improvement Councils and similar bodies, unless they are competent to put their fingers with unerring judgment on the comparatively few major problems on the solution of which all else depends. The advice that they should tender ought to enable action to be taken for the tackling of crucial problems by the best possible teams of investigators that the country can muster, supported by adequate financial resources. The milk and bovine problem ranks, I am convinced, as of the highest importance in providing our country with good fresh food, and nothing is more important in the problem than the breeding aspect. We have always been past-masters at dissipating our energies in this country, but at the present time in our history to do so is a ridiculous luxury. The urgent need for all-out research on a priority basis in many aspects of our national life is for ever nagging at my mind and I am amazed at the negligence of the nation in not tackling the subject in a really comprehensive way. The milk-bovine problem, but one of many needing priority treatment in our inert and complacent country, has served as a frame on which to hang a tirade that was bound sooner or later to take possession of my pen.

Of course there are dangers in every great and necessary undertaking. The danger inherent in a breeding programme is the irreparable loss of genes, those priceless vehicles of the inheritance of potentialities. To suppose that methods and techniques can be found that are infallible and will lead to perfection is the madness of a technically obsessed age, and one that has very little biological common sense. In all our breeding work, no matter if based on an absolutely accurate assessment of the knowledge of the day, we dare not forget that knowledge is not a fixed star and that we do not and cannot envisage the whole firmament. New knowledge sooner or later is bound to dictate a new twist or a new direction in the breeding programme that the wit of science (distilled from the wisdom of the specialists in a hundred different fields) of a particular decade may have set in motion. The new twist or direction that it may become imperative to initiate will almost certainly demand the use of genes not held in the animals or plants begotten of the original programme. In breeding as we build we discard: yet both in plants and animals *what we discard in the furtherance of our comprehensive programme we dare not throw away.* This means that in proportion as we embark upon full-blooded long-term plans, so must plans be made for keeping alive from generation to generation apparently useless and weird plants and animals for the sake of the genes they contain. Some few of these genes may subsequently prove to be inestimable value if properly woven into the living fabrics of our creations.

What is needed are breeding stations of great magnitude and intricacy, of such magnitude and intricacy that they could not lightly be duplicated. The countries of the world should collaborate in the setting up of research stations dedicated to essential problems. In this country we should want all the brains and money we could muster to set up a truly adequate bovine breeding station: we could not set up a multitude of such stations. Other countries should set up their stations. The way for all countries to collaborate best in breeding work is to exchange genes, in other words to exchange segregating breeding material. The practical breeder works on a two-fold basis: first, in strict accord with the known laws of genetics; secondly, on the astute selection of the individuals which appear form his segregating material. This selection is necessarily a function of the breeder's acquired knowledge and acumen and also of the influence of the environment. What suits one characteristic set of conditions may not suit another: an inheritable potentiality which manifests itself in a particular qualitative-quantitative form and degree under one set of conditions may reveal itself in rather a different qualitative-quantitative pattern under totally different circumstances. Today no country can afford the extravagance of unnecessarily duplicating *ad hoc* breeding stations: indeed the world as a whole can ill afford over-duplication. A far better plan would be a world-wide exchange of segregating material in respect of all the plant and animal breeding everywhere in progress. *Genes should be treated as what they are, the common heritage of humanity.*

This chapter has carried me far and into many fields, but it has not carried me far enough into any one field or touched upon a number of fields that are basic to the gigantic problem of feeding all the peoples of the world in a manner adequate to satisfy their nutritional needs: to cater for the essential acceptance coefficients of individuals and to give food its full scope in the cultural development of the human race.

A NEW LOOK FOR ALLOTMENTS

PROFESSOR H. THORPE, Chairman of the Departmental Committee of Inquiry into Allotments, summarised his committee's deliberations (25.2.70) speaking to 160 representatives of 50 local authorities at the Civic Hall, Worsley, Lancashire. He spoke of the leisure garden patterns of the future and recommended a new Leisure Gardens Act. He considered that the National Allotments and Garden Society would not survive unless it adopted a new look leisure gardening policy. There were 1,400,000 plots in 1942 and 600,000 in 1967 and of these one in five plots were vacant, a total of 480,000 plots under cultivation today. 96% of plot holders are male and around 82% are over 40. Prof. Thorpe referred in detail to the figures produced from a questionnaire that was widely circulated. In the reasons for having a plot today 51.5% indicated some importance attached to leisure gardening. A survey of 8,500 Birmingham flat dwellers (private and council) received 15% replies which indicated a need for a garden (some folk prefer a flat to avoid gardening), 58% thought present allotments not attractive enough, 66% would be interested in improved sites, 24% would like a chalet garden. 60% would travel one mile. 37% two miles; size of garden wanted varied, 47% preferred 200 sq. yds. 80% wanted to grow flowers, 18% vegetables, 35% fruit.

Professor Thorpe stressed that good facilities and amenities were required to attract a wider age and class range. He indicated the low amenity provision today—63% of sites had secure gates and fences, 50% piped water. 22% sheds and only 7% have toilets, 5% car parks and 0% a communal hut. 44% of sites have two amenities or less (in contrast to bowling greens and swimming baths). With regard to live stock he felt that it did not fit in with, and often detracted from, gardening. He commended the Land Settlement Association and Worsley

UDC's livestock and gardening sites but preferred separate provision.

He stressed the value of good design, landscaping, amenity and the encouragement of strong community awareness. It was easier to design new sites than redesign the old. The linking of sites with parks had advantages (park rangers and patrol dogs). He criticised the present 'standard cemetary' type of lay out and urged use of trees, shrubs, neat summer houses, plots of different size and shape and open space provision. The Allotments Acts are no guidance for land allocation. They give no security to tenants. He proposed a new formula for established 'leisure gardens' of half an acre per thousand population for local authorities of over 5,000. He suggested that good amenities and maintenances would help build security into sites as past capital investment had been so low that land was ripe for expensive development. He proposed that good private sites become good private Established Leisure Gardens or alternatively the local authority purchase and manage them and that local authorities acquire all charity, field and poor allotments.

The report advocates a Parks and Recreation Department basis for local authority management of established leisure gardens, the abolition of the Statutory Allotment Committees and the establishment of a Leisure Garden Advisory Committees. There was a need for a strong National Gardening movement backed by local associations and realistic membership fees. With regard to the finances of established leisure gardens, the report advocated the continuance of the rate subsidy but that the 2d. limit should be abolished. A fair rent for sites was essential.

Professor Thorpe commented on the extremely low expenditure on allotments by local authorities (in 1965 21.4% spent nothing, 81% spent up to the product of ¼d. rate). Loan sanctions should continue but more money should be made available. The proceeds of sale of surplus statutory allotments or established leisure garden land should be applied to leisure garden development.

In conclusion the Professor said he was concerned to see established good relations and a spirit of goodwill and co-operation, so that all concerned could work together for a viable 'New Look' improvement.

To Allotment Holders and Organizations he had stressed:—

1. *Read* the report.
2. If you believe in it or most of it, *act on it* now.
3. Set in motion now *Operation Spring Clean* on sites—war on weeds, scruffy huts, litter, poor fences and
4. Pull in younger folk and ladies. Make room for some on your committees. Why not determine committees on representation by sex and age groups?
5. Arrange allotment holder's meetings now to discuss *how to improve your site.*
6. *Liaise* with local authorities now about forward steps to be taken.
7. Finally he reminded allotment holders that in future the rule will be *use or lose.*

To Local Authorities he then said:—

1. Start thinking now how *best* you can rationalise your existing allotments system and convert it into a *viable Local Government system* according to guide lines in the report.
2. As an earnest of forward thinking start work now on at least one *fully developed local government site* so that the allotment holder and the general public know what it means. If *professional advice* on design and landscaping is required enquiries to Professor Thorpe at Birmingham University will be given attention. At present he is concerned with new sites at Bristol, Coventry and Birmingham.
3. When Established Leisure Gardens are being set up, provide as many *above the formula* as you can, especially if you have statutory allotments above that quota. Demand for Established Leisure Gardens will rise.
4. Set up eventually a *strong Local Government Advisory Committee* served by *influential* representatives at Councillor, Officer and Association level.
5. Ensure that Allotments under Local Authority Management get a fair crack of the whip in *rate subsidy.* Also take advantage of loan sanction.
6. Devote your *increased revenue* from increased allotment rents to site *improvements* on a realistic scale.

7. Also devote sums derived from any *surrender* or statutory allotment land to imaginative schemes on new sites and improvements on old sites.

8. Encourage *competitions* among your sites and plot holders for the greatest improvement in a year.

9. Vie with other Local Authorities for the distinction of having made *most improvements* in its sites in a year.

10. Induce *important local figures* and the *Civic Trust* to champion allotments of local authorities as they do other forms of recreation for dominantly younger are groups.

11. If you have allowed *livestock* on allotment garden sites in the past plan now for *good livestock sites.*

12. The new local government allotment system will not be built in a day. It should be remembered that relatively *very* little has been *spent* on allotments in many towns in the past and there is a great deal of leeway to make up. The new and improved sites will be assets in the urban landscape. Be bold, be imaginative, have faith in the movement and show it.

APPENDIX III

PLANNING A NEW TOWN

MILTON KEYNES in Buckinghamshire is planned to be a new town of 250,000 people. This city will absorb 15 villages, some of them with considerable rural character and architectual quality. The development is in the charge of a firm of consultant architects and planners—Lord Llewelyn-Davies, Walter Bor and John de Monchaux.

It is intended to keep the villages self-contained and linked by tree lined boulevards which are either two-lane roads or four-lane dual carriage ways according to the density of the traffic. Each village will have a primary school and a middle school and a community centre: each has a few essential shops. Small specially designed buses will take the villagers to any point in the city.

At the heart of the city are the concert hall, the museums, the art gallery, the offices. Distributed around this nucleus and throughout the city are a number of secondary schools, colleges of further education, social centres and an open University. There is a park with lakes and a golf course that follows a canal.

The density—an average of 8 houses to the acre—is quite high so much will depend on the skill of the architects' layout. Stephen Gardiner commenting on the plan in the 'Observer' in April 1970 wrote:

'There must be none of these new town mistakes, these draughty spaces that expose people as crowds, refuse responsibility for them and offer no protection. This is why, for instance, the old closed market is much better than the shopping centre or precinct. In the closed market the richness of this interior, the open stalls, the mass of detail create a balance for people, somehow they get lost.

This is an important architectural point and the designers of the new villages should remember it. People need privacy

225

as they need corners, and the structure of the background should be strong enough, and reticent enough, to receive them.'

This is in line with Stapledon's feelings about 'open spaces.'

APPENDIX IV

LAND USE IN BRITAIN

IT HAS been estimated that in England and Wales, if present trends continue, about six million acres of farmland will be developed for non-agricultural uses before the end of this century. Derelict land produced by mineral workings in the same period will equal the amount produced over the last two centuries. Sand and gravel workings (estimates published in the Jan. 1966 *Newsletter* of the Sand and Gravel Association) are likely to exceed coal as our largest extractive industry by the late seventies. Transporting gravel and sand an extra fifteen miles can double its costs. It will therefore be extracted close to its markets even if this means ignoring amenity and high quality soil. There are, of course, as well as old sites now developed for amenity purposes, many still derelict sites.

The demand for electricity doubled between 1955 and 1963 and is expected to have doubled again by 1970. Millions of tons of pulverised fuel ash are a by-product of power stations. The immense scale on which these by-products are thrown out, including the toxic wastes of nuclear fuels, indicates that economic expansion without restraint may have to be curbed for many other reasons besides preventing land and water from becoming a dumping ground for industry.

It is interesting to note that forests, which are a renewable resource and do not produce toxic wastes, are lagging far behind the demand for timber. Britain produces less than 10% in money terms of her wood requirements. By the year 2,000 home production is intended to meet about 15% of the demand. Yet timber is one of the most expensive cargoes to import. It is possible that, at the present rate of use, the timber supplies of the whole world will be exhausted in the next 100 years. Of course the rate of use is likely to rise! Every edition of the New York Times consumes 15 acres of forest. About 7½% of our land is used for timber—one of the lowest figures in Europe. Forests play a part in the conservation of water, recreation and sanctuaries for wild life. But the profit is not great enough and the return is not sufficiently rapid for a society which estimates values in terms of money to put present needs above future survival. We would rather rip up the earth than employ its ever recurrent fertility.

> 'All is kept infertile by a power
> That sees no wealth upon the grassy slope,
> But digs the mineral and scorns the flower.'
> R. Waller — *The Two Natures*

Many of our uplands—called marginal lands by the economists as they are on the margin between profit and loss—have deteriorated in soil structure because the original forest has been removed and never been allowed to regenerate by the appropriate management. This sort of land accounts for 17 million acres of rough grazing. By a proper agricultural strategy it could be coordinated with lowland farming and the uplands and lowlands worked together, as was often the case in the past.

Some of this land should be used for new towns to soak off the immense pressure on urban areas like South East England where 35% of the people of Britain (18 million) now live. To accommodate these people some of the finest farm land in England has been sterilised. Obviously a national plan is required that distributes population and resources in ecological terms, not in economic terms. But although the government vaguely recognises this and publishes statistics of an alarming and dreary nature, it still allows the principle determinant to be economic—as for example in the plan for the expansion of Ipswich. The argument against building in the nearest marginal area (the Brecklands) was that communications, drainage, building costs etc., could be exorbitant. As Stapledon says, we have been a lazy uninspired nation when it comes to doing the great things, devoid of crusading spirit. We should build in Cumberland and Westmorland, the Solway and mid-Wales with the old youthful pioneering spirit. This would place industry in pleasant surroundings without eating up the best land. All our technological ability should be concentrated on solving the economic problems involved on the assumption that we have no alternative but to preserve our best land, instead of the assumption that we have no alternative but to do what is most immediately profitable. In failing to act swiftly and resolutely on this issue, all our politicians reveal themselves as yesterday's men, still living in the 19th century, and like old military staffs fighting yesterday's battles with so much fervour you would think they were saving us instead of destroying us. But in real war those who still think in the terms of the last war have to be removed from authority. That is why revolutions happen in politics. (The facts quoted in the above are taken from *Man and Environment*. Robert Arvill. Pelican.)

RURAL DEVELOPMENT BOARDS

In selected hill and upland areas in Great Britain, Rural Development Boards have been set up. Their object is to promote programmes covering agriculture, forestry and other uses of land, such as outdoor recreation and tourism. They may acquire land by agreement to provide dwellings for their tenants and employees and give financial assistance to instal electricity, gas or water for any programme drawn up by them which meets the Minister's approval. This goes someway to meet the criticisms raised by Stapledon in chapter eleven (see page 186). On the other hand, Stapledon would presumably have agreed with those who say that the need for these Boards reflects the absence of effective regional government to plan as a whole.

Whether the existing Farm Improvement Scheme with its emphasis on labour-saving buildings and devices does more good or harm is difficult to say. Stapledon believed that farm labour should be subsidised and that capital put into labour-saving devices would be better put into manpower which could, for example, cultivate many fields at the same time when the time is right—which a machine cannot do on its own without someone to drive it.

This year (1970) there has been a move to make the National Agricultural Advisory Service more conservation minded. This is obviously to the good and reflects a certain nervous anxiety in the Government about what is happening to our soils. Indeed an investigation into the state of our soil structures has been set up. Many of the Minister's statements, however, imply that he is determined to square the circle and conceal what is happening to our soils and our environment by a camouflage of pretty trees, coppices and the like on the odd corners of the farm that cannot be cultivated. This attitude would harmonise with the Ministry's idea of quality in food—its appearances that matter. We shall perhaps have quality tests for landscapes as we have quality tests for food that measure the superficial appearances (absence of insect bites etc.) and ignore nutritional values. The fertility of the land can be excluded from conservational assessments in the same way as nutritional values are excluded from the grading of fruit and vegetables.

APPENDIX V

BRINGING INDUSTRY TO VILLAGES

SOME of the snags involved in this have been revealed since the 1940s when it seemed an altogether admirable project. Village industries today are seldom self-sufficient as they were in the Middle Ages: as a consequence raw material has to be brought in from long distances and the finished product exported long distances. The consequence is that the small village roads and lanes are choked. As I have seen this happen and experienced myself the villagers' indignation at their loss of peace and quiet, I wrote to my local planning officer, C. W. Smith, East Suffolk County Council, who is sympathetic towards Stapledon's book, and asked him to comment on Chapter 11. He has done this in a personal, not an official, capacity. He wrote to me:—'I was very happy with the text through the succeeding pages up to page 176. A third of the way down this page is another view which is worthy of support. It says that we must choose with great care the particular villages and small towns to which to bring factories. Again following through this page and the next there is nothing general to disagree with. On page 178 we are told that 'Planners can make a setting favourable to invigoration and growth. . .' It is, however, when we reach page 179 and a quotation from C. H. Gardiner that my views depart from the continuing theme. He says that there is no reason why light industries should not be admitted to the village and the countryside, and that there will be benefit in such an arrangement. The theory may well be sound, and as we come to the top of page 181 there is no harm in saying that the countryside needs new towns and new villages for its own sake and not merely to solve an urban problem. The two needs are said to be compatible.

I must now generalise rather than pick individual points, and it will help you if I say why I cannot agree with the proposals which are made. It is inherent in the proposition that sufficient industry of the right kind exists which can be directed or persuaded into a vast number of small villages. Although the employment benefits are recognised, the tremendous difficulties are not. For example, modern industry is almost always based on heavy vehicles and the village roads cannot cope with such traffic without disastrous effects on their structure, on road safety, and old buildings, and on the environment generally. Furthermore industry usually has special needs resulting in extra electricity lines, unusual water requirements and effluent. The only way to deal with this group of needs is to collect one's industry in a few locations so that the roads can be improved, services provided, and so on.

Of much wider significance is the national policy for the distribution of industry. The limited amount of industry which can be moved is matched against a list of priorities. The first priority is the unemployment areas classified as development areas. Then there are the intermediate or 'grey' areas, the new towns, and expanded towns, which are helping with the distribution of population policies, and below that are some of the rural areas which are 'dealt with sympathetically'. To pretend that anything is left over to serve a nice theory about invigorating villages is frankly nonsense today. Thus one goes back to the statement on page 176 'we must choose with great care the particular villages and towns...' They will indeed be very few and in a County like East Suffolk it may not be possible to justify more than four locations in addition to the established main towns.

Of tremendous help, of course, is the fact that the motor vehicle has widened the catchment areas of employment centres, and with a 15/20 mile radius for journey-to-work, villages are being invigorated by an adventitious population.

A practical and down-to-earth point is the tremendous resistance which we nearly always encounter when there is a chance of introducing an industry into a large village. The nice theories about jobs for sons and daughters are almost never mentioned, whereas the opposition to noise, smells, visual intrusion, traffic and the like, is to the fore. I stress, however, that it is quite exceptional to have the opportunity of encour-

232

aging a moving industry to go to a village. Normally the industrialist would die laughing at the suggestion that he might be sensibly located in a village where there is a limited or non-existant pool of skilled labour, where the services do not exist, the communications are bad, and there is a hostile attitude from the locals. The best we have been able to do is to help the development of small towns such as Halesworth where there is a reasonable infra structure to accommodate growth, and where the decline in agricultural employment in and around the town means that there is a receptive attitude. Nevertheless I stress that the factory which has been attracted is an isolated success story compared with the normal experience of industry directed or baited to the unemployment areas, and the expanding towns. I hasten to add that I agree with these national policies and see no alternative to this selection unless and until there is a great deal more moving industry to play with.

You will readily see that some of the hypotheses from page 188 onwards do not now make a lot of sense. This is where I believe the book should be up-dated because his view is readily understandable in the context of over 20 years ago. At that time industries were commonly in much smaller units and the great amalgamation had not taken place. It was also thought that a great deal more new industry would be developing in such small units and this has not proved to be the case. Also, the decline in some heavy engineering, shipbuilding and coal mining has become understood, and the vast shakedown in the work forces has made it vital to transfer as much new industry as possible into these areas of decline. Tackling this problem has over-ridden a number of post-war ideas which are exemplified in Sir George Stapledon's approach.'

I feel sure that Stapledon would have agreed with Mr. Smith's admirable comments had he been alive today. Later developments have shown that introducing industry only too often destroys the village character (see page 186). It is yet another of the antitheses requiring resolution: Local industry: Traffic congestion. However I have left Stapledon's own text unchanged. It states the principles that must apply when integration is possible without destroying the village character.

APPENDIX VI

DISTRIBUTION OF POPULATION

FIGURES taken from the Registrar General's estimates for 30th June, 1969 which are of interest:

Population of England and Wales:	48,826,800	
Population of South East England:	17,000,000	35.4%
Population of East Anglia:	1,657,130	3.4%
Population of Westmorland:	71,710	
Conurbations make around:	16,486,190	33.8%
Areas outside conurbations with populations of 100,000 or more:	6,500,000	13.4%
50,000 but under 100,000:	10,500,000	21.7%
Rural districts (under 50,000):	10,500,000	21.7%

Note on the new rural population.

Although the drift to the towns of rural people continues, there is a new semi-rural population of commuters and retired people. Many of these select the choicest spots to live in and thereafter the spots are not so choice. To what extent are they prepared to pay for the views they dote on? To what extent should the landowners who sell land for development contribute to the upkeep of the view that has raised their prices? This need is recognised to some extent in the concept of the community price—that it is the community that creates the price of land. The capital gains tax and development levies are justified on these grounds. Nevertheless how much of this money is contributed to the upkeep of the landscape? The community has a right to know how money raised in this way is spent. The high price for land development in choice spots should contribute directly to, and be known to contribute directly to, the conservation of the area. As Stapledon says it is a scandal that land, our most precious commodity, should be sold to the highest bidder as we sell our artistic masterpieces. Taxes on speculation in art and land should go into a special fund for the benefit of art and land.

Those whose creed of agricultural conservation in fact conserves the landscape we all enjoy should not be penalised as they are now. They voluntarily forego immediate gain for the benefit of posterity—the farmer, for instance, who resists the temptation to root up all his hedges and make his land into a prairie for arable crops. He pays a considerable price for his idealism which his less public spirited neighbour does not pay. The recent increase in the fertiliser subsidy (Price Review, 1970) without a compensating subsidy for grazing or organic manures is a good example of the government's urban outlook (fertiliser is an urban product) and indifference to good husbandry. The policy of government should be to reward the ecological conscience — but governments don't appear to have any understanding of what this means.

Many of those who have fled to the sanctuary of rural life —especially the professional commuters—are beginning to understand that, like wild life, they may soon find that their habitat is unable to sustain them. They are beginning to think about the real creative supports of rural life, just as converts to a religion often understand it better than those born into it. These people are beginning to form their own protection societies and to embarrass the local authorities and the government. Their own insight into the urban mind—which is the foundation of their own way of thought—gives them an advantage in coping with its defects. Many of the most ardent and capable conservationists are likely to come from this strata of society—in which I include myself. The culture of today should be fed by all that is most vital both in rural and urban life and traditions.

A good example of this kind of association is the Chiltern Society which has tackled the problems of this outstanding commuter area. Here is a fortified and well informed ecological conscience capable of educating other urban refugees and hammering public opinion.

The situation from the human ecological point of view is thus extremely complex and one can never be sure where wise action will come from. The farmer with powerful self-interest may fight for his right to do what he likes providing it keeps him solvent. The commuters who live around him may fight for his right to keep solvent by good husbandry—fighting his battles while he renounces his ecological conscience. In a situation of such complexity it is essential for everyone to master the principles of human ecology. So I have made a brief list of those which I believe to be most important—the groundwork—in Appendix VII.

SOME BASIC PRINCIPLES OF APPLIED HUMAN ECOLOGY

I BELIEVE that the principles which follow are now those generally current among ecologically minded people, through whatever experiences they have come upon them. They are, I think, dictated by the facts of the matter, i.e. the relation of soil, plant, animal and man to one another: the determining factor is the extent to which man can use what nature provides simply as 'resources' for his civilisation.

In planning the ecological society as a lasting and stable home for mankind, the following fundamental principles should be respected:

One: *Industrial production should be based as far as possible on renewable resources.*

Comment: Non-renewable resources such as fossil fuels, mineral ores etc., must be rationed.

The object of this is to prevent the sources of energy on which our society depends from running out. Agriculture must have first priority in the use of fuels or we shall be back to horses before very long: unless we use steam driven tractors!*

Two: *Productive industries must be designed on a biological model so that residues and wastes are recycled.*

Comment: Industry regards the second half of the growth cycle as unprofitable. The biodegradation of used or discarded material is treated simply as a matter of disposing of rubbish. Yet nature shows us that biodegradation is a positive process of decomposition and works to restore that which has been lost to nature. The biological process of decomposition works against the thermodynamic process of disintegration into forms of energy that cannot be reconstituted into usable natural forms—as in incineration. If wastes are to decomposed,

*It is predicted that oil resources will be exhausted in between 30 and 70 years time.

R

237

they must be treated in such a way that the bacteriological forces of nature are given a suitable habitat for their work. At present our environment is choking in the excrement of plant, animal and man.

Three: *The soil must be managed as a living material, prone to sickness and easy to destroy.*

Comment: Soil is a limited commodity but capable of constant creative renewal if rightly managed. Agriculture is thus the perfect example of the industry on a biological model using renewable resources. (See One and Two.) This characteristic should make it possible to feed mankind indefinately provided the population of the earth does not exceed the capacity of the soil to produce food without wearing it out. The soil is thus like no other material used in industry. If it is confused with industrial machines, and the land is treated like a factory floor, the soil will lose its capacity to work for ever. The future of mankind obviously rests on the recognition of this fact. Considering that one great urban civilisation after another has declined as a result of disregarding, or being ignorant of, this law of the soil, it ought to be written into the constitution of every state.

Four: *A high percentage of mixed farms must be legally enforced.*

Comment: The idea of enforcing systems of husbandry may sound authoritarian but rotations were legally enforced in the past. It follows from Three that soil is our most precious possession and it must be conserved in its optimum creativeness. To rob the soil of creativeness is a crime and legal action to prevent it is thus not unjust. Mixed husbandry has been recognised by all good agrarians as the safest way to preserve soil structure and soil fertility, indefinately. No one should be allowed to keep farm livestock without an appropriate minimum of land to graze each animal and thus, also, to dispose of its manures by fertilising the land instead of contaminating it with wastes as in factory farming. A grazing subsidy should replace the fertiliser subsidy, if subsidies are required. The value of money should be better tied to agricultural produce.

Five: *Nutrition must be treated as the foundation of health.*

Comment: The quality of food must be estimated by its nutritional value and its freedom from elements likely to be poisonous. Quality should be divorced from appearance, convenience and saleability, which are secondary. The evil of the market economy is that it reverses the secondary and the primary: it puts the health of the nation at the mercy of the salesman and the technologist. Even taste can now be faked. The new deficiency diseases (the so-called diseases of civilisation) are due to the abstraction of nutrients from staple foods; this results in a dangerous concentration of the remaining nutrients, as in refined bread and sugar. This has been demonstrated best by Sgn. Capt. T. L. Cleave, Dr. G. D. Campbell and N. S. Painter F.R.C.S., in their book *'Diabetes, Coronary Thrombosis and the Saccharine Disease.'* If quality was commensurate with nutritional value, we should once again value fresh, wholefood as little processed and synthesised as possible. Progress in diet—as in everything else—can only be made if the lethal factors do not offset the positive gains. A welfare service in an unhealthy nation leads to national bankruptcy, as we are witnessing. The greatest tax reducer would be a sound national diet.

Six: *We must strike the balance between rural and urban.*
Comment: This has massive implications and, among other things, involves a new economic calculation of labour-saving on the farm. The ancillary agricultural industries are becoming swollen and impractical. Many factory workers who produce herbicides, pesticides, fertilisers and machines, together with the extensive network of research workers who have to monitor the effects of introducing all these chemicals into the environment, would be better employed on the farm doing the original cultivations which labour saving has displaced. Nitrogen should be made available to crops by good husbandry, not by such gimmicks as putting ammonia gas in the soil. Labour-saving in farming has now reached the point at which it has become an economic fallacy, an unexamined dogma left over from the 19th century. To increase the number of people working on the land is the best way to halt the drift from the land and repopulate the countryside. Many other ways of repopulating the countryside so that it balances the towns and cities are being tried out: light industry, decentralisation of industry and so on. But the core of preserving the

character of the countryside will lie in adequate farm labour, the extensive cultivation of marginal, waste and scenically attractive landscapes, and the design of new villages so that people are not just put into rows of barracks called housing estates. All this is at present economic heresy which leads to seven.

Seven: *Economic arguments must never have priority over ecological arguments.*

Comment: This is obvious. The object of economics is to find the most efficient way of carrying out ends fixed by society. It should not be an end in itself as it is when ends are sacrificed to profit. That 'more at lower price' necessarily enriches us and adds to our variety of choice is another unexamined dogma which usually ends by giving us more of what we don't want at the expense of what we would prefer, thus limiting real choice, as when two apples are needed to provide the nutritional value that was previously found in one. This is good business provided the appearance conceals the reality. But everyone is the loser except the sellers. Similarly, do we really prefer more aircraft at the expense of peace and quiet? Our choice of the good life is restricted not expanded by economic progress as we reckon it today, i.e. in economic not ecological terms.

It follows from the above principles that we must: *Think of the environment as a whole and not of those specific interests which have too much power in the control of national and international affairs.* One can think of a number of over mighty subjects whose investment of money leads to economic expansion without regard to ecology.

Make politicians realise that most of the problems they agitate about are secondary problems and force them to concentrate on primary problems. Even race relations are not important when erosion leads to all races starving.

Determine the optimum population for every region of the earth. This would require very detailed mapping of its resources etc.

Find some way of costing all forms of loss of amenity caused by industry. Intangible values such as freedom from noise, congestion, pollution—disamenities—should be treated as the citizens' rights: no industry should be allowed to deprive the citizen who values these rights of his enjoyment of without compensation. This problem is discussed by Dr. E. J. Nishan: *The Costs of Economic Growth*.

BIBLIOGRAPHY

CHAPTER 2

H. V. Routh: *Humanism: Past, Present and Future;* O.U.P., 1943.

Jacques Maritain: *Redeeming the Time:* The Centenary Press, 1943.

Jacques Maritain: *The Twilight of Civilisation;* Sheed & Ward, 1946.

CHAPTER 3

The Rt. Hon. L. S. Amery, C.H., D.C.L.: *Thoughts on the Constitution;* O.U.P., 1947.

Report of the Machinery of Government Committee (Cmd. 9230): The Ministry of Reconstruction, 1918.

E. S. Russell: *The Directiveness of Organic Activity;* C.U.P., 1945.

Alfred North Whitehead: *Nature and Life;* C.U.P., 1934.

CHAPTER 4

John Hammond: *Animal Breeding in Relation to Nutrition and Environmental Conditions; Biological Reviews,* Vol. 22, 1947.

R. George Stapledon: *Disraeli and the New Age;* Faber & Faber, 1943.

Ananda K. Coomaraswamy: *Figures of Speech and Figures of Thought; Social Series,* Luzac & Co., 1946.

Rudolf Jordan: *Homo Sapiens Socialis;* Central News Agency Ltd., South Africa, 1944.

Sir Charles Sherrington, O.M.: *Man on his Nature;* Cambridge, 1942.

H. J. Muller: *The Gene. Pilgrim Trust Lecture; Proceedings of the Royal Society,* Series B, No. 874, Jan. 1947.

Michael Dillon: *Self. A Study in Ethics and Endocrinology;* William Heinemann, 1946.

E. L. Woodward: *Short Journey;* Faber & Faber, 1942.

Henry Walter Bates: *The Mind and Manners of Wild Animals;* George Routledge and Sons, New University Library.

CHAPTER 5

Innes H. Pearse & H. Crocker: *The Peckham Experiment;* George Allen & Unwin, 1943.

I. A. Richards: *Science and Poetry;* Kegan Paul, Trench & Trubner, 1935.

D. H. Lawrence: *Psychoanalysis and the Unconscious* (1923), *Fantasia of the Unconscious* (1923); Heinemann.

C. H. Gardiner: *The Evesham Custom.* A pamphlet.

CHAPTER 6

Lewis Einstein: *Historical Change;* Cambridge, 1946.

Aldous Huxley: *The Art of Seeing;* Chatto and Windus, 1943.

Emile Cammaerts: *The Flower of Grass;* Cresset Press, 1944.

Herbert Grierson: *Rhetoric and English Composition;* Oliver & Boyd, 1944.

Lord Cherwell: *Philosophy of the Universities;* University Quarterly, Vol. 1, No. 4, Aug., 1947.

CHAPTER 8

C. H. Gardiner: *The Evesham Custom.* A pamphlet.

Innes H. Pearse and Innex H. Crocker: *The Peckham Experiment;* George Allen and Unwin, 1943.

D. H. Lawrence: *Psychoanalysis of the Unconscious* (1923), *Fantasia of the Unconscious* (1923); published by Heinemann.

I. A. Richards: *Science and Poetry;* Kegan Paul, Trench and Trubner, 1935.

APPENDIX

Stephen Gwyn: *Burgundy;* Constable, 1934.

William Morris: *News from Nowhere;* Longmans, Green.

Franklin Kidd and Cyril West: 'Quality in Cox's Orange Pippin Apples', *Agriculture;* Vol. LII (9), Dec., 1946.

Pollard, Keiser and Bryan: *The Apple as a source of Vitamin C;* Long Ashton, Bristol, 1945.

Mamie Olliver: 'The Ascorbic Acid content of Fruits and Vegetables'; *Journal Soc. Chem. India,* Vol. LV, 1936.

George M. Odlum: 'A Breeder's Tabloid'; *Wiltshire Gazette,* 1946.

John Hammond: 'Animal Breeding in Relation to Nutrition and Environmental Conditions'; *Biological Reviews,* Vol. 22, 1947.

R. George Stapledon: *Disraeli and the New Age;* Faber & Faber, London, 1943.

Ananda K. Coomaraswamy: *Figures of Speech and Figures of Thought;* Social Series, Luzac & Co., London, 1946.

Rudolph Jordan, *Homo Sapiens Socialis;* Central News Agency Ltd., South Africa, 1944.

Sir Charles Sherrington, O.M.: *Man on his Nature;* Cambridge, 1942.

H. J. Muller: 'The Gene. Pilgrim Trust Lecture'; *Proceedings of the Royal Society,* Series B, No. 874, Jan. 1947.

Michael Dillon: *Self. A Study in Ethics and Endocrinology;* William Heinemann, 1946.

E. L. Woodward: *Short Journey;* Faber & Faber, London, 1942.

William T. Hornaday: *The Mind and Manners of Wild Animals;* Charles Scribner's Sons, New York & London, 1922.

Henry Walter Bates: *The Naturalist on the Amazon;* George Routledge & Sons (The New University Library), London.

Note. I have been unable to trace the bibliographies for chapters seven, nine, ten, eleven and twelve. Perhaps they were never drawn up: perhaps they have been mislaid. Perhaps they will turn up among Stepledon's papers one of these days.

EDITOR'S RECOMMENDED READING

Other works of Sir George Stapledon published by Faber & Faber.

The Land: Now and Tomorrow.

The Way of the Land.

Disraeli and the New Age.

The Hill Lands of Britain (Out of print).
Prophet of the New Age. Biography of Sir George Stapledon,
    by Robert Waller.

Among new books relevant to Human Ecology are:
G. Borgstrom: *Too Many. A study of earth's biological limita-
    tions;* Macmillan, 1969.
Max Nicholson: *The Environmental Revolution. A guide for
    the new masters of the earth;* Hodder & Stoughton, 1970.
Jean Dorst: *Before Nature Dies;* Collins, 1970.
Hugh Nicol: *The Limits of Man. An inquiry into the scientific
    bases of human population;* Constable, 1967.
Frank Graham Jr.: *Since Silent Spring;* Hamish Hamilton,
    1970.
Robert de J. Hart: *The Inviolabel Hills;* Stuart & Watkins—
    Soil Association, 1969.
Gordon Rattray Taylor: *The Doomsday Book:* Thames and
    Hudson, 1970.

INDEX

Action, negated by culture, 149; must be trained, 150 et seq.

Agriculture, not only an industry, 45-6; common world policy needed for, 47 et seq.; shapes character, 57; should be grouped with town and country planning 73; regionalization of 75; should support largest possible rural population, 86; as school of character and education, 105 et seq., 139; and integration, 139; and machinery, 139-40; and urban industry, 174; and backwaters, 182-3; intrinsic place in national policy, 197; inner meaning of, 202; diversification of production should be the rule, 213

Allotments, better called garden paddocks, 158-167; as leisure gardens 221-224

America, and world reconstruction, 201

Amery, The Rt. Hon. L. S., *Thoughts on the Constitution,* 71 et seq.

Ancestors, we are all, 89-90; and tree of life, 91

Antitheses, chain from individual to species, 77; intellect-instinct, 62; reason-instinct, 87; segregation-integration, 62, 65; inertia-change, 63, 65; complex-simple, 62, 76; lethal-enlivening, 62, 82;

static-dynamic, 65; indolence-activity, 66; social-predatory, 80; knowledge-ignorance, 85; science-art 86; immediate future-remote future, 89; moral antitheses listed, 95; drudgery-enjoyment, 114; quality-quantity, 138; urban-rural, 146 regulations-local knowledge, 191; production-research, 204; local traffic congestion 232

Apprenticeship, balances learning and action, 134; trained not specialized, 140; compulsory, 153-5; national apprenticeships, 153; summary of views, 197 et seq.

Astor and Rowntree, *Mixed Farming and Muddled Thinking,* muddled book, 155-156

Art, function of, 85; decline of, 86; and food, 134, 165, 198, 207; and industry, 198-9

Backwaters, and planning, 182 et seq.

Bacon, Francis, on masters and men, 85; on words, 127; on division of labour, 146, 153; on vocation, 154

Balance, significance of, 46-8; 'correct'. 50; and segregation, 63; balancing antitheses, 64-5; of learning and action, 133-4; and use of land, 162; principle of

246

Ecology, Human (vide also, Stapledon) and full life, 58-9, 108;
why important, 6 et seq.,
method and purpose of 53 et
seq; as a popular word 40, 41;
incompatible with unrestrained
productivity 41; and the stable
state 41; and political action,
41-42; study of environment,
59; heralds era of integration,
64; need for periods of rest, 67;
reacting simply to complexity,
69; and central authority, 78;
and control of evolution, 92,
93; and happiness, 108; errors
of long standing most difficult
to remedy, 121; evils must be
spotted when infant trends,
120; wholly city life dehumanizing, 146; errors in progress,
148 et seq.; efficiency should
be function of happiness, 155;
the human principle in planning, 164, 174; dire effects of
industrial standardization, 185;
rehumanization, 194; some
basic principles of, 237 et seq.
Economics, should not decide all
issues, 49, 50
Edinburgh, Duke of, 41, 42
Education, and acute experience,
49; purpose to arouse interest,
99; and farm life, 105; and
family business, 106; and integration of head, heart, etc.,
109 et seq.; too much intellect,
110; teaching, 110; training,
111; conditioning, 114; as
trinity, 116; why ed. has failed,
116-7; need to ed. subconscious, 117-9; and to train in contemplation, 119-30; obvious
errors most difficult to remedy,
120; examinations as example,
121; general ed. should have
three major aims, 121 et seq.;
new approach and new methods
needed, 121 et seq.; fragmenta-

tion must go, 122; Schools of
Integration at universities, 122-
6; and illiterates, 127-8; and
craftsmanship, 129 et seq.; and
watching, 132; and sensuous
memory, 132-3; and apprenticeship, 134; and the machine,
139; for word-pattern and action-pattern experts, 141;
school leaving age, 142; adult,
142; of scientists, 143; must be
philosophical, 144; must be diversified, 144-5; must include
holidays and life after school,
148 et seq.; and culture, 149;
camp boarding schools, 151-3;
closing of village schools, 151;
needs biological bias, 171; summary of views, 197 et seq.
Efficiency, defeats its own aims,
155-6; human, 156
Einstein, Lewis, on new approach
to teaching, 121
Environment, A. N. Whitehead on,
52; problem of adjustment to,
57; and human ecology, 60;
and paroxysmal change, 65; of
words, 66; and lethal factors,
83; and ideal progress, 87; as
means of controlling evolution,
92; effect on human will, 93-4;
and full life, 96 et seq.; can destroy character, 99; urban must
be counter-balanced by rural,
146; G. M. Trevelyan on, 157;
rate of change, 167; not people
but e. wrong, 179; rehumanization through e., 195
Evolution, and growth of
society, 81; men's control of,
90, 92; and 'will', 94

Facts, and current scientific
method, 56-7; and committees,
71; speculation without facts,
89; fact-loaded curricula, 120-
121; and wisdom, 133-4
Family, link between individual